OECD Reviews of School Resources: Denmark 2016

Deborah Nusche, Thomas Radinger,
Torberg Falch and Bruce Shaw

OECD
BETTER POLICIES FOR BETTER LIVES

This work is published on the responsibility of the Secretary-General of the OECD. The opinions expressed and arguments employed herein do not necessarily reflect the official views of the Organisation or of the governments of its member countries.

This document and any map included herein are without prejudice to the status of or sovereignty over any territory, to the delimitation of international frontiers and boundaries and to the name of any territory, city or area.

Please cite this publication as:
Nusche, D. et al. (2016), *OECD Reviews of School Resources: Denmark 2016*, OECD Publishing, Paris.
http://dx.doi.org/10.1787/9789264262430-en

ISBN 978-92-64-26239-3 (print)
ISBN 978-92-64-26243-0 (PDF)
ISBN 978-92-64-26247-8 (epub)

Series: OECD Reviews of School Resources
ISSN 2413-4333 (print)
ISSN 2413-3841 (online)

The statistical data for Israel are supplied by and under the responsibility of the relevant Israeli authorities. The use of such data by the OECD is without prejudice to the status of the Golan Heights, East Jerusalem and Israeli settlements in the West Bank under the terms of international law.

Photo credits: Cover © VLADGRIN/Shutterstock.com.

Corrigenda to OECD publications may be found on line at: *www.oecd.org/about/publishing/corrigenda.htm.*

Foreword

This report for Denmark forms part of the Organisation for Economic Co-operation and Development (OECD) Review of Policies to Improve the Effectiveness of Resource Use in Schools (also referred to as the School Resources Review, see Annex A for further details). The purpose of the review is to explore how school resources can be governed, distributed, utilised and managed to improve the quality, equity and efficiency of school education. School resources are understood in a broad way, including financial resources (e.g. expenditures on education, school budget), physical resources (e.g. school infrastructure, computers), human resources (e.g. teachers, school leaders) and other resources (e.g. learning time).

Denmark was one of the countries which opted to participate in the country review strand and host a visit by an external review team. The scope for analysis in this report includes public primary and lower secondary education (Folkeskole). Members of the review team were Deborah Nusche (OECD), Thomas Radinger (OECD), Torberg Falch (Norwegian University of Science and Technology), and Bruce Shaw (Ontario Ministry of Education). Deborah Nusche co-ordinated the review between May 2014 and January 2016 and Thomas Radinger co-ordinated the review between February and October 2016. The biographies of the members of the review team are provided in Annex B. This publication is the report of the review team. It provides, from an international perspective, an independent analysis of major issues facing the use of school resources in Denmark, current policy initiatives, and possible future approaches. The report serves three purposes: i) to provide insights and advice to the Danish education authorities; ii) to help other countries understand the Danish approach to the use of school resources; and iii) to provide input for the thematic comparative reports of the OECD School Resources Review.

The involvement of Denmark in the OECD review was co-ordinated by Jon Jespersen, Senior Advisor in the Division for Evidence Informed Policy and Practice in Day Care and Education of the Agency for Education and Quality, in collaboration with Jørn Skovsgaard, Senior Advisor in the Division for International Affairs of the Danish Ministry for Children, Education and Gender Equality. An important part of the involvement of Denmark was the preparation of a comprehensive and informative Country Background Report (CBR) on school resources authored by the Danish Institute for Local and Regional Government Research (KORA) for the Danish Ministry for Children, Education and Gender Equality. The OECD review team is very grateful to the main authors of the CBR and to all those who assisted them in providing a high-quality informative document. The CBR is an important output from the OECD project in its own right as well as an important source for the review team. Unless indicated otherwise, the data for this report are taken from the Danish Country Background Report. The CBR follows guidelines prepared by the OECD secretariat and provides extensive information, analysis and discussion in regard to the national context, the organisation of the education system, the use of school resources and the views of key stakeholders. In this sense, the CBR and this report complement each other and, for a more comprehensive view of the effectiveness of school resource use in Denmark, should be read in conjunction.

The OECD and the European Commission (EC) have established a partnership for the project, whereby participation costs of countries which are part of the European Union's Erasmus+ programme *are partly covered. The participation of Denmark was organised with the support of the EC in the context of this partnership.* The EC was part of the planning process of the review of Denmark (providing comments on the Danish CBR, participating in the preparatory visit and providing feedback on the planning of the review visit) and offered comments on drafts of this report. This contribution was co-ordinated by Joanna Basztura, Country Desk Officer for Poland, Lithuania, Denmark, working within the "Country Analysis" Unit of the Directorate for "Modernisation of Education I: Europe 2020, country analysis, Erasmus+ co-ordination", which is part of the Directorate General for Education and Culture (DG EAC) of the European Commission, until September 2016. The review team is grateful to Joanna Basztura for her contribution to the planning of the review and for the helpful comments she provided on drafts of this report.*

The review visit to Denmark took place on 22-29 April 2015. The itinerary is provided in Annex C. The visit was designed by the OECD (with input from the EC) in collaboration with the Danish authorities. It also involved a preparatory visit by the OECD secretariat on 18-19 February 2015 with the participation of Joanna Basztura, from the EC. The OECD review team met with state secretary Jesper Fisker and held discussions with the relevant divisions of the Ministry of Education, the Ministry of Finance, the Ministry for Economic Affairs and the Interior, the Ministry of Social Affairs, the Ministry of Higher Education and Science, the Danish Evaluation Institute (EVA), Local Government Denmark (LGDK), the Association of Municipal Administrators Responsible for Culture, Day care and Education (BKF), the Danish Association of School Leaders, the Teacher Union (DLF), the Union of Early Childhood and Youth Educators (BUPL), the national parents organisation and student organisation, the Disabled People's Organisation (DPOD), and researchers with an interest in the effectiveness of school resource use. The team also visited six municipalities and schools, interacting with the municipal education departments, school board representatives, school management, teachers and students. The intention was to provide the review team with a broad cross-section of information and opinions on school resource use and how its effectiveness can be improved.

The OECD review team wishes to express its gratitude to the many people who gave time from their busy schedules to inform the review team of their views, experiences and knowledge. The meetings were open and provided a wealth of insights. Special words of appreciation are due to the national co-ordinator, Jon Jespersen and his team. We are grateful to the national co-ordinator for sharing his expertise and responding to the many questions of the review team. The courtesy and hospitality extended to us throughout our stay in Denmark made our task as a review team as pleasant and enjoyable as it was stimulating and challenging. The OECD review team is also grateful to colleagues at the OECD. Eléonore Morena provided key administrative, editorial and layout support. Paulo Santiago and Yuri Belfali provided guidance and support.

The scope for analysis in this report includes public primary and lower secondary education (the Folkeskole). The report is organised in four chapters. Chapter 1 provides the national context, with information on the Danish school system, main trends and concerns, and recent developments. Chapters 2 to 4 look into three dimensions of resource use that Denmark identified as priorities in collaboration with the OECD: i) distribution of school resources; ii) governance of school resource use; and iii) management of the teaching workforce. Each chapter presents strengths, challenges and policy recommendations regarding the effectiveness of school resource use.

The policy recommendations attempt to build on and strengthen reforms that are already underway in Denmark, and the strong commitment to further improvement that was evident among those the OECD review team met. The suggestions should take into account the difficulties that face

* *This document has been produced with the financial assistance of the European Union. The views expressed herein can in no way be taken to reflect the official opinion of the European Union.*

any visiting group, no matter how well briefed, in grasping the complexity of the Danish education system and fully understanding all the issues. This report is the responsibility of the review team. While the team benefited greatly from the Danish CBR and other documents, as well as the many discussions with a wide range of Danish personnel, any errors or misinterpretations in this report are the team's responsibility.

Table of contents

Tables

Figures

Acronyms and abbreviations

AKT	*Adfærd-Kontakt-Trivsel* – Behaviour, Contact and Wellbeing Counsellor
BKF	*Børne- og Kulturchefforeningen* – Association of Municipal Administrators Responsible for Culture, Day Care and Education
BUPL	*Børne- og Ungdomspædagogernes Landsforbund* – Union of Early Childhood and Youth Educators
CBR	Country Background Report
EVA	*Danmarks Evalueringsinstitut* – Danish Evaluation Institute
DLF	*Danmarks Lærerforening* – Danish Union of Teachers
EC	European Commission
ECEC	Early Childhood Education and Care
EU	European Union
KORA	*Det Nationale Institut for Kommuners og Regioners Analyse og Forskning* – Danish Institute for Local and Regional Government Research
FLIS	*Fælleskommunal Ledelsesinformationsystem* – Joint Municipal Information System
GDP	Gross Domestic Product
KL/LGDK	Local Government Denmark
OECD	Organisation for Economic Co-operation and Development
PISA	OECD Programme for International Student Assessment
PPR	*Pædagogisk Psykologisk Rådgivning* – Educational-Psychological Advisory Service
SEN	Special Educational Needs
SFO	*Skolefritidsordning og Fritidshjem* – Leisure and Youth Education
TALIS	OECD Teaching and Learning International Survey
VET	Vocational Education and Training
VISO	*Videns- og Specialrådgivningsorganisation* – Specialised Knowledge and Counselling Organisation

OECD Reviews of School Resources: Denmark 2016

Executive summary

Denmark's public school system (*Folkeskole*) is based on trust, local autonomy and horizontal accountability. Municipalities and schools are responsible for making decisions about how to use and allocate their resources. This provides good conditions for managing resources effectively and for making sure resource decisions meet local needs. At the same time, municipalities and schools are held accountable for and supported in the management of their resources. There is a high level of financial commitment to education. Expenditure per student has always been clearly above average expenditures in the OECD and the EU. Recent policies, however, have acknowledged that better learning outcomes for all students are possible without using more of society's resources on education. Concerning equity in funding, the Danish funding system entails explicit mechanisms for equalisation between municipalities and schools. The country's approach to funding municipalities reduces differences in financial capacity across municipalities. Within municipalities, the fact that students facing some kind of disadvantage need extra resources and follow-up is widely accepted and school funding mechanisms typically take socio-economic characteristics of a school's student body into account.

Despite sustained high investment in education and provisions to ensure needs-based funding for schools, Denmark has a relatively small share of top-performers and there is room to improve the equity of educational outcomes, especially for immigrant students. Against this backdrop, Denmark has been successful in building consensus around the need for change and in implementing a number of reforms. This includes a wide-reaching reform of the *Folkeskole* since 2014, focussing broadly on three main areas of improvement: a longer and more varied school day with longer and better teaching and learning; better professional development for teachers, pedagogical staff and school principals; and few and clear objectives as well as a simplification of rules and regulations. The reform set three national goals for student achievement, equity and wellbeing to provide a clear direction and framework for the systematic and continuous evaluation of the reform. The *Folkeskole* reform is paradigmatic of Denmark's recent goal-oriented approach to policy and reform which holds the potential to create a sense of common purpose within a highly decentralised school system as well as greater transparency about the success of reform initiatives. Other reforms include changes to initial teacher education, the introduction of a new framework for the utilisation of teachers' working hours (Act no. 409), and a policy of inclusion of children with special educational needs in mainstream education.

There is evidence of a growing willingness at all levels of the system to dialogue around pedagogical needs and to build on collaborative work to improve student achievement and wellbeing. However, the shift towards a culture of using data to improve student learning is still in its infancy. Teachers, school leaders and municipalities still face challenges in focussing on improved student learning and there is a need to strengthen the capacity of the different actors to work in a goal-oriented way. Embedding a learning focus in practice is a major cultural shift that needs to be implemented through a range of changes, including the further development of several aspects of teacher professionalism that are still at an early stage of development in Denmark and the strengthening of pedagogical leadership in schools.

Based on its analysis of strengths and challenges, the report identifies the following policy priorities to improve the effectiveness of resource use in the Danish *Folkeskole*.

Continue to pay attention to using resources efficiently and strengthen public reporting about the performance of the school system

Developments in the *Folkeskole* over recent years have the clear potential to contribute to its improved efficiency and effectiveness. The 2014 *Folkeskole* reform aims to further strengthen the focus on learning environments and student performance. Prior to the reform, there was a reduction in expenditure per student and the reform introduces a longer school day for students without a symmetric increase in the number of teachers. The introduction of a new framework for the utilisation of teachers' working time (Act no. 409) has created greater flexibility for schools to use the time and competencies of their teachers. Whether the recent changes lead to greater efficiency and effectiveness will, however, depend on the ability of all actors in the system to use resources efficiently and to adapt to the changes the recent reforms imply. It will, therefore, be key to ensure that all actors continue to work intensively on using resources most effectively to improve student learning in relation to national goals. Knowledge-sharing across schools and municipalities will be particularly important in this regard. Considering changes to teachers' working conditions, strategies to develop and allocate human resources effectively in schools are crucial to ensure the success of the reform. For instance, if teachers do not have the right conditions to prepare and collaborate as they use more of their time on teaching, there could be risks to both quality and equity in schooling.

Denmark should also consider strengthening its reporting about the performance of the school system to the public at large at all levels of the system to build and sustain the overall consensus for investments in the *Folkeskole*. Denmark could develop a system-wide reporting framework that brings together a broader range of financial indicators and outcome indicators. The reporting framework could form the basis for the periodic publication of key national analytical reports in addition to the digital publication of the data (e.g. in the ministry's data warehouse). Municipalities and schools should make efforts to bring together and analyse data on the use of resources and outcomes. Municipalities should be encouraged to consider both financial and pedagogical dimensions in their biannual quality reports and to use data with a greater focus on the effective use of resources. Schools could benefit from a school-level reporting framework which enables them to examine the fiscal impact of their resource and curriculum decisions.

Give attention to all learning goals, monitor the learning outcomes of students at risk of underperformance and further support schools in striving towards excellence

A key challenge in monitoring education systems is to develop indicators and measures of performance that permit a good understanding of how well an education system is achieving its objectives. While national goals are typically comprehensive and broad, monitoring systems may be rather limited in the information they can offer. Schools should be encouraged to supplement standardised national assessment tools with a range of other assessments to obtain relevant information on student learning across the curriculum and to use this information to design differentiated teaching strategies. The ministry could consider introducing broader national measures of student learning to monitor the school system's progress in stimulating students to excellence in higher-order thinking and the development of complex competencies (such as a light monitoring sample survey on a broader range of skills and competencies).

There is also room to give more prominence to monitoring inequities in learning outcomes between specific student groups. Education system targets could pay attention to the achievement of different student groups. It would be important to review how more targeted indicators for the achievement of equity goals could be included in the monitoring strategy for the *Folkeskole* reform. In particular, regular reporting of information on learning outcomes for groups for which there is evidence of systematic underperformance is recommended. Ensuring that key performance indicators in the ministry's data warehouse are systematically disaggregated for different groups at risk of underperformance would be helpful for monitoring equity goals at all levels of the system. Given the high investment in schools enrolling students from socio-economically disadvantaged backgrounds and students with special educational needs, municipalities and the school community should monitor how such funding is used in schools and how this translates into performance for students at risk of underperformance.

The *Folkeskole* reform aims to challenge all students to reach their full potential and to increase the number of high-performing students from year to year. A policy focused on achieving these ends must set high standards for achievement and would involve the use of differentiated approaches to teaching, assessment and evaluation to provide the right level of support and challenge to individual students, professionals and schools. Enhancing school evaluation practice would be key to continuously challenge all schools to improve and the national level could play a stronger role in stimulating more effective self-evaluation in schools and municipalities (e.g. through a national sample programme of external school reviews and/or a central evaluation framework to model good practice).

Promote the better use of data at all levels of the system

Information can only lead to school improvement if it is relevant, available in adequate quantity, and properly interpreted. As the Danish school system is highly decentralised, it is of key importance to address concerns of varying capacity among schools and municipalities to effectively use the available information. For municipal staff, this means developing the capacity to understand, interpret and make decisions based on evaluation and assessment data collected from schools and drawn from the data warehouse together with their own data on resource inputs. Municipal administrators must be able to use school reporting data to engage in meaningful discussion with their schools and school leaders. Ongoing resources should be set apart to make sure municipalities can play their supervision role to its full extent. For school principals and teachers, it means developing the capacity to collect and report data on school budgets and student outcomes to the school community and the municipality in effective ways. School leaders and educators need to be able to transform data into knowledge that meets their own needs and those of their different stakeholders. School leaders need to develop an inquiry habit of mind, become data literate and be able to create a culture of inquiry. Exemplars of good practice in data interpretation, analysis, reporting and communication should be provided nationally to schools and municipalities to promote minimum requirements and municipalities should support their schools in using the available data.

At the national level, it is important to invest in research to increase the number of experts capable to respond to future needs and to offer the best advice available from scientific knowledge. The ministry's initiatives to establish a learning consultant corps and to develop a data warehouse should be sustained and further developed. Both the ministry and Local Government Denmark (KL/LGDK), the association of Danish municipalities, have an important role to play in the management and dissemination of the knowledge and data required to analyse the relationship between inputs and outputs and the effectiveness and efficiency of policies and programmes, and to facilitate both horizontal and vertical connections within the system.

Develop a vision for teacher professionalism and further develop the school leadership profession

Many changes to the education system in Denmark have left teachers struggling with what it means to be an excellent teacher. To support teachers, school leaders and municipal leaders in understanding and supporting the implementation of these changes, Denmark should consider developing a national teacher profile, vision or standards of practice. A national teacher profile would communicate the new expectations regarding teacher practice and put the conditions in place for many of the changes of the *Folkeskole* reform to take shape. Teacher standards would help to provide a framework to guide the development of the profession as whole. They would establish a foundation for teachers to explore their practice and for schools to develop their improvement initiatives. In a decentralised system like Denmark, a national teacher profile could be particularly relevant to promote a common vision and shared expectations.

The effective monitoring and appraisal of teaching is central to the continuous improvement of schools. Denmark should, therefore, also strengthen formal teacher performance appraisal focused on the continuous improvement of teaching practice (e.g. through a low key and low cost process organised internally in schools with some form of external validation) and consider ways to strengthen informal feedback to teachers to improve their practice (e.g. by encouraging collaborative teacher activities in schools).

Both the ministry and the individual municipalities as the employers of school leaders should promote the further development of school leadership, including teacher leadership, in collaboration with the school leader association. The first step should be the creation of a framework to guide the work of school leaders. This framework should clearly focus on the pedagogical role of school leaders while recognising that successful school leadership is always context-dependent. The ministry should consider developing a more strategic approach to the training of school leaders that constitutes a continuum and is available at and targeted to the different stages of a school leaders' career. Opportunities for collaboration, coaching and mentoring between school leaders can also provide useful support and enable school leaders to gain new expertise. Further developing school leader performance management in municipalities is another area for possible policy development.

Assessment and recommendations

Context

An average to above average performance in international student assessments

Danish students participate in the IEA (International Association for the Evaluation of Educational Achievement) Progress in International Reading Literacy Study (PIRLS) in Year 4 and in the Trends in Mathematics and Science Study (TIMMS) in Year 8. In the 2011 round of assessments in mathematics and science, Danish students scored above the TIMMS scale centrepoint, but below the TIMMS Advanced and High International Benchmarks. In the reading assessment, Danish students reached excellent results above the PIRLS scale centrepoint and the PIRLS High International Benchmark. This result places Denmark among the top eleven high-achieving countries. Over time, Denmark has increased its performance in mathematics and science (between 2007 and 2011) as well as in reading (between 2006 and 2011).

At age 15, Danish students participate in the OECD Programme for International Student Assessment (PISA) in mathematics, reading and science. In the PISA 2012 assessment of mathematics, Danish students performed above the OECD average, but performance has steadily decreased since PISA 2003 across assessments. In reading and science, performance was around the OECD average in PISA 2012, and this has remained unchanged since PISA 2003. In problem-solving, Denmark also performed around the OECD average. Denmark has a comparatively small share of low-performing students, but also a relatively low proportion of top-performing students. The difference in performance between the 90th and the 10th percentiles is comparatively small. Across assessments, the share of top-performing students has remained stable in science, but decreased since 2003 in mathematics (from 15.9% to 10%) and reading (from 8.1% to 5.4%). The share of low performing students has been reduced in science and reading, but has increased in mathematics.

Concerns about the performance of disadvantaged students despite a number of features that promote equity

The Danish education system has a number of features that promote equity. This includes a high proportion of students enrolled in early childhood education and care, low levels of year repetition and comprehensive schooling until age 16. Nevertheless, like in other countries, students' socio-economic background has a strong impact on performance in Denmark. For example, in PISA 2012, 16.5% of the variance in mathematics performance in Denmark could be explained by socio-economic background (OECD average: 14.8%). Similar to the average across OECD countries, a more socio-economically advantaged student in Denmark scored 39 points higher in mathematics than a less-advantaged student – the equivalent of nearly one year of schooling. According to PISA 2012, education in Denmark is less equitable than in other Nordic countries where the strength of the relationship between socio-economic background and performance is less pronounced. In Denmark, furthermore, only a small proportion of students beats the odds and manages to overcome difficult socio-economic circumstances (4.9%, compared to an OECD average of 6.4%).

Similar to other Nordic countries with comprehensive schooling systems, performance between schools differs relatively little in Denmark. Between-school differences account for less than 15% of the OECD average total variation in performance in Denmark. By contrast, across OECD countries, 37% of the overall performance differences are observed between schools. The performance differences that do exist between schools are relatively closely related to socio-economic disparities between schools. Performance differences within schools are around the OECD average, but these within-school differences are more strongly related to students' socio-economic status: 65.8% of the total variation in performance is observed within schools (OECD average: 63.3%), and 10.5% of the performance difference can be explained by differences in students' socio-economic status (OECD average: 5.1%).

Students with an immigrant background are particularly at risk of underperformance in Denmark, and more so than in many other OECD countries. In the PISA 2012 mathematics assessment, students with an immigrant background scored an average of 40 points lower than their native peers after accounting for socio-economic background (OECD average: 21 points). Students with an immigrant background in Denmark were 2.43 times more likely to perform in the bottom quarter of the performance distribution than non-immigrant students (OECD average: 1.70 times more likely).

A wide-reaching reform of the Folkeskole and a number of other reforms

In June 2013, the Danish government introduced a reform of the *Folkeskole* based on a broad political agreement to improve public primary and lower secondary education. The reform has been implemented since the 2014/15 school year. As basis of this reform, the government set three national goals: i) the *Folkeskole* must challenge all students to reach their full potential; ii) the *Folkeskole* must lower the significance of social background on academic results; and iii) trust in the *Folkeskole* and student wellbeing must be enhanced through respect for professional knowledge and practice in the *Folkeskole*. These three goals were conceived to set a clear direction and a high level of ambition for the development of the *Folkeskole* and to provide a clear framework for a systematic and continuous evaluation of the reform. The three national goals are operationalised through four clear, simple and measurable targets that form the basis for dialogue and follow-up regarding the development of students' academic performance and wellbeing at all levels. To fulfil the three national goals, the 2014 *Folkeskole* reform focuses broadly on three main areas of improvement: a longer and varied school day with more and improved teaching and learning; better professional development of teachers, pedagogical staff and school principals; and few and clear objectives as well as a simplification of rules and regulations. Other recent changes include a reform of initial teacher education, the introduction of a new framework for the utilisation of teachers' working hours (Act no. 409), and a policy of inclusion of children with special educational needs in mainstream education.

Strengths and challenges

A school system based on trust, local autonomy and horizontal accountability

Resource allocation decisions are based on the principle of autonomy and devolved directly to schools. This provides good conditions for the effective management of resources and gives municipalities and schools the necessary flexibility to use funding to fit their own needs. At the same time, there are mechanisms to ensure that schools do not make resource management decisions in isolation and that schools are held accountable and supported in their resource management. Local stakeholders are involved in budget decisions via the work of the school board. Municipal education offices provide their school leaders with various degrees of help with the more technical aspects of school budgeting. And municipalities play an important role in the delivery of services and can help their schools achieve economies of scale.

Supervision and support are also available for municipalities. Biannual quality reports prepared by the municipalities provide a tool for goal-oriented management of local school systems, horizontal accountability and central supervision. In their preparation of the quality reports, municipalities can draw on data provided in a data warehouse run by the Ministry for Children, Education and Gender Equality. The central level monitors progress towards the goals of the *Folkeskole* reform and follows up with support in the case of underperformance of schools.

The central level has also been taking on an increasing role in collecting and disseminating knowledge of good practice. A newly created "resource centre for the *Folkeskole*" in the Ministry for Children, Education and Gender Equality plays a key role in overseeing a new body of learning consultants and for bringing together evidence from research and practical knowledge from the field. Local acceptance of this central role for knowledge management and support for municipalities and schools through the learning consultants indicates good levels of trust and co-operation between the central and local level in an effort towards making educational practice more evidence-based.

A high level of consensus regarding the need for change, clear national targets for the school system, and a range of tools to monitor goal achievement and reform implementation

The Danish school system has been successful in building consensus around the need for change and in implementing a wide-reaching reform of the *Folkeskole*. The 2014 *Folkeskole* reform has been supported by a broad partnership involving several ministries at the central level and the representative organisations of municipalities, school leaders, parents and students. Despite the challenges that all actors are confronted with in a period of major change following not only the 2014 *Folkeskole* reform, but also the introduction of a new framework for the utilisation of teachers' working hours, changes to initial teacher education, and the inclusion of children with special educational needs, there appears to be wide agreement among the main stakeholders that most of these changes have been necessary to improve the school system.

Denmark has put major emphasis on ensuring that reforms are introduced along with clear goals and targets. The most notable example of this goal-oriented approach is the 2014 *Folkeskole* reform with its three core objectives for student achievement, equity and wellbeing. Similarly, the policy for teacher competency development and specialisation includes clear targets that provide a common objective for actors at all levels. The inclusion process had also been introduced together with a quantitative target and was measured against this benchmark until 2015. This outcome-oriented approach to designing and implementing reforms represents a new way of educational steering in Denmark. It holds the potential of creating greater transparency and a sense of common purpose within a highly decentralised school system.

Furthermore, there is a clear intention to make sure that the central goals are translated into concrete targets at the local and school levels. Evaluation and reporting mechanisms have been introduced to monitor progress towards these goals at the central, municipal and school levels. Key monitoring instruments include the national student assessments, the calculation of "expected" exam grades for all students, the national wellbeing survey, and a survey to monitor the effect of inclusion on wellbeing. The use of the results from these measurements by actors at all levels is being facilitated by increasingly user friendly tools to access the data (e.g. through the development of a data warehouse by the Ministry for Children, Education and Gender Equality). In addition, stakeholder groups have developed their own initiatives to evaluate the impact of the reform on their members and to identify any potential negative effects.

Challenges for maintaining a focus on broad learning goals and scope for improving the monitoring of learning outcomes in terms of equity and excellence

Danish education pursues a broad set of learning goals for all-rounded student development. As emphasised in the *Folkeskole* Act, Danish students are to acquire not only subject-specific knowledge, but also cross-curricular learning goals, the Common Objectives provide a fairly broad curricular frame and the 2014 *Folkeskole* reform again emphasises the importance of cross-curricular learning and complex competencies. However, as in many other countries, there appears to be some lack of alignment in Denmark between these broad goals for student learning and relatively narrow measurements of learning. There seems to be a perception among teachers and school leaders that schools are held accountable primarily based on the results of students on the national tests, an impression that is reinforced by the fact that the main benchmarks for monitoring the *Folkeskole* reform are based primarily on the national test results. Too narrow a focus on discrete learning areas may negatively impact the learning process itself and there are some indications of this being the case in Denmark. Nevertheless, it also needs to be recognised that there are inevitable trade-offs between different goals in school systems, and that the focus on one goal may lead to a smaller focus on other goals.

While the Danish school system has a strong focus on supporting equity, the present monitoring system could pay more attention to monitoring the equity outcomes of the system. The 2014 *Folkeskole* reform sets the goal of lowering the significance of social background on academic results, but it does not include an explicit vision or targeted measures for particular student groups at risk of underperformance. The reform does not set specific benchmarks for reducing educational disadvantage for these groups and there appears to be little differential analysis on the impact of the reform on different student groups. In the monitoring of educational quality, student assessment results are not systematically disaggregated for student groups from different backgrounds. Information on student outcomes reported in the ministry's data warehouse is not systematically broken down for different student groups. As a result, system evaluation does not include measures to assess whether or not equity objectives are being achieved. Similarly, at the level of municipalities and schools, it does not seem to be common practice to analyse results separately for different groups at risk of underperformance.

A stronger focus on excellence might be needed as well considering Denmark's relatively low proportion of top performing students and concerns that highly talented students may not be receiving adequate levels of challenge and support to fully realise their academic potential. With a view of achieving the goal of the 2014 *Folkeskole* reform to "challenge all students to reach their full potential", and of moving more schools "from good to great", the Danish school system would benefit from a stronger focus on monitoring continuous improvement and excellence and on promoting excellence in school practices and outcomes.

High investment in education and explicit equalisation mechanisms in the funding system

Historically, Denmark has allocated a high level of resources to education. Expenditures per student have always been clearly above average expenditures in the OECD and the EU. During the last decade, there has been some variation in the level of total expenditures, but total expenditure has always been at a comparatively high level. Recent policies have acknowledged that better learning outcomes for all students are possible without using more of society's resources on education and it has been possible to implement reforms with clear and high ambitions for improved student performance without a major increase in overall spending.

The funding system of the *Folkeskole* entails several equalisation mechanisms. The national system reduces differences in financial capacity across municipalities. Within municipalities, the mechanisms for school funding typically take socio-economic characteristics of the student body at the school into account. Overall, these mechanisms yield school expenditures per student that are positively related to the share of students with a low socio-economic status at the school. The fact that students facing some kind of disadvantage need extra resources and follow-up is widely accepted. In addition, municipalities can apply to the central government for specific targeted funds for special needs education and students with special needs receive additional resources.

However, there is untapped potential for municipalities to learn from each other from their diversity of approaches on how funding formulas can best contribute to equalise student performance and there is little evaluation of how additional funding for schools with a disadvantaged intake is used and to what extent it contributes to improving learning opportunities for disadvantaged students.

Some concerns related to the decentralised funding model and a lack of transparency on the use of resources at the local and school levels

The national funding system implies that the resources available in each municipality to a large extent depend on national policies. The flexibility of municipalities to influence their own income is limited by the national steering of the income tax rate. At the same time, the central government's influence on expenditure on education is limited as education is only one of many local services the municipalities are responsible for and prioritise across. The present system relies to some extent on the regulation of inputs as illustrated by the maximum class size rule.

Although the 2014 *Folkeskole* reform has changed the focus towards learning outcomes, the measurement of learning outcomes still has to develop and there are at present no attempts to link expenditure decisions to realised outcomes. The decentralised approach to school funding makes it difficult to monitor how resources are being distributed and used at the local and school levels. Hence, there is little knowledge at the local and system level on how resources are used, whether resources are spent efficiently, and to which extent the different priorities set by the municipalities affect the quality and equity of learning outcomes.

Furthermore, expenditure per student clearly varies across municipalities. This stems from differences in socio-economic conditions between municipalities, but also from differences in the decided level of service or differences in productivity, which indicates a potential for efficiency savings in several municipalities.

Potential for efficiency and innovation through private schools, but risk of increasing segregation

Private schools have a long tradition in Denmark and constitute a significant and growing part of compulsory education. According to OECD statistics, the only European countries that have a larger share of students in private lower secondary schools than Denmark are the Netherlands and Spain and between 2008 and 2013, the share of students in private schools in Denmark increased from just under 17% to over 19%. From an efficiency point of view, the coexistence of public and private schools might be beneficial. Private schools might enhance competition and innovation. However, one potential challenge in education systems relying on an extensive offer of private schools is increased segregation of students. Students in private schools are typically from relatively well-educated families with relatively high income. Available data indicate that this is the case on average also for Denmark.

Understanding how schools are competing for students is important for judging whether competition contributes to improved performance of the school system. In Denmark, there are significant information gaps with respect to school quality across private and public schools. If parents care strongly about the peers of their children, this might work in the direction of segregation in the school system. Furthermore, competition between schools does not by itself eliminate an information problem. Research indicates that while choice policies increase the level of information of all parents, the quantity and quality of information seems to be highly correlated with parents' level of education. It is, therefore, important that relevant, fair and comparable information on available school choices is easily accessible for all parents.

A high degree of delayed enrolment in upper secondary education

About half a cohort in Denmark enrols in the voluntary Year 10 of the *Folkeskole*, thereby delaying their enrolment in upper secondary education (youth education). One of the arguments for the public support of Year 10 rests on the possibility for students to improve their qualifications up to a level necessary for upper secondary education. If this is the real motivation for the main part of the students enrolling in Year 10, it reflects that the *Folkeskole* is either not able to provide students with the necessary skills to succeed in upper secondary education, or that the requirements in upper secondary education are too high compared to the quality of the *Folkeskole*. In either of those cases, Year 10 can be seen as some form of year repetition. It is highly questionable whether so much of the year repetition in the last year of compulsory education contributes most effectively to student learning as remedial education is more efficient in early ages than towards the end of compulsory education.

An alternative explanation for the high enrolment in Year 10 is that it provides an opportunity for young people to enhance their wellbeing, to develop broader social and emotional skills and competencies, and to find out what to do later in life. In that case, Year 10 is a year without much learning pressure on core subjects for a majority of the students. While there can be benefits (e.g. in terms of social competencies and clarity about future career choices), it is questionable whether a year without clear learning intentions for core subjects in school contributes to student performance in upper secondary education and labour market attachment for young adults. An additional year in education delays entry into the labour market and there is also a risk that children at this critical age downplay education as a life-long investment.

New opportunities for schools to utilise their teachers' competencies and working time to meet local needs, but also challenges in adapting to the new arrangements

Considering the role of the quality of daily classroom instruction for student learning and achievement, the effective use of teachers and other staff and the quality of their instruction in classrooms is essential. The introduction of a new framework for the utilisation of teachers' working hours (Act no. 409) has increased schools' flexibility in using the time and competencies of their teachers. School leaders now have the flexibility to organise their staff around the learning needs of their school's students and the competencies, strengths, weaknesses, and learning needs of their staff. For instance, school leaders can assign less teaching time to their teachers in favour of having them work with other teachers in their area of expertise or they can use their new autonomy to support beginning teachers in their school. This holds the potential that schools can adjust the use of staff and their time to local needs if school leaders use their new autonomy well and if teachers adjust to the new realities. The introduction of longer school days as part of the 2014 *Folkeskole* reform provides some further potential opportunities for schools and students. Teachers are typically required to be present for a longer time at school which may help students learn and facilitate greater collaboration between teachers and other staff.

However, as can be expected with any reform, the report notes some concerns with the initial implementation of the new organisation of teachers' working time. While it was the government's intention that teachers should change their way of working, such a change in work organisation is likely to take more time. Whether the change of working time arrangements actually leads to a more efficient organisation of teachers' work and responsibilities will depend on the ability of teachers and school leaders to adapt to the new arrangement. For instance, if teachers do not have the right conditions to prepare and collaborate as they use more of their time on teaching, there could be risks to both quality and equity in schooling. Strategies to develop and allocate human resources effectively in schools are, then, crucial to ensure the successful implementation of the new working time arrangement.

Conditions in place to focus on goal-oriented teaching and learning, but challenges in moving from a teaching to a learning focus and in making better use of the available data

Denmark has put the conditions in place for school staff and leaders to focus on pedagogy which alters student learning outcomes. One of the most fundamental changes over the past 15 years has been the introduction of a set of Common Objectives, a set of binding learning progressions, achievement targets and curricular guidelines. The introduction of a set of national assessments and a student wellbeing survey constitute a further important step. A range of data are thus increasingly available at the municipal, school and individual student levels to use when setting goals and monitoring progress toward the achievement of these goals. The *Folkeskole* reform has strengthened this focus on outcomes further.

Evidence also points to a growing willingness at all levels of the system to dialogue around pedagogical needs and to build on collaborative work to improve student achievement and wellbeing. At the national level, this is evident in the establishment of a learning consultant corps, the development of a website of educational resources and initiatives to share research. In municipalities, there seems to be a genuine attempt to make school leader collaborative work the norm. And schools seem to be increasingly organised in a way that grants opportunities for collaboration, teamwork and peer learning. School leaders and teachers seem to recognise the value of having educators with expertise work directly with teachers to improve teaching practice.

The shift towards focussing on student learning is, however, still in its infancy in terms of implementation in classrooms, schools and municipalities across the country. Stakeholders reported that important progress had been made both in the availability of relevant data and the focus of professionals on the assessment of outcomes, but they also reported that further progress was needed in using this data effectively for accountability and improvement purposes. Teachers identified a need to come to an understanding of the new goal-oriented way of working with the curriculum and how it changes how they teach and assess students. Many municipalities are still reluctant to follow up on school performance and goal attainment despite the fact that school performance is now more transparent. And school leaders tend to use more informal leadership strategies rather than evaluation, documentation and other forms of data. Embedding a learning focus in practice is a major cultural shift that needs to be implemented through a range of changes with regards to initial teacher education, professional development, performance management and leadership.

Several aspects of teacher professionalism still at the early stages of development and scope to further strengthen pedagogical leadership

Considering the decentralised nature of education in Denmark, not all municipalities and schools may provide their teachers with the support they need to develop their practice. There does not appear to be a shared understanding of the standards of teacher practice and there is little discussion regarding excellent teaching within schools, municipalities or at the central level. There is no formal and systematic induction to provide new teachers with the additional support they may need for coping in the early years of their career. The availability of induction processes depends on local contexts and, while some municipalities and schools pay special attention to new teachers, such practices appear to be as yet the exception rather than the norm. There is neither a standard certification of new teachers that is based on a specific set of criteria, nor a formal appraisal of a teacher's readiness to assume a teaching role or a probationary period for newly qualified teachers. And while there are teacher appraisal practices at a local level, performance appraisal of practicing teachers is not mandatory. Occasionally, municipalities require their school leaders to appraise their teaching staff, but no formal appraisal process appears to be occurring systematically. If teacher appraisal takes place, it does not always seem to involve classroom observations, to have strong links to professional development, or to have substantial impact on teaching practices. As a result, not all teachers receive feedback on how to improve. The underperformance of a teacher may not be detected and, therefore, be addressed, to the detriment of students.

Also the management of the school leadership profession reveals a number of challenges. There is no common understanding of effective leadership that could guide the management and development of the profession. This leads to a lack of clarity among school leaders in terms of expectations and on how to improve their leadership practice. School leaders are not required to undertake specific training for their function, even if they may participate in such training. And while there are practices of school leader performance management at the level of municipalities, practices vary and not all school leaders benefit from sufficient support and feedback. There seems to be a great deal of focus on pedagogical leadership as well as a desire on the part of school leaders to carry out this work, but school leaders feel they are lacking training and experience to work in this manner. The lack of strong school leadership raises concerns regarding the quality of school improvement efforts overall and specifically how effective leaders are at developing the competency of the teaching staff in individual schools. The lack of strong leadership is also of concern considering the significant changes the Danish education system is undergoing.

Policy recommendations

Continue to pay attention to using resources efficiently

Developments in the *Folkeskole* over the last years have the clear potential to contribute to improved efficiency and effectiveness of the Danish school system. The 2014 *Folkeskole* reform aims to further strengthen the focus on learning environments and student performance. There has been a reduction in expenditure per student up to the *Folkeskole* reform and the reform has increased the school day of students without a symmetric increase in the number of teachers. The introduction of a new framework for the utilisation of teachers' working time (Act no. 409) has created greater flexibility for schools to use the time and competencies of their teachers. Whether the recent changes lead to greater efficiency and effectiveness will, however, depend on the ability of all actors in the system to use resources efficiently and to adapt to the changes the recent reforms imply. It will, therefore, be key to ensure that all actors continue to work intensively on using resources most effectively to improve student learning in relation to national goals. Knowledge-sharing across schools and municipalities will be particularly important in this regard. There is, for example, a lot of potential for municipalities to learn from each other regarding the effective design of school funding formulas to create synergies and to avoid double efforts. LGDK and the association of municipal administrators responsible for culture, day care and education (*Børne- og Kulturchefforeningen* [BKF]) have the potential to play a key role here. Considering changes to teachers' working conditions, strategies to develop and allocate human resources effectively in schools are crucial to ensure the success of the reform.

Strengthen public reporting about the performance of the system and analyse the effectiveness of resource use in municipalities and schools

To move the school system towards excellence while further narrowing equity gaps requires strong public consensus regarding fiscal effort and inclusiveness. The Ministry for Children, Education and Gender Equality has already undertaken considerable steps to make data from its central monitoring system available for use by different stakeholders, and municipalities and schools in particular. To build and sustain the overall consensus for investments in the *Folkeskole*, Denmark should consider strengthening its reporting about the performance of the school system also to the public at large at all levels of the system. Data on inputs and outcomes should be easily publicly available. Denmark could develop a system-wide reporting framework that brings a broader range of financial indicators and outcome indicators together. The reporting framework could form the basis for the periodic publication of key national analytical reports in addition to the digital publication of the data (e.g. in the ministry's data warehouse). The system of the Ministry of Social Affairs and the Interior to monitor municipal service performance could be extended to include information on different outcomes of the school system.

Municipalities and schools should make efforts to bring together and analyse data on the use of resources and outcomes. LGDK should pursue its plans to develop the municipalities' common business management system (FLIS) into a data hub that brings together information on resources and outcomes. Individual municipalities should be encouraged to consider both financial and pedagogical dimensions in their biannual quality reports and to use data with a greater focus on the effective use of resources to meet the goals of the education system and the *Folkeskole* reform. At the school level, a school-level reporting framework could be introduced that enables schools to examine the fiscal impact of their resource and curriculum decisions and that creates greater transparency about resource use decisions in schools. Schools should be encouraged by their municipalities to consider the impact of their resource use decisions as part of their self-evaluations.

Consider reducing enrolment in Year 10

The OECD review team formed the impression that the goals of Year 10 are not clearly defined and that the large enrolment rate in Year 10 only weakly contributes to the educational outcomes in Denmark, even if there may other benefits (e.g. social and emotional skills). The review team suggests that public support for Year 10 should be more focused on those in real need to increase their skills. The obligation for municipalities to provide Year 10 to all students, including students from advantaged socio-economic backgrounds to spend a "leisure time" year, should be reconsidered. The target group for Year 10 could be better defined (e.g. it could be an offer targeted at students achieving below a specific skill level as measured by the final school results in Year 9) and students' right to enrolment could be linked to certain criteria. It appears highly inefficient that a large share of 16-17 year-old youth spend an additional year of education with low focus on improving basic or vocational skills. It should also be considered to implement stricter criteria in order for private schools to receive public financial support for Year 10 education.

For some students it seems necessary to improve their skills before they are ready to enrol in upper secondary education. For these students, Year 10 takes the form of year repetition. Considering that the empirical evidence clearly suggests that remedial education is more efficient the earlier it is introduced for students, the enhanced provision of targeted remedial education at an earlier stage in the *Folkeskole* should be a priority. The 2014 *Folkeskole* reform has the clear goal of improving the skills of students. This should reduce the need for Year 10 education as a means for skill upgrading, and contribute to more students transferring directly from the *Folkeskole* to upper secondary education. Denmark should consider establishing a national goal to gradually decrease enrolment in Year 10.

Ensure that school competition can happen with regard to school quality rather than student composition

Information on school performance and school quality seems necessary in order for the relatively large share of private schools in Denmark to contribute to improved performance of the school system. For example, if parents choose schools based on the degree to which students perform relative to the national goals, there can be competition based on school quality. Without information on school quality, school choice will be based on other factors.

If school choice is based primarily on peer composition in schools, the large degree of private schools will contribute to school segregation. In addition, parents are likely to be interested in a variety of other factors at schools, such as cultural and sport activities.

In the present system, there is a risk that schools compete along these dimensions and that parents put larger weights on such issues than they ideally would prefer, simply because they have very limited information on the learning environment and school quality. In this context, developing a shared vision of school quality, refining both external and internal evaluation of school quality and performance and improving parents' access to relevant information will be important to ensuring that the large share of private schools can be used more strategically to improve performance.

Equity concerns in the use of information about school quality also need to be taken into account. In most countries, upper middle-class and middle-class families are those most aware of how to use the education system for their own interest and benefit and those more likely to use information about school achievement to place their child in the best performing schools.

Give attention to all learning goals in the evaluation and assessment framework

A key challenge in monitoring the quality and progress of education systems is to develop indicators and measures of system performance that permit a good understanding of how well the system is achieving its objectives. While national goals are typically comprehensive and broad, monitoring systems may be rather limited in the information they can offer. For monitoring to be meaningful, it must be well-aligned to the type of learning that is valued. Denmark should, therefore, consider introducing broader national measures of student learning to monitor the school system's progress in stimulating students to excellence in higher-order thinking and in the development of complex competencies. System-level attention to broader learning goals can also help communicate to municipalities and schools a shared focus on the broader aims of the *Folkeskole*.

A great deal of assessment research in recent years has focused on "authentic" forms of assessment that would be able to capture the type of learning that is valued in today's societies. These alternative forms of assessment are more effective at capturing more complex achievements, but they are also more costly to implement on a large scale than closed-ended test formats. One option for Denmark would, therefore, be to consider introducing a light monitoring sample survey to supplement the current national monitoring system with information on broader competency goals. Such a sample survey can provide stable trend information and monitor a broader range of student knowledge and skills at a lower cost compared to a full cohort test. In addition, the central level should continue communicating to schools the importance of supplementing standardised national assessment tools with a range of other assessments to obtain relevant information on student learning across the curriculum and to use this information to design differentiated teaching strategies. Denmark should continue to develop teachers' assessment capacities and support professional learning communities that work with assessment data in non-threatening ways.

Pay special attention to monitoring the learning outcomes of students at risk of underperformance and further support schools in striving towards excellence

Denmark should give more prominence to monitoring inequities in learning outcomes between specific student groups. Attention to equity issues when monitoring results and goal achievement at the system level can inform policies and help target support more effectively. For example, education system targets could pay attention to the achievement of different student groups and it would be important to review how more targeted indicators for the achievement of equity goals could be included in the monitoring strategy for the *Folkeskole* reform. Overall, the value of annual monitoring reports could be further enhanced by regularly reporting information on student learning outcomes for underperforming groups of students. This would allow tracking the education system's progress in responding to the needs of diverse groups. National research into how student background characteristics and school contextual characteristics are associated with student performance can identify the type of information that is most pertinent to collect systematically.

Ensuring that key performance indicators in the ministry's data warehouse are systematically disaggregated for different groups at risk of underperformance would be helpful for monitoring equity goals at all levels of the system, including municipalities and schools. Feeding such disaggregated information back to municipalities and schools should also enhance their focus on equity outcomes and strategies in their own self-evaluations and development and improvement planning. In addition, given Denmark's high investment in schools enrolling students from socio-economically disadvantaged backgrounds and students with special educational needs, it would be important to monitor specifically how such funding is used at the school level and how this translates into performance for these students. Municipalities should collect data, track resources spent on different student groups and monitor how these resources support teaching and learning for students at risk of underperformance. School boards should discuss the use of resources and the achievement levels for different student groups with their school management. The central level could also commission thematic studies on the use of resources for equity and inclusion in Danish schools.

As part of the 2014 *Folkeskole* reform, the Danish government aims to challenge all students to reach their full potential and to increase the number of high-performing students from year to year. A policy focused on achieving these ends must set high standards for achievement. Using differentiated approaches to teaching, assessment and evaluation can help to provide the right level of support and challenge to individual students, professionals and schools. At the level of individual students, excellence could be supported through further attention to monitoring student progress and providing differentiated feedback for improvement. At the level of professionals and schools, Denmark could consider introducing differentiated supervision mechanisms. This would involve maintaining close attention to helping underperforming schools improve, but at the same time focussing on schools that are already achieving average or good results so as to raise ambitions and move towards excellence. Enhancing school evaluation practice would be key to continuously challenge all schools to improve. The national level could play a stronger role in stimulating more effective self-evaluation at the school and local level and establish and manage a national sample programme of external reviews of schools, possibly in partnership with LGDK and individual municipalities across Denmark.

Promote the better use of data at all levels of the system

Information can only lead to school improvement if it is relevant, available in adequate quantity, and properly interpreted. As the Danish school system is highly decentralised and relies on resource management and evaluation competencies of all its agents, it is of key importance to increase the capacity at all levels to ensure the effective use of available information, particularly in schools and municipalities. Such capacity building must respond to the diverse needs of different stakeholders and consider equity issues inherent in the use of data and information. Some municipalities and schools may be more likely than others to fully use the available data.

For municipal staff, this means developing the capacity to understand, interpret and make decisions based on evaluation and assessment data collected from schools and drawn from the data warehouse together with their own data on resource inputs. Municipalities should be able to use school reporting data as a basis for engaging in meaningful discussions with their schools. This capacity needs to be sustained over time and ongoing resources should be set apart to make sure municipalities can play their supervision role to its full extent. For school principals and teachers, it means developing the capacity to collect and report data on school budgets and student outcomes to their school community and their municipality in effective ways. School leaders need to develop an inquiry habit of mind, become data literate and be able to create a culture of inquiry. Exemplars of good practice in data interpretation, analysis, reporting and communication should be provided nationally to schools and municipalities to make sure some minimum requirements are met and municipalities should support their schools and school leaders in using the available data. However, school professionals need to develop not only the capacity to use, interpret and follow up on results obtained from nationally provided evaluation and assessment tools, but also to develop valid and reliable tools which meet their own specific local needs.

National expertise could also be further developed. It has become increasingly important to invest in higher education and research to increase the number of experts capable to respond to future needs and to offer the best advice available from scientific knowledge and scholarly work. Both the Ministry for Children, Education and Gender Equality and LGDK have an important role to play in the management and dissemination of knowledge and data required to analyse the relationship between inputs and outputs and the causal links between interventions and outcomes. They can facilitate both horizontal and vertical connections within the system to increase the coherence of the evaluation and assessment framework and to properly align efforts and resources on priorities. The ministry's initiatives to establish a learning consultant corps and to develop a data warehouse are both promising in encouraging and facilitating the use of data. Both initiatives should be sustained and further developed.

Develop a vision for teacher professionalism and support effective teaching through systematic formal and informal teacher feedback and appraisal

Many changes to the school system in Denmark have left teachers struggling with what it means to be an excellent teacher. To support teachers, school leaders and municipal leaders in understanding and supporting the implementation of these changes, Denmark should consider developing a national teacher profile, vision or standards of practice. Such a national teacher profile would communicate the new expectations regarding teacher practice putting the conditions in place for many of the changes of the 2014 *Folkeskole* reform. Teacher standards would establish a foundation for teachers to explore their practice and for schools to develop their improvement initiatives. A national teacher profile would help to provide a framework to guide the development of the profession as whole. In a decentralised system like Denmark, a national teacher profile could be particularly relevant to promote a common vision and shared expectations.

The effective appraisal of teaching is central to the continuous improvement of schools. It is, therefore, also recommended that Denmark strengthen formal teacher performance appraisal focused on the continuous improvement of teaching practice. Formal teacher appraisal would serve both as a form of developmental feedback for teachers and as a mechanism for feedback for schools, municipalities and potentially the Ministry for Children, Education and Gender Equality. Developmental appraisal could be a low-key and low-cost process that is organised internally in schools. To guarantee a systematic application of developmental evaluation across Danish schools, it would, however, be important to undertake the external validation of the respective school processes. Municipalities have a key role to play here. The development of a national sample programme of external reviews of schools through the Ministry for Children, Education and Gender Equality could be a further instrument of external validation. An alternative approach entails the introduction of stronger national parameters and regulations that suggest a range of tools and guidelines for implementation of formal teacher appraisal. Denmark should, furthermore, consider ways to strengthen informal feedback to teachers to improve their practice. This very much depends on the extent to which schools are successful in establishing a culture of learning and continuous improvement. Collaboration has a key role to play as most collaborative teacher activities include an element of feedback to teachers and quite often teacher self-assessment of their practice.

Develop the school leadership profession and provide support for school principals and their deputies

Denmark should pay particular attention to the development and management of its school leadership profession, from recruitment and initial training to professional development and performance management. This includes both the Ministry for Children, Education and Gender Equality and the individual municipalities as the employers of school leaders. Denmark's school leader association should be thoroughly involved in the process of developing the profession.

The first step in the further development of the profession should be the creation of a framework to guide the work of school leaders (both formal school leaders and informal teacher leaders). Considering the importance of pedagogical leadership for teaching and learning, the framework should have a clear focus on competencies related to this leadership style, but also recognise that successful school leadership is always context-dependent. Once developed, a Danish leadership framework could serve as a basis for continued collaboration among school leaders, as a reference point for school leadership consultants, as a catalyst for the development of personal learning objectives with a learning plan for individual school leaders and a basis for reflection and introspection on the part of individual school leaders. Denmark should also consider developing a more strategic approach to the training of school leaders that ideally represents a continuum and is available at and targeted to the different stages of a school leaders' career. Opportunities for collaboration, coaching and mentoring between school leaders can also provide useful support and enable school leaders to gain new expertise.

The wide range of responsibilities that school leaders are often expected to fulfil bears a risk of placing too high expectation on school leaders. School leaders should, therefore, have the support they need from their employer as well as distributed leadership structures. Further developing school leader performance management in municipalities is another area for possible policy development.

Chapter 1

School education in Denmark

This chapter presents an overview of the political, economic, social and demographic context in Denmark. It also provides a brief description of the Danish school system for international readers. It presents evidence on the quality and equity of the Danish school system and describes current policy priorities and recent developments, including the 2014 reform of the Folkeskole, the introduction of a new framework for the utilisation of teachers' working time, and the policy of inclusion of children with special educational needs in the regular school system.

The statistical data for Israel are supplied by and under the responsibility of the relevant Israeli authorities. The use of such data by the OECD is without prejudice to the status of the Golan Heights, East Jerusalem and Israeli settlements in the West Bank under the terms of international law.

Context

Geography and population

Denmark – not counting the self-governing Faroe Islands and Greenland – covers about 43 000 km^2 (that is ten times smaller than Sweden and eight times smaller than Germany) and consists of the Jutland Peninsula and 391 islands, most notably Zealand (*Sjælland*), Funen (*Fyn*), Lolland-Falster and Bornholm. The Jutland Peninsula (including *Vendsyssel-Thy*) accounts for 69% of Denmark's total area (Statistics Denmark, 2015a).

In January 2015, the country had a population of 5.7 million people with over one million living in the capital Copenhagen and just over half a million living in the three other major cities Aarhus (261 570), Odense (173 814) and Aalborg (110 495). Population density in Denmark is relatively high compared to other European countries with 131 persons per km^2. In the other Nordic countries, population density is considerably lower, at 17 persons per km^2 in Norway, 18 persons per km^2 in Finland and 24 persons per km^2 in Sweden (Eurostat, 2016b; Statistics Denmark, 2015a).

Since 1970, Denmark has seen a slow, but steady increase in the size of the population as the number of births has been higher than the number of deaths and the number of immigrants has been higher than the number of emigrants (population growth rate of 0.4% in 2007 and in 2012, OECD, 2015a) (Statistics Denmark, 2015a). While the Danish population has been growing in size, it has also been ageing. Between 2004 and 2014, the share of the elderly population aged 65 or above increased from 15.0% to 18.2%, while the share of young people aged less than 15 decreased from 18.8% to 17.4% in the same period (OECD, 2015a; OECD, 2015c). Almost one in four Danes is now over 60, while this was only the case for one in five in 2000 (Statistics Denmark, 2015a).

Concerning the school-age population, Denmark has had a slightly different trend than other EU or OECD countries since 1990, but today shares the experience of a declining school-age population. As can be seen from Figure 1.1, the number of school-age children has fluctuated more in Denmark than across the OECD and EU27 area.

Between the early and the mid-1990s, the number of children aged 6-16 (the age bracket for compulsory education in primary and lower secondary education) declined sharply, but from the mid-1990s until 2005 it increased again steeply and above 1990 levels (see Figure 1.2). Since then, the school-age population has again been slowly decreasing and outside the capital area of Copenhagen only a few municipalities have experienced growth in the number of school-aged children over the last years. Between 2008 and 2014, the number of 6-16 year-olds dropped by 4.5%, on average across municipalities, and in some municipalities by close to 30% (Statistics Denmark, 2016a, 2016b; Houlberg et al., 2016). According to demographic forecasts, this development is likely to continue in the years to come, even if the trend may reverse again in the long run as the number of 0-4 year-olds has started to grow again (see Figure 1.1) (OECD, n.d.). These demographic changes continuously challenge educational planning to adjust school capacities to the changing number of students.

Figure 1.1. **Trend in school-age population: Denmark, EU27, OECD**

1990 = 100

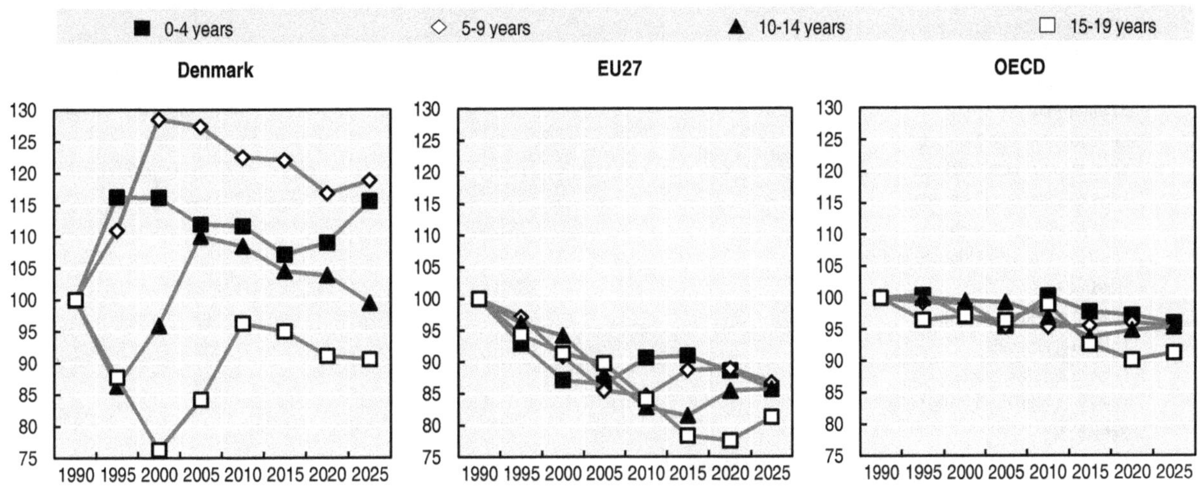

Source: OECD (n.d.), *Historical Population Data and Projections* (1950-2050), OECD statistical database, *http://stats.oecd.org.*

Figure 1.2. **Trend in school-age population in the *Folkeskole*, 6-16 year-olds**

1990 = 100

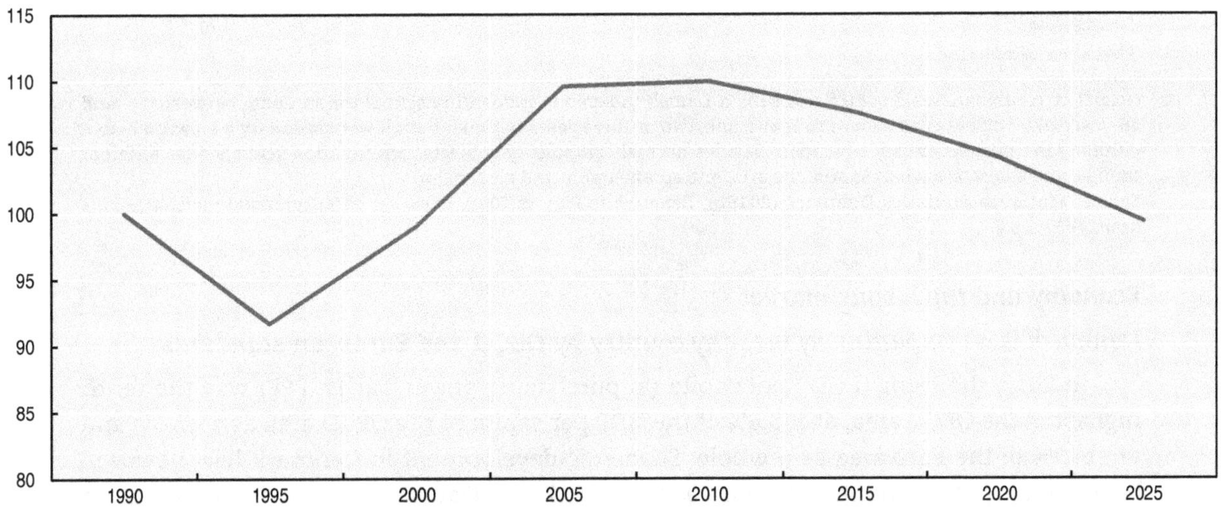

Source: Statistics Denmark (2016a), StatBank Denmark FOLK2: Population 1 January by Sex, Age, Ancestry, Country of Origin and Citizenship, *www.statbank.dk/statbank5a/SelectVarVal/Define.asp?MainTable=FOLK2&PLanguage=1&PXSId=0&wsid=cftree*; Statistics Denmark (2016b), StatBank Denmark FRDK115: Population Projections 2015 for the Country by Ancestry, Sex and Age, *www.statbank.dk/statbank5a/SelectVarVal/Define.asp?MainTable=FRDK115&PLanguage=1&PXSId=0&wsid=cftree.*

In 2014, immigrants and their descendants made up 11.6% of the total Danish population. The largest group originated from Turkey, followed by Poland, Germany and Iraq. The level of immigration is, however, relatively low when compared to countries such as neighbouring Germany and Sweden (Statistics Denmark, 2015a). Students with an immigrant background similarly made up 10.7% of all students in public primary and lower secondary education (Statistics Denmark, 2016c).

Table 1.1 provides some statistics about the average 15-year-old in Denmark. The year 2000 comprises 69 000 boys and girls, with boys slightly outnumbering girls.

Table 1.1. **The average Danish 15-year-old in 2015**

Origin (%)	
Immigrants	3
Descendants	8
Danish origin	89
Siblings (%)	
Lives together with 0 siblings	19
Lives together with 1 siblings	49
Lives together with 2 siblings	25
Lives together with 3 siblings	6
Lives together with 4 siblings and over	2
Housing (%)	
Lives in one-family houses	67
Lives in apartments	20
Lives in terraced houses	12
Lives with both mother and father	72
School (%)	
Goes to public primary and lower secondary school (*Folkeskole*)	72
Goes to private school	16
Goes to continuation school	11
Leisure (%)	
Plays computer games daily	59
Does sports	23
Never does sports	9
Streams music	70
Plays a musical instrument	26

Note: The continuation school (*Efterskole*) is a Danish independent boarding school for students between 14- and 18-years-old. Students can choose to spend one, two or three years to finish their lower secondary education before enrolling in upper secondary education. Besides normal compulsory subjects, continuation schools offer different profiles and subjects, such as sports, the arts, entrepreneurship and citizenship.
Source: Statistics Statistics Denmark (2015b), *Denmark in Figures 2015*, *www.dst.dk/pukora/epub/upload/19006/denmark2015.pdf*.

Economy and the labour market

Denmark is a comparatively wealthy country by OECD and European standards

In 2012, the Danish GDP per capita (at purchasing power parity, PPP) was the tenth highest in the OECD area, at 115.6% of the GDP per capita of the OECD area as a whole and at 116.1% of the Euro area as a whole. Economic development in Denmark has, however, been somewhat stagnant. Between 2002 and 2012, the Danish economy increased at an average growth rate of only 0.36%, compared to 1.11% in the Euro area and 1.72% in the OECD group of countries. Denmark was one of only five countries with an annual growth rate below 1% within the OECD. The financial and economic crisis has not left Denmark untouched and GPD per capita decreased by 0.8% in 2008 and by a historic 5.7% in 2009 (OECD, 2014a), but after five years of slow recovery, the Danish economy seems to be picking up: GDP grew by 1.8% in 2015 and growth is expected to remain at just under 2% in 2016 and 2017, supported by investment and a pick-up in world trade (OECD, 2015f).

The Danish labour market has not yet fully recovered from the financial and economic crisis that started in 2008

The employment rate for Denmark for the population aged 15 and over fell from 62.5% in the 4th quarter of 2007 to 59.1% in the 4th quarter of 2014, and is projected to increase only slightly to 59.8% by the 4th quarter of 2016. The current job gap – that is the difference in the share of the population aged 15 years and over that is currently employed with pre-crisis employment levels – is still 3.3 percentage points and Denmark has yet to regain its pre-crisis employment rate (OECD average: 1.4 percentage points, EU15 average: 2.5 percentage points). This post-crisis reduction in employment is largely related to an increase in unemployment, from 3.6% in the 4th quarter of 2007 to 6.3% in the 4th quarter of 2014. However, the unemployment rate is still lower than the OECD and the EU15 averages (OECD average: 5.5% in 4th quarter 2007 and 7.1% in 4th quarter 2014; EU15 average: 7.3% in 4th quarter 2007 and 11.4% in 4th quarter 2014). Youth unemployment peaked at over 14% in the years following the financial and economic crisis, but has since fallen again (11.2% in 4th quarter 2014). However, youth unemployment remains higher than before the crisis (6.8% in 4th quarter 2007), even if it is still lower than the OECD and EU28 averages (14.7% and 21.5% respectively, in 4th quarter 2014). The percentage of young people aged 15-29 who are neither employed nor in education or training – the so-called NEET rate – has increased since 2007, but remains comparatively low (OECD, 2015g). In 2014, 11.5% were NEET in Denmark, compared to 15.8% on average across OECD countries (OECD, 2015c).

Inequality and poverty

As illustrated in Figure 1.3, Denmark has the lowest level of inequality in disposable income among OECD countries for which data are available. The Gini coefficient, a common measure of income inequality that scores 0 when everybody has identical incomes and 1 when all the income goes to only one person, stands at 0.249. This compares to 0.315 on average across OECD countries. The gap between the average income of the richest and the poorest 10% of the Danish population is also comparatively low. The richest 10% earn about 5 times more than the poorest 10%, compared to almost ten times more on average across OECD countries. Nevertheless, as in many other countries, income

Figure 1.3. **Income inequality across OECD countries and emerging economies (Gini coefficient), 2013 or latest available year**

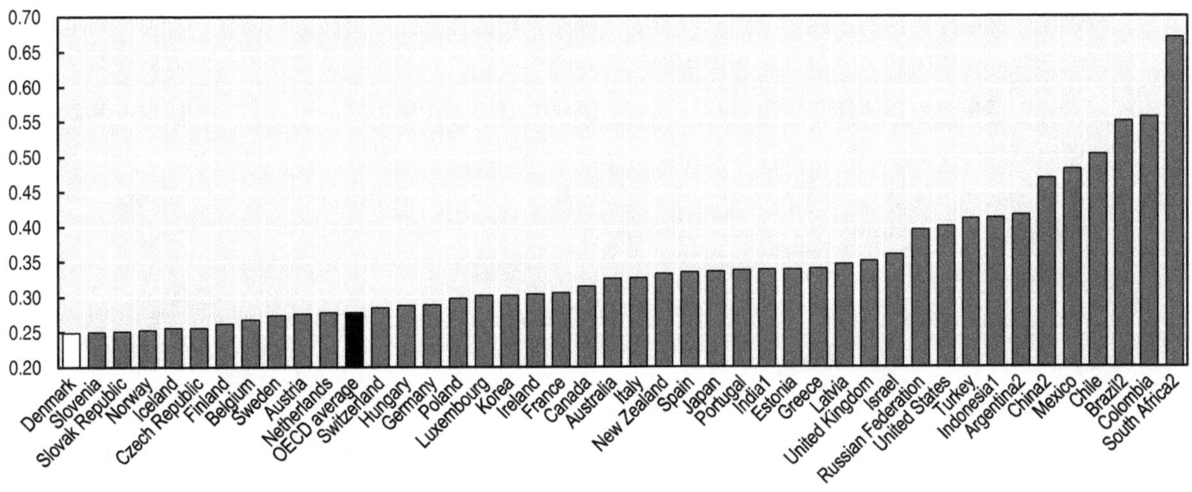

1. Secondary data sources – Consumption based.
2. Secondary data sources – Income based.

Note: Data refer to 2014 for China, 2013 for Finland, Hungary, India, Israel, the Netherlands and the United States, 2011 for Brazil, Canada, Chile and Turkey, 2010 for Indonesia, 2009 for Japan, and 2012 for the other countries. Gini coefficients are based on equivalised incomes for OECD countries, Colombia, Latvia and the Russian Federation, per capita incomes for Argentina, Brazil, China and South Africa, and per capita consumption for India and Indonesia. Income-based and consumption based data are from secondary data sources, are not strictly comparable and should be interpreted with caution.

Source: OECD (2015e), *In It Together: Why Less Inequality Benefits All, http://dx.doi.org/10.1787/9789264235120-en.*

inequality has been on the rise in Denmark. Between 2007 and 2011, incomes in real terms at the top increased while incomes at the bottom fell (OECD, 2015e).

Poverty in Denmark is also very low. Only about 1 in 20 people in Denmark is affected by poverty defined as the share of people living with less than half the median income in their country annually (OECD average: about one in ten people). The financial and economic crisis did not affect poverty in Denmark as it did in other countries. When measured in terms of "anchored" poverty, i.e. when fixing the real low income benchmark to pre-crisis levels, the poverty rate actually decreased by 0.4 percentage points between 2007 and 2012 (OECD, 2015e). Only a small proportion of Danish children (6.3%) fall below the country's relative poverty line, but those who do, fall almost 30% below that line, much more than in many other countries (UNICEF Office of Research, 2013).

Governance and administration

The Local Government Reform of 2007

Denmark reorganised its public sector through a Local Government Reform in 2007. This reform reduced the number of municipalities from 271 to 98 and abolished the 14 counties replacing them with five regions (see Annex 1.1). Except for some smaller islands, most of the 98 municipalities have a minimum size of 20 000 inhabitants. The reform also redistributed responsibilities from former counties to municipalities, leaving the municipalities responsible for most welfare tasks, and reduced the number of levels of taxation from three to two as regions were not granted the authority to levy taxes. Regional revenues consist of block grants and activity-based funding from the central government and the municipalities. In addition, to ensure that the local government reform would not result in changes in the distribution of the cost burden between the municipalities, the grant and equalisation system was reformed to take into account the new distribution of tasks (Blöchliger and Vammalle, 2012) (see Danish Ministry for Economic Affairs and the Interior, 2014, for further details on governance). The reform sought to primarily improve the quality of municipal services, but also to address efficiency concerns (e.g. by creating economies of scale). Many of the 271 municipalities that existed prior to 2007 were considered too small to provide effective local services, in particular in the health sector.

Since the local government reform, municipal responsibilities include all of the following:

- social services
- childcare and compulsory education, including special needs education and special pedagogical assistance for small children
- special needs education for adults
- preventive health care and rehabilitation and long-term care for the elderly
- nature and environmental planning
- local business services and promotion of tourism
- participation in regional transport companies and maintenance of the local road network
- libraries, schools of music, local sports and cultural facilities
- and the responsibility for employment, shared with the central government.

The new regions took over the responsibility for health care from the counties, including hospitals and public health insurance covering general practitioners and specialists. In addition, the regions are responsible for regional development and the operation of highly specialised social services (e.g. special needs education for children with functional physical and mental impairments, and secure institutions for juvenile offenders).

The central government was given a clearer role in overseeing efficiency in the provision of municipal and regional services. Employment services became a shared responsibility between the central government and the municipalities. Tax collection was transferred to the central government as was part of collective transport and road maintenance. The central government assumed a stronger role in nature and environmental planning. Finally, responsibility for culture was transferred to the central government (in practice, subsidising a number of private cultural institutions of national character) (Blöchliger and Vammalle, 2012; Houlberg et al., 2016).

Regarding responsibilities for education, the local government reform transferred the responsibility for general upper secondary education from the counties to the central state. As vocational education was already a state task, the central state has been responsible for all upper secondary education since the reform. Upper secondary schools generally have the status of self-governing institutions. The reform allocated full responsibility for both mainstream and special needs compulsory education to the municipalities to facilitate a more effective use of resources (Houlberg et al., 2016). Municipalities that do not have sufficient capacity to offer special needs education rely on special needs education organised through the regions.

Multi-party politics

Danish national governments are often characterised by minority administrations that rely on the informal help of one or more supporting parties. This means that Danish politics is largely based on consensus with parties often striving for broad coalitions on important issues and decisions. Since 1909, no single party has held a majority in parliament.

Political authority in the municipalities lies with the municipal council consisting of 9 to 31 counsellors. The counsellors are elected for a fixed four-year term on the basis of a proportional voting system. The head of the council is the mayor, who is elected by and among the local counsellors (Houlberg et al., 2016; Statistics Denmark, 2015b).

Public finances

A fiscally highly decentralised country

In 2011, the sub-central share of total public expenditure amounted to 62.8%, compared to 31% on average across OECD countries. The sub-central share of revenues was 28.9% (OECD average: 15%) (see Figure 1.4) (OECD, 2013a). The financial framework on the overall tax and expenditure levels for all local authorities is decided annually between the Ministry of Finance and Local Government Denmark (KL/LGDK), the association of Danish municipalities. For 2014, the frame for municipal service expenditures was agreed to be DKK 230.5 billion. Annual agreements do not set parameters for individual municipalities, but LGDK co-ordinates the budgeting processes of individual municipalities to keep the collective budget of all municipalities within the agreed limit.

Local expenditures by municipalities are mainly financed through local taxes and general grants from the central government (71% and 26% respectively, of the total municipal revenues in 2014). General grants are distributed to individual municipalities through the Ministry of Social Affairs and the Interior according to an equalisation mechanism to adjust for socio-economic differences between municipalities (e.g. considering differences in tax

Figure 1.4. **Fiscal decentralisation in OECD countries**

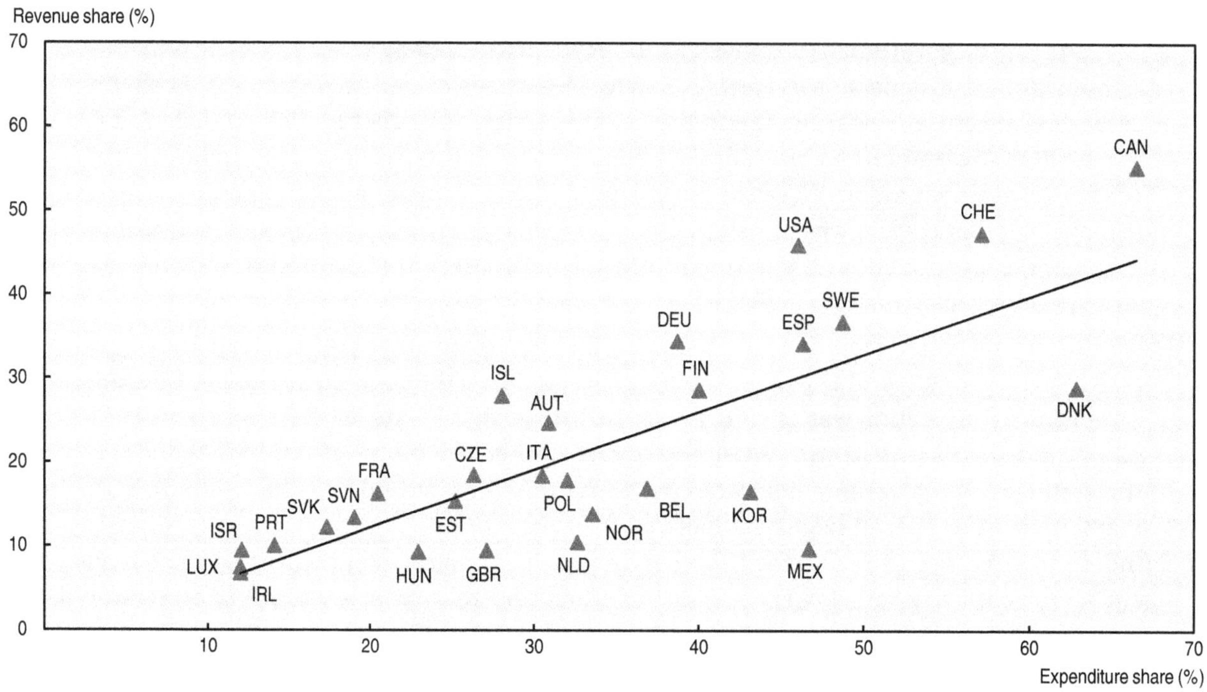

Source: OECD (2013a), *Fiscal Federalism 2014: Making Decentralisation Work*, *http://dx.doi.org/10.1787/9789264204577-en*.

base and demography). Within the overall framework of national legislation and the annual financial agreement, municipalities are autonomous to decide about the allocation of resources between different public services according to their needs (see Country Background Report for further details, and Chapter 2 for an analysis of school funding) (Houlberg et al., 2016).

Public finances under pressure

Like in many other countries, increasing social expenditures and decreasing tax revenues as a result of the financial and economic crisis have put pressure on public finances in Denmark, leading to a public budget deficit between 2009 and 2013. However, the public deficit remained one of the lowest among European countries and, in 2014, the deficit turned into a surplus again. Only three other EU countries recorded a budget surplus in that year, Germany, Estonia and Luxembourg. A surplus or a deficit on public finances impacts the level of public debt and, therefore, a country's future scope for fiscal policy and economic development. In 2014, public debt in Denmark amounted to 45.2% of GDP, compared to 86.8% in the EU28 and 91.9% in the Euro zone. Denmark, therefore, complied with the criteria of the European Economic and Monetary Union that prescribe that the public deficit of EU member countries must not exceed 3% and that public debt must not exceed 60% of GDP (Eurostat, 2016a).

In 2012, the Danish parliament introduced multi-annual expenditure ceilings for the central government, municipalities and regions through a budget law (Act no. 547). For municipalities, the budget law foresees financial sanctions of up to DKK 3 billion in case of overspending for both individual municipalities that contribute to the overspending and for all municipalities collectively. While municipalities had overrun their budgets in 2009, they have kept their total service expenditure within the expenditure ceiling in both the budgets and the final accounts since 2011 and, in fact, underran their budgets by DKK 4 to 6 billion annually between 2011 and 2013. Municipalities have been pursuing an agenda of efficiency and expenditure reduction over the past years and have cut municipal service expenditure by DKK 12 billion between 2009 and 2013, i.e. 5% of the total service expenditures (Houlberg et al., 2016).

To improve public finances and to increase the supply of labour, Denmark has put in place a number of macro-structural reforms and initiatives in recent years, including reforms of disability pensions, a flexi-job scheme, a cash benefit system, a sickness benefit system along with a tax reform, a pension package, a growth package, and a comprehensive youth unemployment package (European Commission, 2016).

Structure and governance of the school system

Structure of the school system

The Danish school system is organised in three stages: non-compulsory day care for children from age 0-5, compulsory primary and lower secondary education for children from age 6-16, and upper secondary education for young people aged 16-19 (see Annex 1.2 for a diagram of the Danish education system and Houlberg et al., 2016 and Eurydice, 2016 for further information). This report focuses on public municipal primary and lower secondary education, i.e. the *Folkeskole*, only.

- All children in Denmark from the age of 26 weeks to the beginning of compulsory education have the right to receive **non-compulsory day care.** Day care can be provided through private child-minders and public or private nurseries, kindergartens and age-integrated institutions (Eurydice, 2016). Participation in early childhood education and care is very high by international standards: more than 95% of children aged 3 to 5 attend early childhood education and care (OECD average: 74.0% of 3-year-olds, 87.6% of 4-year-olds, and 94.8% of 5-year-olds) (OECD, 2015c).
- The entire period of **compulsory education** is provided in one single integrated structure. Since 2009, all children aged 6 begin their schooling with one year of compulsory pre-school (Year 0). Children then continue with 9 years of schooling which they complete with a compulsory school leaving examination. In Years 8 to 10, students have the option of changing to continuation schools (*Efterskole*), i.e. private boarding schools offering lower secondary education. Parents are free to decide if their children complete compulsory education at a *Folkeskole*, a private school or through home schooling (Eurydice, 2016). The majority of children attend a *Folkeskole*, but the share of students going to private schools has been increasing over the last few years (see Table 1.2). In 2013, 4.8% of all students in the *Folkeskole* attended a special needs school, compared to 5.8% in 2010 (Houlberg et al., 2016).
- With completion of Year 9, students have the option of attending a **voluntary Year 10** if they wish (e.g. if they do not feel prepared for upper secondary education or if they need more time to choose an upper secondary programme). In 2013/14, 37 975 students decided to take a tenth year, 17 316 of which chose to do so at a public municipal school (Danish Ministry For Children, Education and Gender Equality, 2016a).
- **Upper secondary education,** or youth education as it is called in Denmark, is divided into general programmes qualifying students primarily for access to tertiary education

Table 1.2. **Distribution of students in primary and lower secondary education (Years 0-9) across school types**

	2010	2011	2012	2013	2014	Share of students in 2014 (%)	Percentage change between 2010 and 2014 (%)
Public municipal *Folkeskole*	559 609	552 792	550 710	545 549	543 753	80.80	-2.8
Private independent schools	95 142	100 022	102 638	104 866	107 581	15.99	13.1
Continuation schools (*Efterskole*)	10 647	10 727	10 342	9 940	10 357	1.54	-2.7
Special schools	9 345	8 962	8 405	8 496	8 121	1.21	-13.1
Daily treatment centres	2 682	2 092	1 898	2 039	1 933	0.29	-27.9
Youth schools (SFO)	1 703	1 591	1 575	1 567	1 202	0.18	-29.4
All primary and lower secondary schools	679 128	676 186	675 568	672 457	672 947	100.00	-0.9

Note: Figures as on 1 September of each year. Year 10 not included.
Daily treatment centres are special schools connected to 24-hour care centres for children and young people with social and behavioural difficulties.
Source: Danish Ministry for Children, Education and Gender Equality (2016a), Elevtal – Grundskole [Number of Students – *Folkeskole*] (EGS) Database, *http://statweb.uni-c.dk/databanken/uvmDataWeb/MainCategories.aspx*.

and vocational programmes qualifying students primarily for a career in a specific trade or industry. In 2013, 56.7% of upper secondary students were enrolled in a general programme and 43.3% of students in a vocational programme (OECD average: 53.6% and 46.4% respectively) (OECD, 2015c). In 2011, the government set itself the goal that 95% of each cohort should complete upper secondary education by 2015 as part of the government platform *A Denmark that Stands Together*.

- Students can choose between four **general upper secondary programmes** with different curricula. The three-year Upper Secondary School Leaving Examination (STX) programme and the two-year Higher Preparatory Examination (HF) programme offer a broad range of subjects in the fields of humanities, natural and social sciences. The three-year Higher Commercial Examination (HHX) and Higher Technical Examination (HTX) programmes focus on a combination of business and socio-economic studies and technological and scientific students with general subjects respectively.
- **Vocational education and training (EUD)** includes a vast range of programmes and is based on the dual training principle, i.e. periods in school alternating with periods of practical training in an enterprise: basic vocational education and training (EGU), vocational education and training (VET), vocational and general upper secondary education (EUX) and some maritime programmes. The EGU programme is a short basic vocational programme that combines practical training with theoretical education at a school. VET programmes also combine theoretical education at a secondary vocational college and practical training at a company in a number of different specialisations (e.g. carpentry, gardening, retail). Students must enter into a training agreement with a company approved by the social partners to complete this programme. The EUX programme is a combination of the VET and STX programmes and enables students to gain a vocational specialisation as well as a general upper secondary school leaving certificate (Houlberg et al., 2016).

After the end of the school day and during some school holidays, children and young people can attend different **leisure or youth clubs** at public or private schools (*Skolefritidsordning og Fritidshjem* [SFO] and *Fritids- og ungdomsklubber*) that offer a range of social and creative activities depending on their age.

Distribution of responsibilities

The Ministry for Children, Education and Gender Equality is responsible for the overall framework and objectives of day care,[1] primary and lower secondary education, and upper secondary education. Within these general frameworks and national legislation, the financial and organisational operation of day care and public primary and lower secondary education, the *Folkeskole*, is the full responsibility of the municipalities (for a depiction of the governance of the *Folkeskole*, see Figure 1.5). Upper secondary schools have the status of self-governing institutions (see Houlberg et al., 2016, Appendix 3, for further details).

Figure 1.5. **Governance of the *Folkeskole***

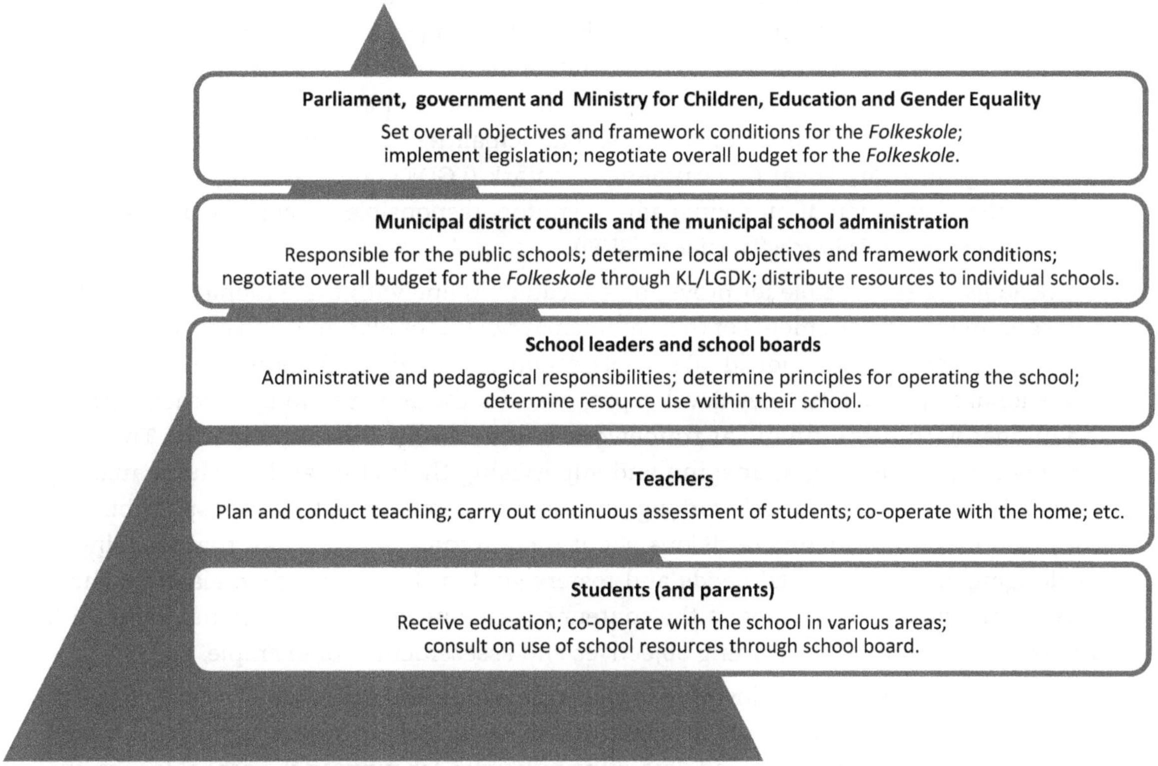

Source: Based on Houlberg, K. et al. (2016), *OECD Review of Policies to Improve the Effectiveness of Resource Use in Schools: Country Background Report for Denmark, www.oecd.org/edu/school/10932_OECD%20Country%20Background%20Report%20Denmark.pdf.*

Public primary and lower secondary education is regulated through the *Folkeskole* Act.[2] The *Folkeskole* Act sets out the overall goals of the *Folkeskole*, the responsibilities of the different layers of governance, the subjects to be taught and the learning goals for teaching in each subject ('Common Objectives'). The Ministry for Children, Education and Gender Equality has the overall responsibility for setting the legal and financial governance framework, steering the *Folkeskole*, monitoring the overall quality of education, and ensuring that municipalities and schools carry out the government's education policies. The ministry also sets national requirements and regulations for municipalities and schools (e.g. on assessment and evaluation, such as the implementation of national assessments in schools and the production of biannual quality reports by municipalities according to specified criteria).

Stakeholders influence the national policy making process through their interest associations (e.g. the early childhood and youth educator, teacher and school leader unions

[BUPL, *Danmarks Lærerforening* and *Skolelederforeningen*], the School and Parents Organisation [*Skole og Forældre*], and the Association of Danish Students [*Danske Skolelever*]). In its work, the Ministry for Children, Education and Gender Equality also co-operates with other ministries (e.g. for teacher education and professional development, for transitions across levels of education, and for inclusion), most notably with the Ministry of Higher Education and Science responsible for tertiary education and with the Ministry of Social Affairs and the Interior responsible for children with special needs.

Within the framework set by the *Folkeskole* Act and the regulations issued by the Ministry for Children, Education and Gender Equality, municipalities have full financial and organisational responsibility for the *Folkeskole*. Municipalities determine how their schools are organised, set local goals and objectives, determine the financial framework for their schools, specify the exact parameters for education (e.g. curricular plans, number of classes taught, additional classes, teacher-student ratios, etc.), supervise their schools and follow up on results. They can also launch their own special initiatives and programmes (e.g. organising local learning consultants). Municipalities can seek the support of their interest organisation, Local Government Denmark (LGDK), and exchange experiences through the association of municipal administrators responsible for culture, day care and education (*Børne- og Kulturchefforeningen* [BKF]).

Schools are responsible for providing education in line with the national aims for the *Folkeskole* and the requirements of their municipality, and for planning and organising their education programme. At individual schools, school principals hold the administrative and educational responsibility. They develop proposals for the activities in their school and for the budget within the financial framework laid down by the municipality. They are responsible for selecting, managing and supervising their staff and teachers, making decisions about their teachers' working time, and distributing tasks and responsibilities. They also make all concrete decisions about their students and ensure that teaching is challenging, meets students' needs and fosters student learning. Schools and teachers have relatively large autonomy on the content of teaching within the national framework that sets requirements for learning objectives and assessments, for example.

The school community is involved in the organisation and operation of schools through school boards made up of parents, students and teachers. School boards approve the school budget and teaching materials, and determine principles for running the school (e.g. on the organisation of teaching, the length of the school day, the offer of optional subjects, collaboration between the school and the home, information for parents about their children's progress). School boards are consulted by the municipality on issues relating to their school. Optional pedagogical councils made up of all school staff with pedagogical functions can provide an advisory function for the school leadership at all schools. Student councils provide a platform for student voice in schools (Eurydice, 2016; Houlberg et al., 2016).

Compared to other OECD countries, schools in Denmark have an average level of decision-making power, while the local level plays a comparatively large role and the central level plays a comparatively small role. According to data collected for the OECD *Education at a Glance 2012* publication, lower secondary schools make 44% of key decisions (OECD average: 41%), the local level makes 34% of the decisions (OECD average: 17%), and the central level makes 22% of the decisions (OECD average: 36%) (see Figure 1.6).[3] Similar to many other OECD countries, schools hold a high degree of autonomy for the organisation of instruction (89%, OECD average: 75%). Decision-making for personnel management is shared

Figure 1.6. **Decisions taken at each level of government in public lower secondary education, 2011**

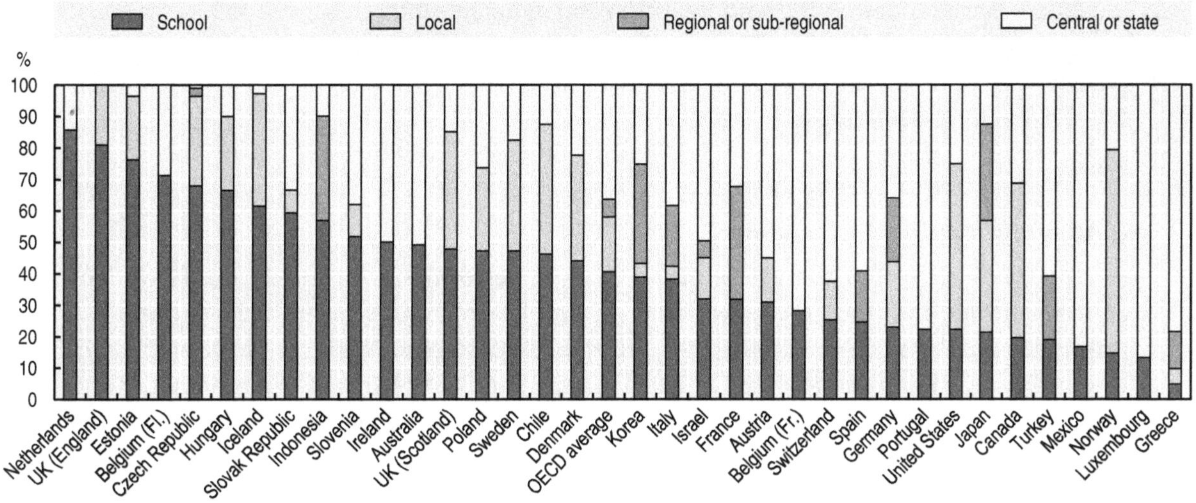

Note: Countries are ranked in descending order of the percentage of decisions taken at the school level.
Source: OECD (2012), *Education at a Glance 2012: OECD Indicators, http://dx.doi.org/10.1787/eag-2012-en,* Table D6.1.

across all three levels, while decision-making for planning and structures is shared between the local and the central level only. For resource management decisions, only schools and the local level are involved in decision-making (OECD, 2012, see Annex 1.3).[4]

While the national level has traditionally played a less important part in the governance of the *Folkeskole*, it has sought to take on a more prominent role in driving the quality of the education system by supporting a culture of performance management, evaluation and assessment and local capacity building (see Chapter 3). Examples for tools and processes put into place to facilitate soft steering include national performance goals and measures for student achievement and wellbeing; national learning progressions and curricular guidelines in the form of Common Objectives; compulsory examinations after Year 9; national assessments and student plans; reporting and documentation requirements in the form of biannual quality reports; the establishment of a learning consultant corps; the development of IT infrastructure that encourages the use of data;[5] and the development of specialised institutions, such as the Danish Evaluation Institute (*Danmarks Evalueringsinstitut*, EVA) and specific units in the Ministry for Children, Education and Gender Equality that work to strengthen the role of evaluation and assessment and performance management. These tools and processes constitute the framework within which municipalities, schools, principals and teachers operate. For example, Common Objectives, national assessments and student plans all influence the ways in which teachers should plan their teaching (Houlberg et al., 2016).

At a national level, Denmark has created a number of institutions to monitor and evaluate the quality of education in the *Folkeskole*. This includes a school council (*Skolerådet*), an advisory council that provides guidance on questions of academic performance, student progress, and the pedagogical and didactic development of the *Folkeskole*, and the Danish Evaluation Institute (EVA), an independent agency conducting both officially commissioned and independent evaluations. The Quality and Supervision Agency (*Kvalitets- og Tilsynsstyrelsen*) responsible for administering national and international assessments, producing quality support materials and supervising public and private providers was replaced with an Agency for Education and Quality (*Styrelsen for Undervisning og Kvalitet*) in

April 2015. For the *Folkeskole*, the new agency is primarily responsible for supporting quality and capacity development activities in areas such as the new learning consultant corps, including consultants working with inclusion and bilingual children as well as international supervisors, and the development and operation of assessments and examinations (Shewbridge et al., 2011; Houlberg et al., 2016). The agency is also responsible for the quality supervision for the *Folkeskole*.

Main features of the school system

Quality and equity of education

Denmark shows an average or above average performance in international student assessments depending on the subject and year level. Danish students participate in the IEA (International Association for the Evaluation of Educational Achievement) Progress in International Reading Literacy Study (PIRLS) in Year 4 and in the Trends in Mathematics and Science Study (TIMMS) in Year 8. In the 2011 round of assessments in mathematics and science, Danish students scored above the TIMMS scale centrepoint, but below the TIMMS Advanced and High International Benchmarks.[6] Compared to its Nordic neighbours, Denmark outperformed Norway and Sweden in mathematics, and Norway in science, but stayed behind Finland in both mathematics and science, and behind Sweden in science. In the reading assessment, Danish students reached excellent results above the PIRLS scale centrepoint and the PIRLS High International Benchmark. This result places Denmark among the top eleven high-achieving countries. Danish students outperformed their Norwegian and Swedish peers, but remained behind the results of Finnish students. Almost all Danish Year 4 students reached a basic level of achievement in mathematics, science and reading (low benchmark), and a number of Danish students perform very highly (high and advanced benchmarks) (See Table 1.3). Over time, Denmark has increased its performance in mathematics and science (between 2007 and 2011) as well as in reading (between 2006 and 2011) (Martin et al., 2012; Mullis et al., 2012a; Mullis et al., 2012b).

At age 15, Danish students participate in the OECD Programme for International Student Assessment (PISA) in mathematics, reading and science. In the PISA 2012 assessment of mathematics, Danish students performed above the OECD average, but performance has steadily decreased since PISA 2003 across assessments. In reading and science, performance was around the OECD average in PISA 2012, and this has remained unchanged since PISA 2003 (OECD, 2014b). In problem-solving, Denmark also performed around the OECD average (OECD, 2014c).

Denmark has a comparatively small share of low-performing students, but also a relatively low proportion of top-performing students, and the difference in performance between the 90th and the 10th percentiles is comparatively small (see Table 1.4). For instance, in mathematics in PISA 2012, 16.8% of 15-year-olds performed below proficiency level 2, believed to be the mark of basic competency necessary for a successful transition to the labour market or tertiary education (OECD average: 23%), and 10% of 15-year-olds performed at proficiency level 5 or above (OECD average: 12.6%). The performance difference between the 90th and the 10th percentiles was 214 score points (OECD average: 239). Across assessments, the share of top-performing students has remained stable in science, but decreased since 2003 in mathematics (from 15.9% to 10%) and reading (from 8.1% to 5.4%). The share of low performing students was reduced in science and reading, but increased in mathematics (OECD, 2014b).

Table 1.3. Performance of Danish students in TIMMS and PIRLS

Percentage of students in primary education reaching international benchmarks in mathematics, science and reading

International benchmark/Domain	Denmark (%)	International median (%)
Low		
Mathematics (TIMSS)	97	90
Science (TIMSS)	95	92
Reading (PIRLS)	99	95
Intermediate		
Mathematics (TIMSS)	82	69
Science (TIMSS)	78	72
Reading (PIRLS)	88	80
High		
Mathematics (TIMSS)	44	28
Science (TIMSS)	39	32
Reading (PIRLS)	55	44
Advanced		
Mathematics (TIMSS)	10	4
Science (TIMSS)	8	5
Reading (PIRLS)	12	8

Source: Martin, M.O. et al. (2012), *TIMSS 2011 International Results in Science, http://timssandpirls.bc.edu/timss2011/downloads/T11_IR_Science_FullBook.pdf;* Mullis, I.V.S. et al. (2012a), *PIRLS 2011 International Results in Reading, http://timssandpirls.bc.edu/pirls2011/downloads/P11_IR_FullBook.pdf;* Mullis, I.V.S. et al. (2012b), *TIMSS 2011 International Results in Mathematics, http://timssandpirls.bc.edu/timss2011/downloads/T11_IR_Mathematics_ FullBook.pdf.*

Table 1.4. Selected indicators of quality and equity in Danish education, based on PISA 2012 for mathematics and reading and PISA 2006 for science

	Denmark	OECD average
Percentage of top performers		
Mathematics	10	12.6
Reading	5.4	8.4
Science	6.8	8.4
Percentage of low performers		
Mathematics	16.8	23
Reading	14.6	18
Science	16.7	17.8
Difference in performance between the 90th and 10th percentiles (in score points)		
Mathematics	214	239
Reading	216	242
Science	238	239
Percentage of variance in performance explained by socio-economic status		
Mathematics	16.5	14.8
Reading	15.3	13.1
Science	15.7	14
Percentage of immigrant students who are low performers in mathematics	42	36
Percentage of students who repeated a year	4.7	12.4

Note: Top performers = students performing at PISA level 5 and above; low performers = students performing below PISA level 2.

Source: OECD (2014b), *PISA 2012 Results: What Students Know and Can Do (Volume I, Revised edition, February 2014): Student Performance in Mathematics, Reading and Science, http://dx.doi.org/10.1787/9789264208780-en;* OECD (2013c), *PISA 2012 Results: Excellence through Equity (Volume II): Giving Every Student the Chance to Succeed, http://dx.doi.org/10.1787/9789264201132-en;* OECD (2013e), *PISA 2012 Results: What Makes Schools Successful (Volume IV): Resources, Policies and Practices, http://dx.doi.org/10.1787/9789264201156-en.*

Although the Danish education system has a number of features that promote equity, including a high proportion of students enrolled in early childhood education, low levels of year repetition and comprehensive schooling until age 16, students' socio-economic background has a strong impact on performance in Denmark (see Table 1.4 and Figure 1.7). For example, in PISA 2012, 16.5% of the variance in mathematics performance in Denmark can be explained by socio-economic background, close to the OECD average of 14.8% (see Figure 1.7). Also similar to the average across OECD countries, a more socio-economically advantaged student in Denmark scores 39 points higher in mathematics – the equivalent of nearly one year of schooling – than a less-advantaged student. According to PISA 2012, education in Denmark is less equitable than in other Nordic countries, where the strength of the relationship between socio-economic background and performance is less pronounced. In Norway, only 7.4% of the variance in mathematics performance can be explained by socio-economic background, in Iceland only 7.7%, in Finland only 9.4%, and in Sweden only 10.6%. In Denmark, furthermore, only a small proportion of students beats the odds and manages to overcome difficult socio-economic circumstances and to exceed expectations (4.9%, compared to an OECD average of 6.4%) (OECD, 2013c).

Figure 1.7. **Student performance and equity, PISA 2012**

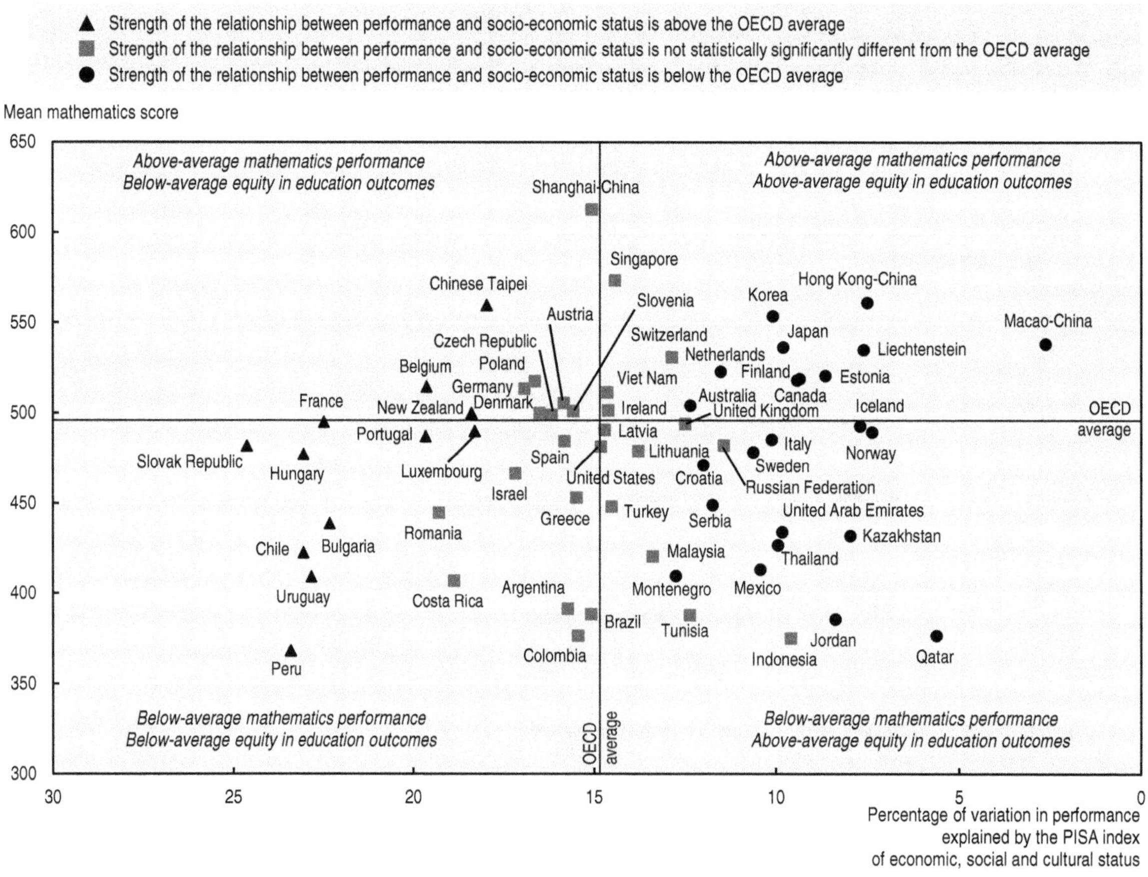

Source: OECD (2013c), *PISA 2012 Results: Excellence through Equity (Volume II): Giving Every Student the Chance to Succeed, http://dx.doi.org/10.1787/9789264201132-en.*

Performance differs relatively little between schools in Denmark. Similar to other Nordic countries with comprehensive schooling systems, between-school differences account for less than 15% of the OECD average total variation in performance in Denmark. By contrast, across OECD countries, 37% of the overall performance differences are observed between schools. The performance differences that do exist between schools are relatively closely related to socio-economic disparities between schools: 70.9% of the performance differences between schools are explained by the socio-economic status of students and schools (OECD average: 62.8%). Performance differences within schools are around the OECD average, but these within-school differences are more strongly related to students' socio-economic status: 65.8% of the total variation in performance is observed within schools (OECD average: 63.3%), and 10.5% of the performance difference can be explained by differences in students' socio-economic status (OECD average: 5.1%). A one-unit increase in the PISA index of economic, social and cultural status is associated with a score-point difference of 31, one of the highest among OECD countries (OECD average: 19 points) (OECD, 2013c).

Students with an immigrant background are particularly at risk of underperformance in Denmark, and more so than in many other OECD countries. In the PISA 2012 mathematics assessment, students with an immigrant background scored an average of 66 points lower than their native peers before accounting for socio-economic background (OECD average: 34 points), and an average of 40 points after accounting for socio-economic differences (OECD average: 21 points). In fact, students with an immigrant background in Denmark were 2.43 times more likely to perform in the bottom quarter of the performance distribution than non-immigrant students (OECD average: 1.70 times more likely) (OECD, 2013c). Children with an immigrant background also participate less in early childhood education and care, which may contribute to later performance gaps. Children with an immigrant background in Denmark were roughly half as likely to participate in early childhood education and care as their non-immigrant peers, a fact holding true even after accounting for children's socio-economic background (OECD, 2015d, Figure 4.14; European Commission/EACEA/Eurydice/Eurostat, 2014).

PISA 2012 also asked students to evaluate their sense of belonging at school as well as their happiness at and satisfaction with school. These subjective evaluations provide a good indication of whether education systems are able to foster overall student wellbeing. According to PISA 2012, in Denmark, a larger than average proportion of students agreed or strongly agreed with the statements that they feel happy at school and that they are satisfied with their school, and a larger than average proportion of students disagreed or strongly disagreed with the statements that they feel like an outsider and that they feel awkward and out of place at their school. However, a smaller than average share of students agreed or strongly agreed with the statements that they feel like they belong at school and that things are ideal at their school (see Tables 1.5 and 1.6) (OECD, 2013d).

Attainment, adult skills and labour market outcomes

Education attainment in Denmark is high and has been historically so. In 2014, 79.6% of 25-64 year-olds had attained at least an upper secondary education and, 35.8% of 25-64 year-olds had completed a tertiary degree (OECD average: 76.3% and 33.6% respectively). Among 55-64 year-olds, 71.6% had completed at least an upper secondary education and 29.1% had attained a tertiary qualification (OECD average: 66.2% and 25.1% respectively); among younger Danes (aged 25-34), 84.1% held at least an upper secondary qualification and 42.1% held a tertiary qualification (OECD average: 82.7% and 40.7%) (OECD, 2015c).

Table 1.5. **Students' sense of belonging at school, based on PISA 2012**

Percentage of students who reported to "agree" or "strongly agree" with the following statements:

	Denmark	Finland	Iceland	Norway	Sweden	OECD average
I make friends easily at school	84.4	85.5	85.6	85.6	86.8	86.9
I feel like I belong at school	77.4	84.3	88.2	87.1	78.6	81.3
Other students seem to like me	87.7	87.6	91.2	88.7	88.8	89.2
I feel happy at school	86.1	66.9	90.4	86.9	85	79.8
Things are ideal in my school	38.5	51	75.2	71.4	36.7	61.1
I am satisfied with my school	81.5	73.4	85.1	73.9	76.6	78.2

Source: OECD (2013d), *PISA 2012 Results: Ready to Learn (Volume III): Students' Engagement, Drive and Self-Beliefs, http://dx.doi.org/10.1787/9789264201170-en.*

Table 1.6. **Students' sense of belonging at school, based on PISA 2012**

Percentage of students who reported to "disagree" or "strongly disagree" with the following statements:

	Denmark	Finland	Iceland	Norway	Sweden	OECD average
I feel like an outsider (or left out of things) at school	93	90.9	90.4	91.6	89.5	88.8
I feel awkward and out of place in my school	90.5	85.5	89	87.7	90.2	87.6
I feel lonely at school	92.7	91.3	91.8	90.5	90.5	91.1

Source: OECD (2013d), *PISA 2012 Results: Ready to Learn (Volume III): Students' Engagement, Drive and Self-Beliefs, http://dx.doi.org/10.1787/9789264201170-en.*

Results from the OECD 2012 Programme for the International Assessment of Adult Competencies (PIAAC) show that the skills of the adult Danish population aged 16-65 are slightly below the international average in literacy and above the international average in numeracy and problem solving, but generally lower than in other Nordic countries in all domains (see Table 1.7). Younger adults aged 16-24 performed less well than the 16-65 year-old population in PIAAC 2012 and scored only around or below the OECD average in all domains: performance in literacy was higher, but was still below the OECD average; performance in numeracy was lower at around the OECD average; and performance in problem-solving in technology-rich environments was higher, but also only around the OECD average. The proportion of low-skilled adults in Denmark is comparable to the OECD average, but higher than in other Nordic countries in literacy, and lower than the OECD average and comparable to other Nordic countries in numeracy (OECD, 2013b).

Like in all other OECD countries, people with high qualifications have the highest employment rates in Denmark, and, like in most countries, the lowest risk of being unemployed. In 2014, the percentage point difference in employment rates between people aged 25-64 with tertiary qualifications and those with below upper secondary education amounted to 24.6 percentage points (OECD average: 27.6 percentage points). And while 8.2% of people with below upper secondary education were unemployed in 2014, this applied to only 4.4% of tertiary graduates (OECD average: 12.8% and 5.1% respectively) (OECD, 2015c).

Among the younger generation (25-34 year-olds), employment rates decreased for all levels of attainment between 2000 and 2014, and unemployment rates for all levels of attainment increased in the same period. However, employment rates remained higher and unemployment rates remained lower than the OECD and the EU21 average in 2014. Compared to other Nordic countries, Danish young people with low qualifications (i.e. below upper secondary education) fare better on the labour market than their Finnish peers, but worse than low-qualified young people in Norway. 57% of 25-34 year-olds in Denmark were employed in 2014, compared to 52% in Finland, 65% in Sweden and 61% in Norway. While

Table 1.7. **Adult skills, PIAAC 2012**

	Denmark	Finland	Norway	Sweden	OECD average
Mean proficiency score (16-65 year-olds)					
Literacy	271	288	278	279	273
Numeracy	278	282	278	279	269
Percentage scoring at Level 2 or 3 in problem-solving in technology-rich environments (16-65 year-olds) (%)	39	42	41	44	34
Mean proficiency score (16-24 year-olds)					
Literacy	276	297	275	283	280
Numeracy	273	285	271	278	271
Percentage scoring at Level 2 or 3 in problem-solving in technology-rich environments (16-24 year-olds) (%)	50.4	61.9	61.7	54.9	50.7
Proportion of low-skilled adults (16-65 year-olds) with skills at or below Proficiency Level 1 (%)					
Literacy	15.7	10.6	12.3	13.3	15.5
Numeracy	14.2	12.8	14.6	14.7	19
Proportion of adults opting out of the computer-based assessment, failing the ICT core, or without computer experience (%)	14.1	18.4	13.5	12	24.4

Note: In the problem-solving in technology-rich environments domain, adults at Level 3 can complete tasks involving multiple applications, a large number of steps, impasses, and the discovery and use of ad hoc commands in a novel environment. They can establish a plan to arrive at a solution and monitor its implementation as they deal with unexpected outcomes and impasses. At Level 2, adults can complete problems that have explicit criteria for success, a small number of applications, and several steps and operators. They can monitor progress towards a solution and handle unexpected outcomes or impasses. The division between Level 2 and above and Level 1 and below in problem solving in technology-rich environments in the figures showing the distribution of the population by proficiency level has been made for ease of presentation. It does not reflect a judgment that Level 2 in problem solving represents a performance benchmark in any sense.

Source: OECD (2013b), *OECD Skills Outlook 2013: First Results from the Survey of Adult Skills, http://dx.doi.org/10.1787/9789264204256-en.*

14.7% of 25-34 year-olds in Denmark with below upper secondary education were unemployed in 2014, this was the case for 18.1% in Finland, 18.9% in Sweden, and for 11.8% in Norway. On the other hand, unemployment among young tertiary graduates is higher in Denmark than in other Nordic countries. In 2014, the unemployment rate of 24-35 year-old Danish tertiary graduates reached 7.2%, close to the OECD average of 7.5% and lower than the EU21 average of 8.7%, but higher than that for young Fins (6.2%), Norwegians (3.4%) and Swedes (3.9%) (OECD, 2015c).

Among 25-64 year-olds with upper secondary or post-secondary non-tertiary education as their highest level of attainment, graduates from vocational education and training (VET) have better labour market outcomes than graduates from general programmes. In 2014, 81% of individuals with a vocational upper secondary or post-secondary non-tertiary qualification were employed, 20 percentage points more than individuals with a general upper secondary education (OECD average: 77% and 7 percentage points difference). Unemployment also affects graduates from VET programmes less than graduates from general programmes (6.6% compared to 12.1%). These differences may be explained, at least in part, by the fact that people who study non-vocational tracks generally pursue education at the next education level, while those who study vocational tracks at the upper secondary level generally enter the labour market once they have obtained this qualification. Furthermore, a potential drawback may be that the skills that individuals acquire through VET might be of limited use in a rapidly changing labour market which may make it more difficult to adapt to changes in work environments (OECD, 2015c).

Policy priorities and recent developments

Education as part of the 2011 and 2015 government programmes

In November 2011, the Danish government led by the Social Democrats released its government programme entitled *A Denmark that Stands Together* (the full programme is available on the following website *www.stm.dk/multimedia/Regeringsgrundlag_uk_2011.pdf*). The programme established the key priorities for education, such as improving early childhood education and care and reforming primary and lower secondary schools in co-operation with teachers and parents. The programme set a number of objectives as well as measurable goals and targets: to increase the number of young people completing a vocational education and training programme; to reform education and training to increase growth and the labour supply; to launch an economic programme that includes funding for improvements in education; and to invest in research. The specific goals and targets stated that by 2020, 95% of a cohort should achieve an upper secondary education, 60% of a cohort should achieve a tertiary education, and 25% of a cohort should achieve a long tertiary education (OECD, 2015b).

In June 2015, the newly elected Danish government led by the Liberal Party (*Venstre*) published a new government programme with the name *Together for the Future* (the full programme can be accessed on *www.stm.dk/multimedia/Regeringsgrundlag_2016.pdf*). The new government programme set out the government's vision of improving day care by focussing on smoother transitions from day care to early childhood education and care/ pre-school and by placing day care under the responsibility of the Ministry for Children, Education and Gender Equality. The government reaffirmed its commitment to the 2014 *Folkeskole* reform (see below) and promised stability for primary and lower secondary schools in this respect, but it also stated plans to put in place further measures to ensure the effective implementation of the reform. According to the programme, the government planned to review the process of inclusion in the *Folkeskole* and the collaboration between schools and youth clubs. The programme also set out plans to ensure that all students benefit from further learning opportunities through homework or other educational challenges. The government, furthermore, set out its plans to provide better opportunities for children with special needs by offering students with learning difficulties the opportunity to take part in a crash course to be ready for school, by giving children with special needs more freedom to choose private primary and lower-secondary schools, and by strengthening collaboration between schools and local associations. In upper secondary education/youth education, the government programme set out the goal of facilitating young people's choices between general and vocational programmes and of reducing school dropout through greater coherence across upper secondary programmes.

The 2014 reform of the Folkeskole

In June 2013, the Danish government introduced a reform of the *Folkeskole* based on a broad political agreement by the major political parties to improve public primary and lower secondary education.[7] The reform has been implemented since the 2014/15 school year.

As basis of the *Folkeskole* reform, the government set three national goals that should contribute to setting a clear direction and a high level of ambition for the development of the *Folkeskole* while ensuring a clear framework for a systematic and continuous evaluation:

1. The *Folkeskole* must challenge all students to reach their full potential.
2. The *Folkeskole* must lower the significance of social background on academic results.

3. Trust in the *Folkeskole* and student wellbeing must be enhanced through respect for professional knowledge and practice in the *Folkeskole*.

These three national goals for the development of the *Folkeskole* are operationalised through a number of clear, simple and measurable targets:

- At least 80% of students must achieve "good" results (mark 3 or higher) at reading and mathematics in the national assessments. The baseline is the share of students achieving mark 3 or higher in the national assessments in 2012.[8]
- The number of high-performing students in Danish and mathematics must increase from year to year. The baseline is the percentage of students achieving the top mark 5 in the national assessments in 2012.[9]
- The number of low-performing students in reading and mathematics, independent of social background, must decrease from year to year. This target should focus on the percentage of students with parents with only compulsory or unknown education performing poorly in the national assessments.[10]
- The wellbeing of students as measured by a national survey must increase.[11]

The targets are measurable on national, municipal, school and class levels and are envisaged to become the basis for dialogue and follow-up regarding the development of students' academic performance and wellbeing at all levels.

To fulfil the three national goals, the *Folkeskole* reform focuses broadly on three main areas of improvement:

- A longer and varied school day with more and improved teaching and learning (e.g. through more classes in Danish and mathematics, more classes in foreign languages and natural sciences/technology, greater involvement of local sports clubs, cultural centres and associations, a clarification and simplification of the Common Objectives, greater freedom for schools to offer electives, the introduction of elite sports and talent music classes, a review of the school leaving examination, and competency development for school boards to increase parental involvement).
- Better professional development of teachers, pedagogical staff and school principals (e.g. through the introduction of a requirement that all teachers must be fully qualified for the subjects they teach by 2020, through the provision of additional earmarked funding (DKK one billion) for the professional development of teachers and pedagogues (a profession similar to early childhood and care staff in other countries, but supporting all stages of human development more broadly) between 2014 and 2020, through the introduction of a national programme for the training and development of principals and the availability of DKK 60 million for the professional development of principals between 2013 and 2015, and the creation of a national body of approximately 80 learning consultants to advise municipalities and schools on quality development).
- Few and clear objectives and simplification of rules and regulations (e.g. through the annual publication of a written status account that forms the basis for the ongoing dialogue between the government, the municipalities and other stakeholders, through quality supervision and a revision of the results-based quality oversight process of the Ministry for Children, Education and Gender Equality, the municipal quality reports and individual student plans, facilitation of the common management of several schools and schools and youth clubs, and the expansion of school councils into Youth Education Guidance and Counselling).

Act no. 409 on the utilisation of teachers' working time

In April 2013, the Danish parliament passed an Act specifying the framework for the utilisation of teachers' working hours (Act no. 409). The Act was passed following the inability of the Danish Union of Teachers (DLF) and Local Government Denmark (LGDK) representing the municipalities as employers to reach a collective agreement and the four week long lockout of *Folkeskole* teachers by LGDK in spring 2013. As prospects for reaching an agreement seemed unrealistic and as the parliament considered it irresponsible to let the dispute continue, the parliament passed Act no. 409 to end the conflict, even though working conditions in Denmark are traditionally agreed upon between employers and employees without the interference of legal regulation.

Act no. 409 revised the previous agreement on teachers' working time that had given all teachers a certain amount of preparation time for each class irrespective of their subject or experience. Act no. 409 intends to facilitate a better use of human resources in schools by encouraging teachers to use their preparation time in a more targeted and effective way, and to enable school leaders to move resources to where they are needed. For instance, under the new framework, school principals can give newly qualified teachers fewer and more experienced teachers more teaching hours. Under Act no. 409 and following the 2014 *Folkeskole* reform, it is expected that, on average, teachers teach about two clock hours more per week within their regular working hours (18.3 hours a week compared to 16.3 hours a week prior to the new framework). Spreading the annual standard of 1 680 working hours over 42 weeks, a Danish teacher works, on average, 40 hours a week (Astrup Bæk, 2014; KL, 2012).

Following the implementation of Act no. 409, the majority of municipalities have issued guidelines on the implementation of the law and school leaders typically announce these guidelines to their staff (e.g. regarding mandatory hours of presence and possibilities to work from home). More than half of the municipalities have introduced attendance requirements that require teachers to be present at school for a certain duration each day irrespective of their number of teaching hours. Various municipalities have introduced an upper limit for the number of teaching hours a teacher is supposed to perform. In general, it appears that municipalities have increased the number of classes taught per teacher, and those municipalities with already high rates of teaching hours per teacher continue to have comparatively high rates of teaching hours per teacher (Houlberg et al., 2016; Danish Ministry of Education, 2014; Danish Ministry of Education, 2013).

Reforms to upper secondary education (youth education)

Since the early 2000s, Denmark has implemented various reforms in the area of secondary education. Although this report focuses on primary and lower secondary education only, this section briefly outlines these reforms as contextual information for the analysis.

In 2003, the Danish parliament passed a reform of Danish upper secondary academically-orientated programmes to improve the quality of the four general upper secondary programmes (STX, HHX, HTX and HF) and to make curricula more coherent. The reform restructured programmes into a common curriculum over half a year followed by specialised curricula over the subsequent years.

In 2008, Denmark introduced a reform in vocational education and training (VET) to reduce dropout rates in these programmes. The reform redefined the structure of VET programmes into 12 main study areas with new plans of action and learning. Under the new system, students were enabled to choose among programmes with different degrees of work-based learning and institutions were given greater flexibility to tailor programmes to students' individual needs. Since 2010, students can combine a VET programme with a general academic examination to gain access to tertiary education.

Alongside the reform of the *Folkeskole*, Denmark has been implementing a further reform of vocational upper secondary education called "Better and more attractive vocational education and training programmes" (*Bedre og mere attraktive erhvervsuddannelser*). This reform came into force in 2015 and seeks to improve the quality and attractiveness of VET programmes. The following objectives are to be reached by 2020:

- to increase the proportion of young people entering a VET programme directly after finishing primary and lower secondary education to at least 25%
- to increase the share of students completing their VET programme
- to provide more professional development to teachers and staff
- to offer flexible VET education that caters to students with different levels of abilities
- to improve counselling to students before and during VET programmes to ensure successful transition to the labour market or higher education
- to collaborate closely with companies providing training places for apprentices (OECD, 2015b).

A further reform of general upper secondary education was in preparation at the time of drafting the report to create a coherent school system for children from age 0 to 18 and to achieve the goal of a 95% completion rate of upper secondary education among young people (Houlberg et al., 2016). The main elements of the reform proposed by the former government envisaged a reduction of the number of study combinations, a strengthening of the teaching of mathematics and natural sciences, and the assessment of students' ability to co-operate and generate new ideas. In September 2015, the Minister for Children, Education and Gender Equality formed a new commission to look into how the transition from the *Folkeskole* to upper secondary education can become more relevant for the labour market and ensure a better balance between the number of youth that choose a general upper secondary education and those that choose a vocational pathway.

Changes to initial teacher education and funding for professional development

In 2012, Denmark implemented a major reform to its teacher education. Since 2013, teacher education in the form of bachelor's degree programmes has been structured around modules that are geared towards competency objectives for each teaching practice. University colleges (*Professionshøjskoler*) have been granted greater autonomy in setting programme structures and in determining the content of modules for the development of different teacher profiles. In 2010, the Danish Ministry of Education initiated a recruitment campaign to attract more of the best students to the teaching profession (OECD, 2015b).

As already stated, the 2014 *Folkeskole* reform also includes the development of the teaching profession and school leadership as one of its core elements to achieve its overall targets. As part of the *Folkeskole* reform, DKK one billion have been made available for the competency development of teachers between 2014 and 2020 to ensure that teachers are qualified for the subjects they teach. Municipalities must ensure that 85% of teachers are fully qualified by 2015 and that at least 90% are fully qualified by 2018. Funds are distributed across municipalities based on the number of children in primary and lower secondary education. Municipalities can use funds for a range of priority areas, including competency in the main subject, inclusion, classroom management, specialist competencies in areas such as reading, mathematics and Danish as a second language, and other priority areas such as the use of ICT Information and Communication Technologies) in classrooms (Undervisnings Ministeriet, 2013).

Private foundations have provided further funding for the professional development of teachers and school principals. For example, the A P Møller Foundation (*A P Møller Fonden*) made available DKK one billion in 2013 for the professional development of teachers and school principals. Schools, municipalities, associations and other actors in the *Folkeskole* can apply twice a year for funding (for further information, see *www.apmollerfonde.dk/Folkeskolen.aspx*).

Greater inclusion of children with special educational needs

Denmark has committed itself to the greater inclusion of children with special needs in the mainstream *Folkeskole* in line with international conventions such as the UN Convention on the Rights of Persons with Disabilities which Denmark ratified in 2006 and the Salamanca Statement on Inclusive Education which Denmark signed in 1994. As a large share of funding for the *Folkeskole* had been allocated to special needs education without clear evidence for benefits in terms of student learning, inclusion has also been seen as a way to make more efficient use of resources. To achieve greater inclusion, Denmark has implemented a number of measures in recent years.

In 2012, the central government and the municipalities represented by Local Government Denmark (LGDK) set clear targets and principles for the inclusion of children with special needs in mainstream education. Accordingly, Denmark seeks to raise the share of children in mainstream education, to improve academic performance and to maintain student wellbeing. A goal was set to increase the share of children included in mainstream schools to 96% by 2015. To support municipalities in achieving this goal, the central government and LGDK agreed on a number of initiatives, including: a new legislation on inclusive education in the *Folkeskole*;[12] the continuous monitoring of the inclusion process; the creation of a National Inclusion Counselling Unit/Inclusion Development; an outgoing consulting unit that should support better inclusion in day care, school and leisure time facilities; the creation of a Centre for Inclusive Education and Special Needs Education; information campaigns; and the establishment of an Expert Monitoring Group for Inclusive Education (Danish Ministry of Education, 2013). The expert monitoring group has been tasked to monitor the transition rates and to analyse challenges and initiatives at the level of schools and municipalities, also concerning the use of human resources and special learning environments and resources; to identify the main problems and best practices in relation to the specific implementation of inclusion, for example in relation to specific groups of students; and to formulate recommendations for practical implementation that can immediately be used by the different actors, as well as suggestions for specific adjustments. To create incentives for inclusion, many municipalities have decentralised the financial responsibility for special needs education to the school level. Whereas special needs education was typically financed through common pools in the municipality before this change, schools are now often required to transfer funds if they decide to exclude a student with special needs (Houlberg et al., 2016). In June 2016, the Danish government and LGDK agreed to create inclusive learning environments by focussing more on the individual child rather than the overall inclusion target of 96%.

The goal of inclusive education was reaffirmed in a government action plan on disability – *One Society for All* – which focuses on the overall scheme for policies concerning disability and which covers actions and initiatives in all relevant domains as well as the 2014 *Folkeskole* Reform (Danish Ministry of Education, 2013).

Targeted programmes for bilingual students

The integration of bilingual students with an immigrant background is a further policy priority in Denmark. Following national legislation, the Danish municipalities have implemented a number of initiatives to increase the performance and wellbeing of bilingual students. For instance, municipalities have put in place measures for early language stimulation in day care, for additional teaching in Danish as a second language (e.g. in a reception class, individual instruction or through team teaching), for the integration of Danish as a second language as a dimension in all subjects, for mother tongue instruction, and for the transition of bilingual students to upper secondary education. Following a change in legislation in 2006, a number of municipalities have also established transportation programmes to reduce the concentration of bilingual students in particular schools and school districts (Houlberg et al., 2016). In addition, the central government has established a task force for teaching bilingual children (now part of the learning consultant corps) that provides guidance to municipalities and schools on effective strategies to strengthen the language proficiency and academic results of bilingual students. This unit also provides guidance to municipalities on effective strategies to improving the language proficiency of bilingual children in day care, including through early language stimulation.

Consolidation of the school offer

Since 2009, several municipalities have consolidated their school offer to react to demographic changes and possibly as a consequence of the 2007 Local Government Reform. The school offer has been consolidated in both merged municipalities and municipalities that were not merged. The probability of school closure seems influenced by the number of students, population size, population density and the number of public schools. Municipalities have closed down smaller schools or reorganised the management of schools by joining several schools under the same school leadership. However, one challenge that municipalities face in the consolidation of their school offer is the possibility for private schools to emerge and to replace the public school that has been closed.

Between 2007 and 2013, a total of 270 out of 1 580 municipal schools, i.e. more than one in five schools, were closed, and the average size of a *Folkeskole* across municipalities increased from 362 students to 442 students. In line with this trend towards fewer and larger schools, the average class size from 2009 to 2013 increased from 20.1 to 21.4 students per class. Considering demographic developments, this trend of school consolidation is likely to continue in the future (Houlberg et al., 2016).

Notes

1. Until the change of government in 2015, the Ministry of Children, Gender Equality, Integration and Social Affairs was responsible for setting the overall framework and policies for day care.
2. The Danish *Folkeskole* was founded in 1814. Until the end of the 20th century, only five major changes were made to the *Folkeskole* Act (1903, 1937, 1958, 1975, and 1993). Since the beginning of the 21st century, the *Folkeskole* Act has undergone a number of comprehensive changes. Most recently, a new comprehensive reform of the *Folkeskole* has been implemented since the school year 2014/15.

3. This indicator presents results from data collected in 2011 on decision making at the lower secondary level of education and updates the previous survey on this topic, which took place in 2007. This indicator shows where key decisions are made in public institutions at the lower secondary level of education. The indicator does not capture the totality of decisions made within a school system. Instead, a representative set of 46 key decisions, organised across four domains, are considered. Responses were compiled in each country by a panel of experts representing different levels of the decision-making process at the lower secondary level. Information on the composition of these panels and the methods and process used to complete the survey can be found in the "Notes on methodology" in Annex 3, available at *www.oecd.org/edu/eag2012*.

4. The four domains of decision-making defined by the OECD (2012) comprise the following areas: **Organisation of instruction:** student admissions; student careers; instruction time; choice of textbooks; choice of software/learningware; grouping of students; additional support for students; teaching methods; day-to-day student assessment. **Personnel management:** hiring and dismissal of principals, teaching and non-teaching staff; duties and conditions of service of staff; salary scales of staff; influence over the careers of staff. **Planning and structures:** opening or closure of schools; creation or abolition of a year level; design of programmes of study; selection of programmes of study taught in a particular school; choice of subjects taught in a particular school; definition of course content; setting of qualifying examinations for a certificate or diploma; accreditation (examination content, marking and administration). **Resource management:** allocation and use of resources for teaching staff, non-teaching staff, capital and operating expenditure, professional development of principals and teachers.

5. For example, the Ministry for Children, Education and Gender Equality has set up a new data warehouse to facilitate educational monitoring to which municipalities and schools need to report certain data. The data warehouse includes around 35 indicators, such as results from national examinations and assessments, results from surveys on student wellbeing, and transition rates to upper secondary education.

6. The TIMSS achievement scales range from 0–1 000, although student performance typically ranges between 300 and 700. The scale centrepoint of 500 corresponds to the mean of the overall achievement distribution and functions as a point of reference that remains constant from assessment to assessment. 100 points on the scale correspond to the standard deviation. Along the scale, TIMSS reports achievement at four points as international benchmarks: Advanced International Benchmark (625), High International Benchmark (550), Intermediate International Benchmark (475), and Low International Benchmark (400).

7. For further details, see *http://eng.uvm.dk/~/media/UVM/Filer/English/PDF/131007%20folkeskolereformaftale_ENG_RED.pdf* and *www.uvm.dk/~/media/UVM/Filer/English/PDF/140708%20Improving%20the%20Public%20School.ashx?smarturl404=true*.

8. In 2013/14, 74% of students in Year 2, 71% of students in Year 4, 72% of students in Year 6 and 76% of students in Year 8 achieved good results in Danish; in mathematics 64% of students in Year 3 and 69% of students in Year 6 achieved good results. In 2011/12, 73% of students in Year 2, 66% of students in Year 4, 69% of students in Year 6 and 74% of students in Year 8 achieved good results in Danish; in mathematics, 63% of students in Year 3 and 66% of students in Year 6 achieved good results (Danish Ministry for Children, Education and Gender Equality, 2016b).

9. In Danish, the share of high-performing students in Year 2 increased from 7% in 2011/12 to 8% in 2012/13, but remained stable in 2013/14. In Year 4, the share of high-performing students increased from 6% in 2011/12 to 7% in 2012/13 and to 8% in 2013/14. In Year 6, the share of high-performing students increased from 6% in 2011/12 to 7% in 2012/13 and remained stable in 2013/14. In Year 8, the share of high-performing students increased from 8% in 2011/12 to 9% in 2012/13 and to 11% in 2013/14. In mathematics, the share of high-performing students in Year 3 remained stable at 4% between 2011/12 and 2012/13 and increased to 5% in 2013/14. In Year 6, the share of high-performing students increased from 4% in 2011/12 to 6% in 2012/13 and remained stable in 2013/14 (Danish Ministry for Children, Education and Gender Equality, 2016b).

10. In Danish, the share of poor-performing students in Year 2 decreased from11% in 2011/12 to 10% in 2012/13 and remained stable in 2013/14. In Year 4, the share of poor-performing students decreased from 14% in 2011/12 to 12% in 2012/13 and remained stable in 2013/14. In Year 6, the share of poor-performing students decreased from12% in 2011/12 to 11% in 2012/13 and remained stable in 2013/14. In Year 8, the share of low-performing students decreased from 10% in 2011/12 to 9% in 2012/13 and remained stable in 2013/14. In mathematics, the share of poor-performing students in Year 3 remained stable at 15% between 2011/12 and 2013/14. In Year 6, the share of poor-performing students decreased from 17% in 2011/12 to 16% in 2012/13 and remained stable in 2013/14 (Danish Ministry for Children, Education and Gender Equality, 2016b).

11. The first wellbeing survey was carried out in 2014/15. Results are available on the website of the data warehouse of the Danish Ministry for Children, Education and Gender Equality (2016b).

12. Following a legislative change, special needs education now includes children in special classes or special schools as well as children with special needs in regular classes with the need for instruction in a special class of more than nine teaching hours per week. Children who need less than nine teaching hours of special instruction per week can benefit from individualised teaching in mainstream classes, a temporary subdivision of classes, additional lessons and other types of professional support, from two teachers in a class, from teacher assistants, or from individual support.

References

Astrup Bæk, T. (2014), *Kommunernes økonomiske Implementering af Folkeskolereformen – Afrapportering på Spørgeskemaundersøgelse* [The Economic Implementation of the Folkeskole Reform by the Municipalities – Survey Reporting], KORA, Copenhagen, *www.kora.dk/media/3100094/10842-kommunernes-oekonomiske-implementering-af-folkeskolereformen.pdf.*

Blöchliger, H. and C. Vammalle (2012), "Denmark: The Local Government Reform", in *Reforming Fiscal Federalism and Local Government: Beyond the Zero-Sum Game*, OECD Publishing, Paris, *http://dx.doi.org/10.1787/9789264119970-8-en.*

Danish Ministry for Children, Education and Gender Equality (2016a), Elevtal – Grundskole [Number of Students – *Folkeskole*] (EGS) Database, *http://statweb.uni-c.dk/databanken/uvmDataWeb/MainCategories.aspx.*

Danish Ministry for Children, Education and Gender Equality (2016b), *Datavarehuset* [Datawarehouse], *www.uddannelsesstatistik.dk.*

Danish Ministry for Children, Gender Equality, Integration and Social Affairs (2013), *Disability Policy Action Plan 2013: One Society for All*, Danish Ministry for Children, Gender Equality, Integration and Social Affairs, Copenhagen, *http://sim.dk/media/946360/8_disability_policy_action_plan_2013_-_one_society_for_all.pdf.*

Danish Ministry for Economic Affairs and the Interior (2014), *Municipalities and Regions – Tasks and Financing*, Danish Ministry for Economic Affairs and the Interior, Copenhagen, *http://english.sim.dk/media/670682/municipalities_and_regions_-_tasks_and_financing__june_2014.pdf.*

Danish Ministry of Education (2014), *Improving the Public School – Overview of Reform of Standards in the Danish Public School (Primary and Lower Secondary Education)*, Danish Ministry of Education, Copenhagen, *www.uvm.dk/~/media/UVM/Filer/English/PDF/140708%20Improving%20the%20Public%20School.ashx?smarturl404=true.*

Danish Ministry of Education (2013), *Agreement between the Danish Government (the Social Democrats, the Social-Liberal Party and the Socialist People's Party), the Liberal Party of Denmark and the Danish People's Party on an Improvement of Standards in the Danish Public School (Primary and Lower Secondary Education)*, Danish Ministry of Education, Copenhagen, *http://eng.uvm.dk/~/media/UVM/Filer/English/PDF/131007%20folkeskolereformaftale_ENG_RED.pdf.*

European Commission (2016), Europe 2020 in Denmark, *http://ec.europa.eu/europe2020/europe-2020-in-your-country/danmark/country-specific-recommendations/index_en.htm.*

European Commission/EACEA/Eurydice/Eurostat (2014), *Key Data on Early Childhood Education and Care in Europe, 2014 Edition. Eurydice and Eurostat Report*, Publications Office of the European Union, Luxembourg, *http://eacea.ec.europa.eu/education/eurydice/documents/key_data_series/166EN.pdf.*

Eurostat (2016a), *Government Finance Statistics*, *http://ec.europa.eu/eurostat/statistics-explained/index.php/Government_finance_statistics#Further_Eurostat_information.*

Eurostat (2016b), Population Density, *http://ec.europa.eu/eurostat/web/population-demography-migration-projections/population-data/main-tables#.*

Eurydice (2016), *European Encyclopedia on National Education Systems, Eurypedia: Denmark*, *https://webgate.ec.europa.eu/fpfis/mwikis/eurydice/index.php/Denmark:Redirect.*

Houlberg, K. et al. (2016), *OECD Review of Policies to Improve the Effectiveness of Resource Use in Schools: Country Background Report for Denmark*, Det Nationale Institut for Kommuners og Regioners Analyse og Forskning (KORA) [Danish Institute for Local and Regional Government Research], Copenhagen, *www.oecd.org/edu/school/10932_OECD%20Country%20Background%20Report%20Denmark.pdf.*

KL (2012), *Rapport om KL's Srategiprojekt om Effektiv Anvendelse af Lærernes Arbejdstid* [Report on KL's Strategy Project on the Effective Use of Teachers' Working Time], KL, Copenhagen, *www.kl.dk/ImageVault/Images/id_58304/scope_0/ImageVaultHandler.aspx*.

Martin, M.O. et al. (2012), *TIMSS 2011 International Results in Science*, International Association for the Evaluation of Educational Achievement (IEA), Amsterdam and TIMSS and PIRLS International Study Center, Boston, *http://timssandpirls.bc.edu/timss2011/downloads/T11_IR_Science_FullBook.pdf*.

Mullis, I.V.S. et al. (2012a), *PIRLS 2011 International Results in Reading*, International Association for the Evaluation of Educational Achievement (IEA), Amsterdam and TIMSS and PIRLS International Study Center, Boston, *http://timssandpirls.bc.edu/pirls2011/downloads/P11_IR_FullBook.pdf*.

Mullis, I.V.S. et al. (2012b), *TIMSS 2011 International Results in Mathematics*, International Association for the Evaluation of Educational Achievement (IEA), Amsterdam and TIMSS and PIRLS International Study Center, Boston, *http://timssandpirls.bc.edu/timss2011/downloads/T11_IR_Mathematics_FullBook.pdf*.

OECD (2015a), "Country statistical profile: Denmark", *Country statistical profiles: Key tables from OECD*, *http://dx.doi.org/10.1787/csp-dnk-table-2015-1-en*.

OECD (2015b), "Denmark", in *Education Policy Outlook 2015: Making Reforms Happen*, OECD Publishing, Paris, *http://dx.doi.org/10.1787/9789264225442-21-en*.

OECD (2015c), *Education at a Glance 2015: OECD Indicators*, OECD Publishing, Paris, *http://dx.doi.org/10.1787/eag-2015-en*.

OECD (2015d), *Immigrant Students at School: Easing the Journey towards Integration*, OECD Publishing, Paris, *http://dx.doi.org/10.1787/9789264249509-en*.

OECD (2015e), *In It Together: Why Less Inequality Benefits All*, OECD Publishing, Paris, *http://dx.doi.org/10.1787/9789264235120-en*.

OECD (2015f), *OECD Economic Outlook, Volume 2015 Issue 2*, OECD Publishing, Paris, *http://dx.doi.org/10.1787/eco_outlook-v2015-2-en*.

OECD (2015g), *OECD Employment Outlook 2015*, OECD Publishing, Paris, *http://dx.doi.org/10.1787/empl_outlook-2015-en*.

OECD (2014a), *National Accounts at a Glance 2014*, OECD Publishing, Paris, *http://dx.doi.org/10.1787/na_glance-2014-en*.

OECD (2014b), *PISA 2012 Results: What Students Know and Can Do (Volume I, Revised edition, February 2014): Student Performance in Mathematics, Reading and Science*, OECD Publishing, Paris, *http://dx.doi.org/10.1787/9789264208780-en*.

OECD (2014c), *PISA 2012 Results: Creative Problem Solving (Volume V): Students' Skills in Tackling Real-Life Problems*, OECD Publishing, Paris, *http://dx.doi.org/10.1787/9789264208070-en*.

OECD (2013a), *Fiscal Federalism 2014: Making Decentralisation Work*, OECD Publishing, Paris, *http://dx.doi.org/10.1787/9789264204577-en*.

OECD (2013b), *OECD Skills Outlook 2013: First Results from the Survey of Adult Skills*, OECD Publishing, Paris, *http://dx.doi.org/10.1787/9789264204256-en*.

OECD (2013c), *PISA 2012 Results: Excellence through Equity (Volume II): Giving Every Student the Chance to Succeed*, OECD Publishing, Paris, *http://dx.doi.org/10.1787/9789264201132-en*.

OECD (2013d), *PISA 2012 Results: Ready to Learn (Volume III): Students' Engagement, Drive and Self-Beliefs*, OECD Publishing, Paris, *http://dx.doi.org/10.1787/9789264201170-en*.

OECD (2013e), *PISA 2012 Results: What Makes Schools Successful (Volume IV): Resources, Policies and Practices*, OECD Publishing, Paris, *http://dx.doi.org/10.1787/9789264201156-en*.

OECD (2012), *Education at a Glance 2012: OECD Indicators*, OECD Publishing, Paris, *http://dx.doi.org/10.1787/eag-2012-en*.

OECD (n.d.), *Education GPS*, *http://gpseducation.oecd.org*.

OECD (n.d.), *Historical Population Data and Projections (1950-2050)*, OECD statistical database, *http://stats.oecd.org*.

Shewbridge, C. et al. (2011), *OECD Reviews of Evaluation and Assessment in Education: Denmark 2011*, OECD Publishing, Paris, *http://dx.doi.org/10.1787/9789264116597-en*.

Statistics Denmark (2016a), StatBank Denmark FOLK2: Population 1 January by Sex, Age, Ancestry, Country of Origin and Citizenship, *www.statbank.dk/statbank5a/SelectVarVal/Define.asp?MainTable=FOLK2&PLanguage=1&PXSId=0&wsid=cftree.*

Statistics Denmark (2016b), StatBank Denmark FRDK115: Population Projections 2015 for the Country by Ancestry, Sex and Age, *www.statbank.dk/statbank5a/SelectVarVal/Define.asp?MainTable=FRDK115&PLanguage=1&PXSId=0&wsid=cftree.*

Statistics Denmark (2016c), StatBank Denmark UDDAKT20: Educational Activity in Basic School by Education, Age, Ancestry, National Origin, Sex, Type of Institution from Basic School, Region and Status, *www.statbank.dk/statbank5a/SelectVarVal/Define.asp?MainTable=UDDAKT20&PLanguage=1&PXSId=0&wsid=cftree.*

Statistics Denmark (2015a), *Statistical Yearbook 2015*, Statistics Denmark, Copenhagen, *www.dst.dk/en/Statistik/Publikationer/VisPub?cid=20195.*

Statistics Denmark (2015b), *Denmark in Figures 2015*, Statistics Denmark, Copenhagen, *www.dst.dk/pukora/epub/upload/19006/denmark2015.pdf.*

Undervisnings Ministeriet (2013), *Pejlemærker for Kompetenceudviklingen i Folkeskolen [Milestones for the Development of Competences in the Folkeskole]*, Undervisnings Ministeriet [Ministry of Education], Copenhagen, *www.uvm.dk/~/media/UVM/Filer/Udd/Folke/PDF13/Nov/131127%20UVM%20Pejlemaerker%20for%20kompetenceudviklingen%20i%20folkeskolen.pdf.*

UNICEF Office of Research (2013), *Child Well-being in Rich Countries: A Comparative Overview*, Innocenti Report Card 11, UNICEF Office of Research, Florence, *www.unicef-irc.org/publications/683.*

ANNEX 1.A1

The Danish education system

Figure 1.A1.1. **The Danish education system**

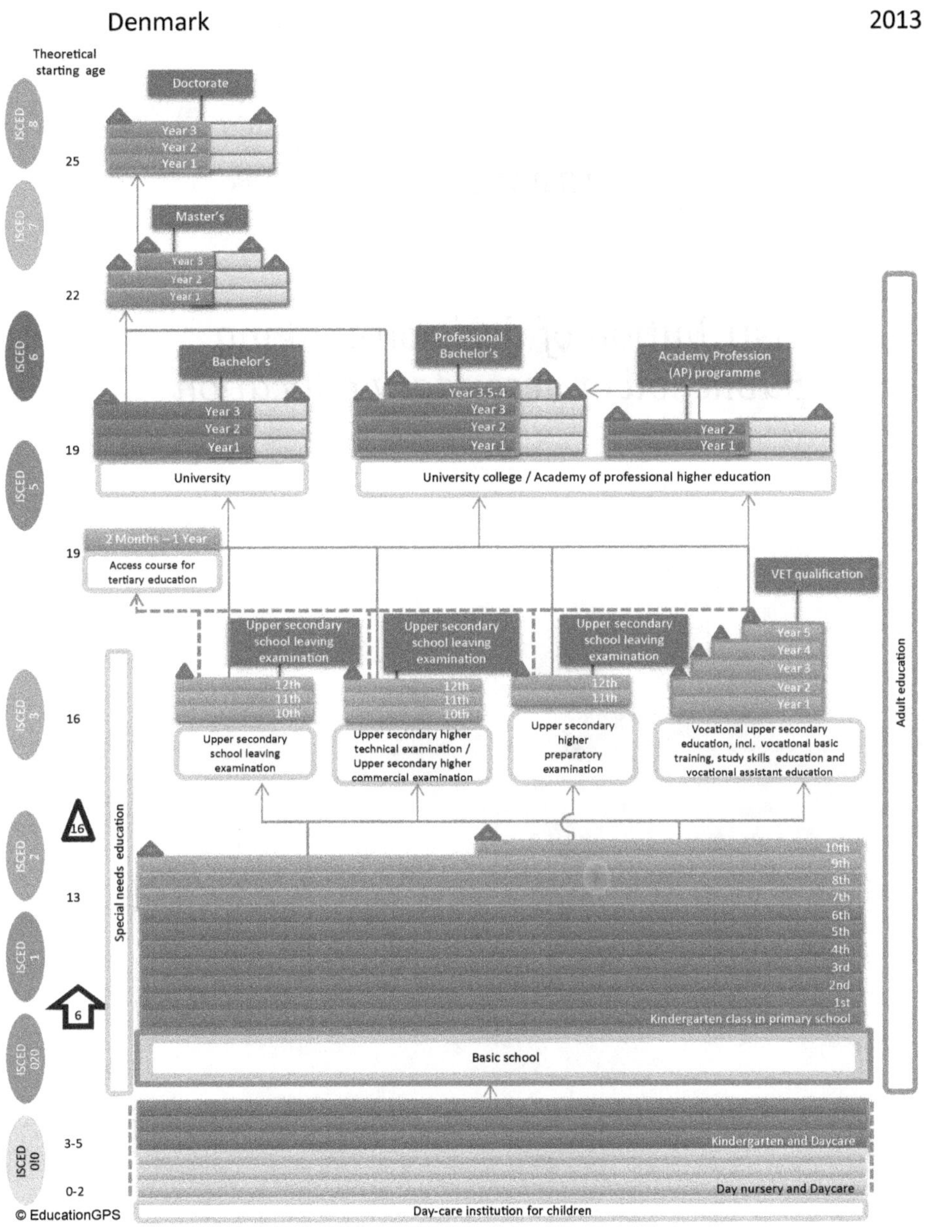

Key:

- Starting/ending age of compulsory education
- Recognized exit point of the education system
- Typical student flow
- Transfer from a programme to another
- Programme designed for part-time attendance
- Vocational/Professional orientation
- Single structure education (integrated ISCED levels)
- May be provided within one school structure
- Transfer at crossing lines is not possible
- Name of diploma, degree or certificate

Source: OECD (n.d.), *Education GPS, http://gpseducation.oecd.org*.

ANNEX 1.A2

Distribution of decision-making in public lower secondary education

Figure 1.A2.1. **Decisions taken at each level of government in public lower secondary education, by domain, 2011**

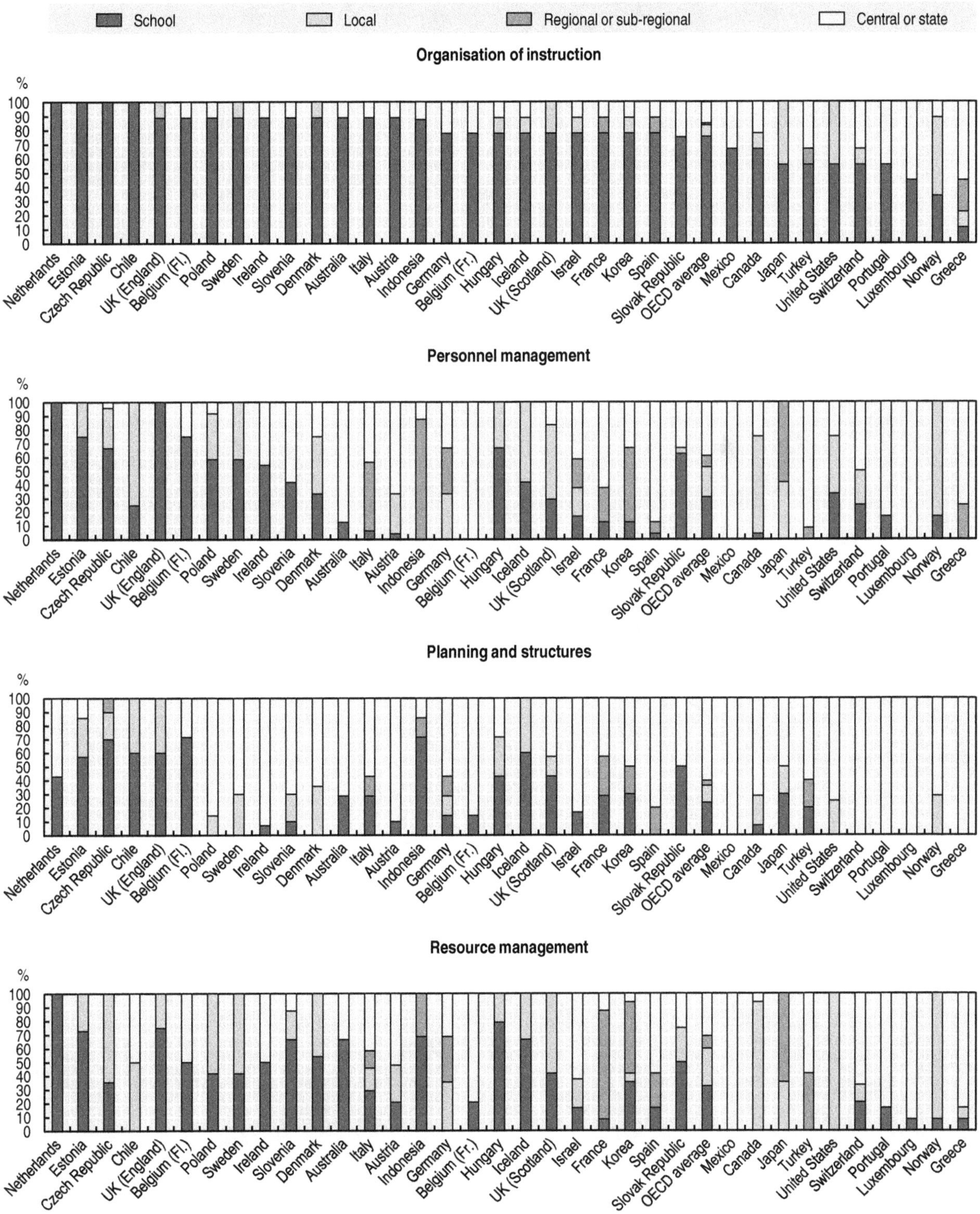

Note: Countries are ranked in descending order of the percentage of decisions about organisation of instruction taken at the school level.
Source: OECD (2012), *Education at a Glance 2012: OECD Indicators*, *http://dx.doi.org/10.1787/eag-2012-en*, Table D6.2a and D6.2b.

Chapter 2

Distribution of school resources in Denmark

This chapter discusses how resources are used and distributed in the Danish school system. It includes descriptions and analyses of expenditures, teacher resources, and the school structure and offer. The central government plays a strong role in the funding of the municipalities, while the municipalities prioritise between local services and allocate resources to individual schools. Schools typically decide how resources are used. The chapter highlights the traditionally high investment in the Folkeskole and the presence of explicit equalisation mechanisms in the funding of municipalities and schools. But it also points out some concerns related to the decentralised funding model and the potential for greater system learning about effective funding formulas. The chapter discusses the potential benefits of a strong private schooling sector in terms of innovation, but also the risks of private schooling to increase segregation. Furthermore, the chapter highlights the benefits of local teacher recruitment for matching teachers to local needs and the increasing flexibility of schools to use their human resources according to their needs under the new framework for the utilisation of teachers' working time. But it also point out concerns about the attractiveness of the teaching profession and the organisation of teachers' career development. The chapter concludes with a number of policy recommendations to consider.

The statistical data for Israel are supplied by and under the responsibility of the relevant Israeli authorities. The use of such data by the OECD is without prejudice to the status of the Golan Heights, East Jerusalem and Israeli settlements in the West Bank under the terms of international law.

Context and features

Distribution of funding

Expenditure per student

The *Folkeskole* is financed by the municipalities and the central government. The expenditure per student is relatively high compared to other countries, both at the primary and lower secondary level (see Figure 2.1). In 2012, the most recent comparison available, the expenditure per student was 32.8% and 30.8% above the OECD and EU21 averages for primary education, and 19% and 14.1% above the averages of the OECD and EU21 areas for lower secondary education. Although primary and lower secondary education are typically provided under the same roof in the *Folkeskole*, expenditures are slightly higher at the lower secondary level than at the primary level, presumably because of longer school days for students at the lower secondary level. This is similar to other countries.

Figure 2.1. **Annual expenditure per student, 2012**

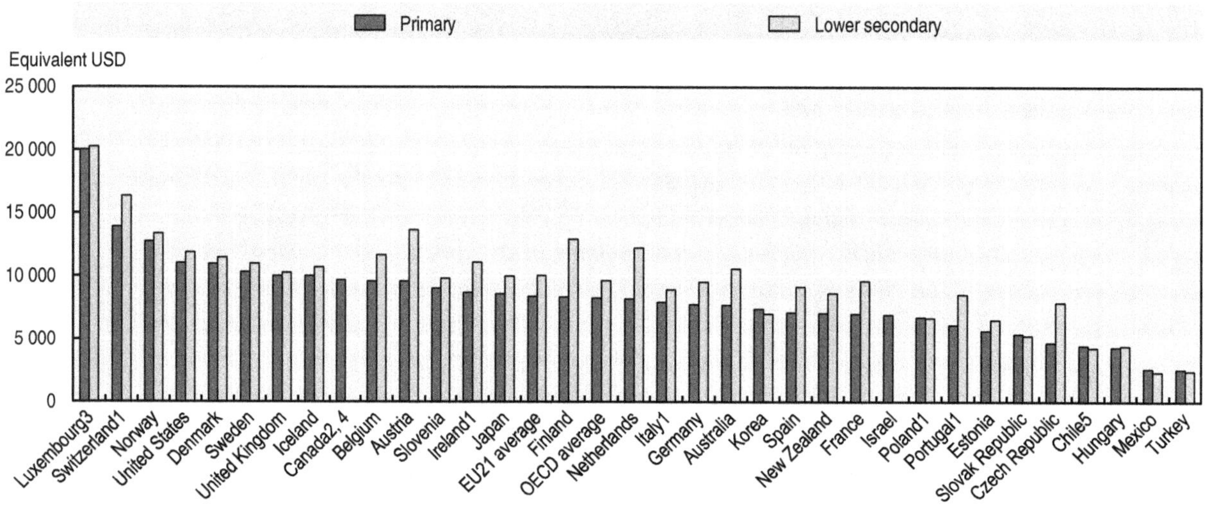

1. Public institutions only.
2. Data for lower secondary education is included in data for primary education.
3. Pre-primary and primary education include reimbursements from local authorities for previous years.
4. Year of reference 2011.
5. Year of reference 2013.

Note: Expenditure is measured in equivalent USD converted using PPPs for GDP and includes expenditure in private schools.
Source: OECD (2015), *Education at a Glance 2015: OECD Indicators*, *http://dx.doi.org/10.1787/eag-2015-en*, Table B1.1a.

Denmark is a rich country. An alternative measure of the degree to which a country prioritises education is the share of GDP spent on education. Denmark was the highest spending country in this respect in 2012, spending a larger share of GDP on primary and lower secondary education than all other OECD countries (see Figure 2.2). The figure includes both public and private spending.

Figure 2.2. **Spending on primary and lower secondary education, 2012**

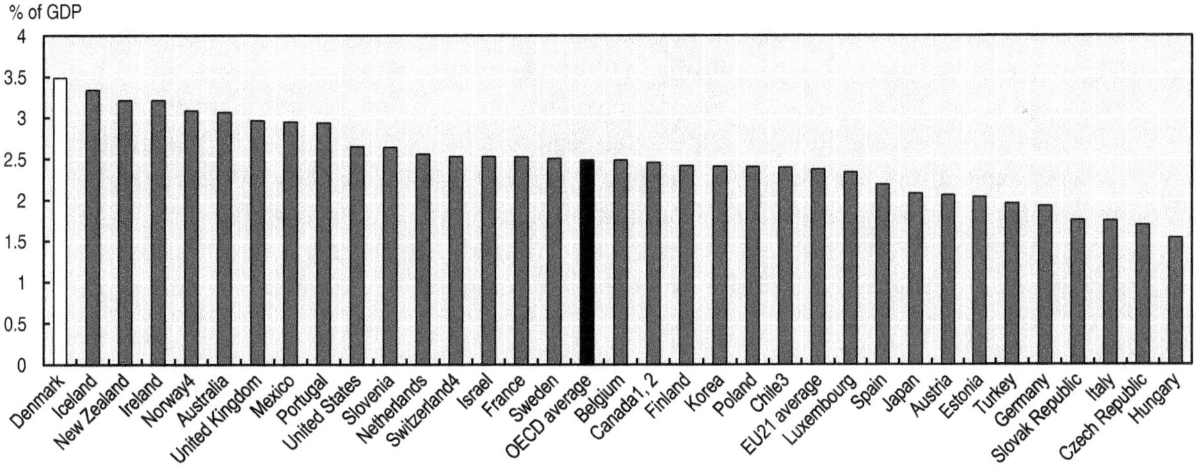

1. Only primary education.
2. Year of reference 2011.
3. Year of reference 2013.
4. Public expenditure only.

Note: Expenditure on primary and lower secondary education as a percentage of GDP, include public and private sources of funds.
Source: OECD (2015), *Education at a Glance 2015: OECD Indicators, http://dx.doi.org/10.1787/eag-2015-en*, Table B2.1.

In recent years, there has been some variation in expenditure per student in Denmark. According to the OECD Education at a Glance, expenditure per student in primary education declined sharply compared to the other EU and OECD countries in 2010 and 2011 (Figure 2.3). In 2012, the latest comparison available, relative per student expenditure for primary education increased again, but was still below the pre-2010 levels. This development is a combination of the official numbers for Denmark and other countries, both working in the same direction. The changes are more modest for lower secondary education, where Denmark is more in line with several other countries (see also Figure 2.3).

Figure 2.3. **Development in international relative expenditure per student, 2005-12**

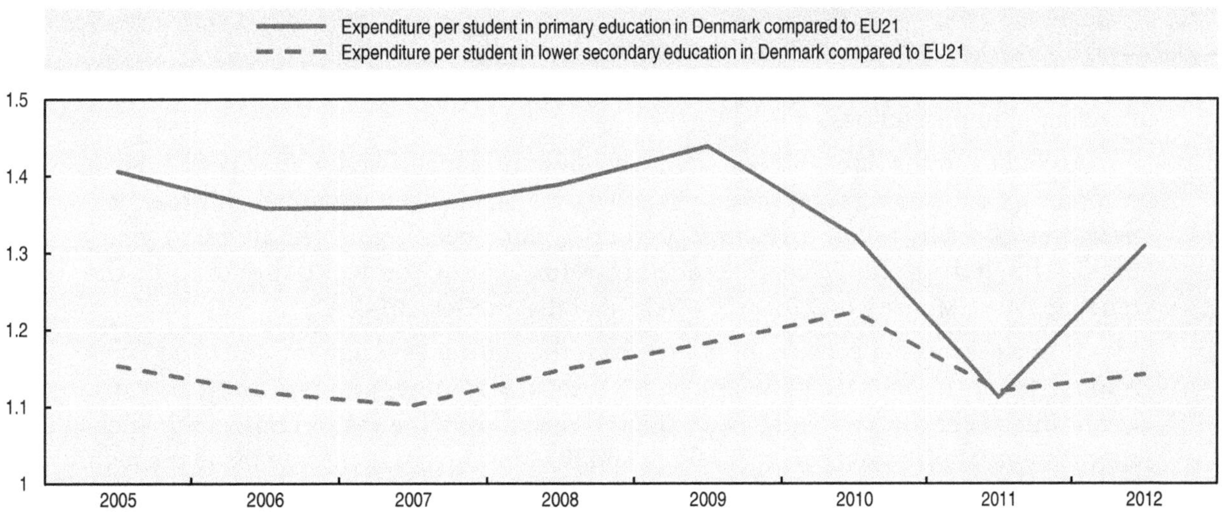

Source: OECD (2008, 2009, 2010, 2011, 2012, 2013a, 2014a, 2015), *Education at a Glance: OECD Indicators*, OECD Publishing, Paris, Table B1.1a.

According to the municipal accounts in Denmark, covering the whole *Folkeskole* (public primary and lower secondary schools, including special schools, but excluding private schools), there was a reduction in real expenditure per student in the period 2009-13 (Figure 2.4). However, the expenditures in 2013 were extraordinarily low because of the lockout of all teachers for about one month (see Chapter 1). Taking the lockout into account, it seems like real expenditure per student has been on a rising path since 2012. The trend of reduced expenditure per student in the public schools was followed by markedly higher expenditures in 2014 and 2015. Expenditure per student in real terms was 4.7% higher in 2015 than in 2012, but still 3.3% below the level in 2009. The block grant from the central government to the municipalities increased permanently in 2014 as a result of the 2014 *Folkeskole* reform.

Figure 2.4. **Development in real expenditure per student in the *Folkeskole*, 2007-15**

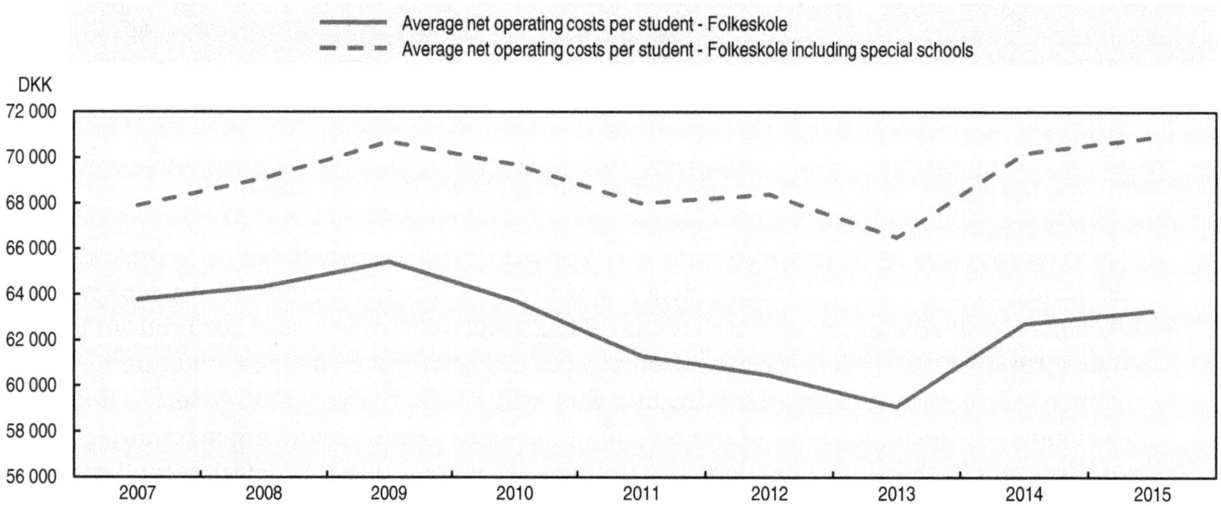

Note: Figures for 2007-14 are accounting information from accounting functions 3.22.01. Folkeskoler [Folkeskole], 3.22.07. *Specialundervisning i regionale tilbud* [Special education in regional institutions], 3.22.08. *Kommunale specialskoler og fra 2014 tillige 3.22.09. Efter- og* [Municipal special schools and from 2014 onwards also continuation schools].
Figures for 2015 are budget numbers.
Source: Ministry of Social Affairs and the Interior (2016), Key Figures, *www.noegletal.dk* (accessed 24 February 2016); Statistics Denmark (2016), StatBank Denmark, *http://statistikbanken.dk* (accessed 24 February 2016).

Funding of municipalities

According to the *Folkeskole* Act, municipalities are responsible for all expenditures in compulsory education, except if stated otherwise by law. Municipalities are the main providers of public sector services in Denmark, and spending on children and young people (including the *Folkeskole*) accounts for 26% of the total spending of the municipalities (Ministry of Economic Affairs and the Interior, 2014).

Municipal income consists of grants from the central government and local taxes. About 71% of the municipal revenues are local tax income, grants from the central government account for about 26% of the revenues, while the rest are mainly financial transactions (Ministry of Economic Affairs and the Interior, 2014). Income tax is the main local tax income source. The main part of income tax in Denmark goes to the municipalities. The rules determining how taxable income is collected are decided nationally, while the municipalities in principle decide the tax rate (see below). The local income tax rate varies between municipalities from 23% to 28%.

The central government allocates different kinds of grants to the municipalities. However, there are very few specific or earmarked grants to the *Folkeskole*. Those that do exist concern relatively small amounts compared to the overall spending level in schools (for example for the competency development of teachers). The *Folkeskole* is almost exclusively financed by the unconditional block grant from the central government in addition to local taxes.

An important mechanism to keep the balance between central regulations and local autonomy are the annual negotiations between the central government and Local Government Denmark (KL/LGDK), the interest group and member authority of the Danish municipalities. Negotiations take place in the spring. In these negotiations, the Ministry of Finance is responsible for setting the total spending level and the total level of grants. The Ministry of Social Affairs and the Interior is responsible for determining the grant system and for monitoring the overall performance of the municipalities, while LGDK co-ordinates tax rates. The agreement sets the goals for the coming fiscal year with regard to both the municipal economic performance and the development of the different municipal services. It lays down the overall framework for the economy for the coming year and the level of overall service expenditure and capital investments.

It is a general agreement which enables the municipalities to prioritise expenditure and taxes in relation to local needs taking into account the overall framework agreed upon. The agreement is not legally binding, but the system is based on observance of the rules it includes. Negotiations include both the level of the grants from the central government and changes in the local income tax rate. This effectively puts limitations on the local freedom to change the tax rate (Lotz et al., 2013). Setting the grant level is important for the overall fiscal policy of the central government, while agreeing on changes in the local income tax rate is important for the budgeting process of the individual municipalities.

If the total municipal expenditure increases more than determined in the agreement, the central government has in the past often enforced sanctions that reduce the general grants the following year (Lotz et al., 2013). Such a sanction system was institutionalised by a budget law from 2012 (Houlberg et al., 2016) (also see Chapter 1). Even though these sanctions are related to the overall economic performance and not the economic performance in individual municipalities, Lotz et al. (2013) argue that the sanction regime has reduced the flexibility of local tax policy.

Negotiations decide the total grant level, but do not directly determine the grant level for each individual municipality. The allocation of the unconditional lump-sum grant follows a budget allocation model decided by the Ministry of Social Affairs and the Interior, which takes certain characteristics of the individual municipalities into account. The model includes population size, age composition, and an index of the socio-economic structure of the municipalities. The factors in the model are designed so as to reflect the expenditure needs facing municipalities on which they have little or no influence. The age group 6-16 years has a relatively high weight in the model as it directly influences the expenditure needs in the *Folkeskole*. The age-related expenditure need has a weight of about 68%, and the socio-economic expenditure need has a weight of about 32%. Important socio-economic characteristics in the system are unemployment, the education level of the population, and housing conditions (Table 2.1).

The aim of the grant system is not to equalise service levels across municipalities as this is a matter of local politics. It is rather designed to give municipalities a similar financial basis so that all municipalities are able to provide a similar service level in all of their remits.

Table 2.1. **Criteria and weights for socio-economic needs in the national equalisation scheme, 2014**

Criterion	Weight
20-59 year-olds without employment over 5%	19
25-49 year-olds without vocational training	16
Rented apartments	5
Psychiatric patients	5
Families in certain types of housing	15
Children in families where the parents have no or little education	8
Individuals 65 years old and older living alone	2.5
Individuals with a low income in three out of four years	8
Number of individuals with intellectual disabilities	5
Number of immigrants and descendants	3
20-59 year-olds with basic skills	5
Estimated annual reduction of the population	2
Children with single parents	4
Children who have moved to another municipality at least three times	2.5

Source: Ministry for Economic Affairs and the Interior (2014), *Municipalities and Regions – Tasks and Financing, http://english.sim.dk/media/670682/municipalities_and_regions_-_tasks_and_financing__june_2014.pdf*; Houlberg, K. et al. (2016), *OECD Review of Policies to Improve the Effectiveness of Resource Use in Schools: Country Background Report for Denmark, www.oecd.org/edu/school/10932_OECD%20Country%20Background%20Report%20Denmark.pdf*, Chapter 3.

The equalisation system takes the municipal tax base into account, thus working as an income tax sharing system. Variations in the tax base across municipalities lead to variations in the potential level of service provision for a given tax rate. The equalisation scheme distributes central government grants to reduce the differences in municipal income related to the tax base, but it does not fully compensate for low tax bases in order to retain incentives for increasing private income in the municipality. The present system implies that if the tax base increases, the municipal revenues increase (for unchanged tax rates), but at a smaller rate than the increase in the tax base as the grants from the central government will decline. If, however, a municipality increases the tax rate, the increased revenues go without reductions to the municipality since the equalisation scheme is only related to the tax base.

Expenditure per student in the municipal accounts (including students with special needs) varies from DKK 58 424 to above DKK 100 000 (Figure 2.5) in 2014. The vast majority of the municipalities, however, have expenditure per student in the order of DKK 60 000 to DKK 80 000, with an average of DKK 70 000. Expenditure per student in the *Folkeskole* varies across municipalities for a number of reasons. Expenditure might be high because inhabitants have a high income, because the municipality chooses to have a relatively high income tax rate, because of characteristics that increase the expenditure needs and thus the grants from the central government, and/or because a municipality chooses to prioritise the *Folkeskole* compared to other local public services.

Since 2013, the implementation of the 2014 *Folkeskole* reform has been an important part of the negotiations between the central government and LGDK. The central government steers in relation to the national goals set with the reform (see Chapters 1 and 3). The high degree of local autonomy in the system implies that the central government does not set specific goals for individual municipalities. However, the central government has recently established mechanisms that make it easier to monitor individual municipalities. This includes the development of a data warehouse and the obligation for schools and municipalities to produce biannual quality reports (see Chapter 3).

Figure 2.5. **Density of expenditure per student across municipalities, including special needs education, based on municipal budgets for 2014 (2015 prices)**

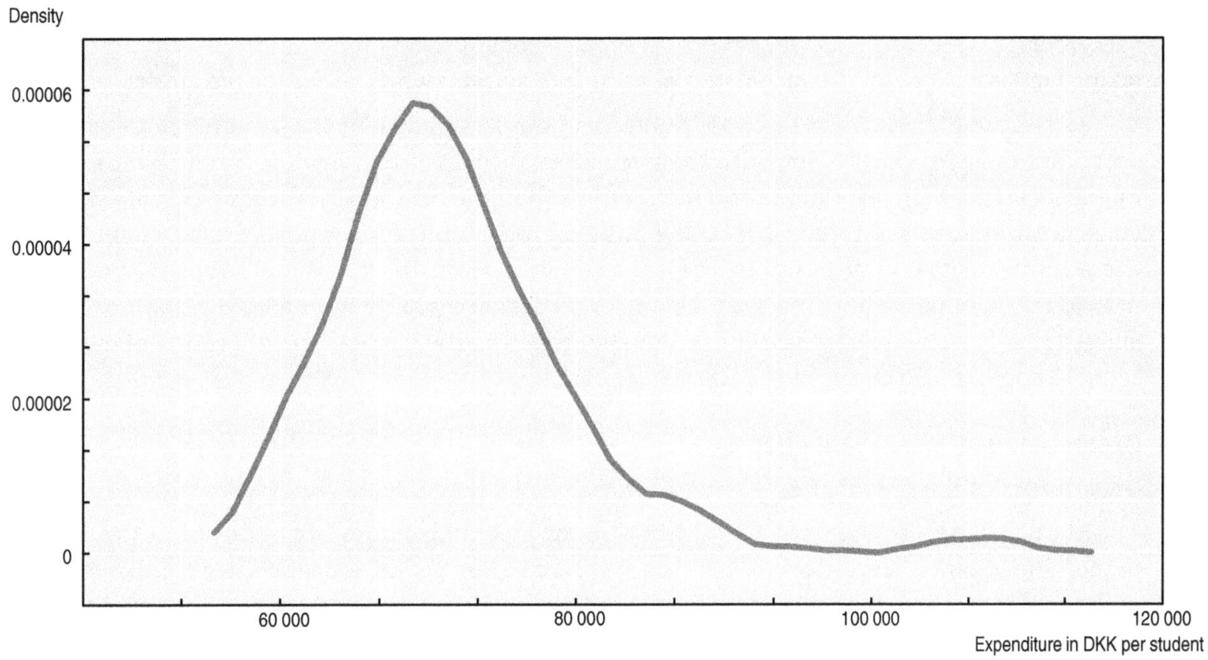

Source: Statistics Denmark (2016), StatBank Denmark, *http://statistikbanken.dk* (accessed 24 February 2016); Danish Ministry for Children, Education and Gender Equality (2016c), *Datavarehuset* [Datawarehouse], *www.uddannelsesstatistik.dk*.

Funding of schools

Municipal councils allocate funds to individual schools. A variety of models and mechanisms are used for this allocation in different municipalities. Some municipalities simply allocate a given amount per student, while most municipalities take the socio-economic background of students or neighbourhoods into account in some way. The way in which socio-economic conditions is taken into account and the relative weight of different socio-economic characteristics vary greatly across municipalities. Typically, funding mechanisms take school size into account. Some municipalities relate funding to the number of students, while others use measures on the required number of classes according to the national maximum class size regulations (which set a maximum class size of 28 students)

Danish municipalities have detailed register data on their inhabitants, which provides them key information about the socio-economic background of each individual student. Thus, there is large local freedom in how to operationalise socio-economic measures as a way to calculate school funding. Municipalities vary in the variables they include in the socio-economic measure. In addition, some municipalities use a measure of the socio-economic composition in the school, while other municipalities use a measure of the socio-economic composition in the school catchment area. In the latter case, schools are responsible for funding the education costs of all students living in the catchment area, including students enrolled in private schools and special schools for students with special needs. Enrolment in private schools is a free choice by parents, whereas for enrolment in special schools the local *Folkeskole* and/or the municipality are involved in the decision.

Since the 2007 local government reform (see Chapter 1), approaches to funding support for students with special educational needs have changed. Based on interviews conducted in Denmark, the OECD review team formed the impression that municipalities rely to a decreasing extent on earmarked funding to individual students and more on general funding. Following an approach of general funding, resources for students with special needs are allocated across schools with respect to general criteria measuring the socio-economic background of students. That way, schools have the flexibility to optimally use these resources, taking factors such as the characteristics of peers into account when allocating resources.

As described in Chapter 1, school principals have a high degree of autonomy in using school funding, in consultation with their school's school board. Individual municipalities might set some more regulations and instructions than the central government, but, above all, school principals are restricted by the national regulations for class size, regulation of the amount of teaching hours in the school year and in the different subjects, and individual students' right to receive teaching in accordance with their needs. Principals are obliged to recruit the relevant teacher competency within the budget. The allocation of the school budget is also discussed by the school board.

Organisation of the school offer

Governance of the school offer

Municipalities in Denmark are responsible for providing compulsory education to all of their inhabitants. This involves ensuring that all children get an education in accordance with the law, starting from 1 August of the year they turn six (enrolment in Year 0) until the end of Year 9, which is typically the year they turn 16. This responsibility includes all children, including children with special needs. Compulsory education does not necessarily need to be provided in the municipal *Folkeskole*, but can also take place in a private school or in private homes. However, every child has the right to be enrolled in the municipal *Folkeskole* free of charge. Children also have the right to enrol in Year 10 free of charge, which implies that municipalities have public schools with a pedagogical offer for Year 10 (see below).

This system of governance relies on a balance between local autonomy on the one hand, and central authority and regulation on the other. The national level defines the space for local autonomy within nationally specified frames and guidelines. The municipalities are obliged to follow all the central regulations since Denmark does not have a formal federal system. The central government has the overall responsibility for education, regulating the content of education through the *Folkeskole* law and different regulations.

The municipalities are multi-purpose local governments. They provide several of the main services of the welfare state, including health care, social services, care for the elderly, cultural services, local infrastructure, and local industrial and economic development. Within their budget, they prioritise between different services (see Chapter 1). This system implies that some municipalities might prioritise spending on education more than others. The municipalities are autonomous in making a wide range of decisions, including decisions on the organisation of the school offer, the number of schools, whether students with special needs should be enrolled in regular schools or in special schools, the pedagogical organisation of schools and the number of classes.

National regulations only set some minimum standards. For example, classes shall not exceed 28 students and students with special needs have the right to special assistance and support. All children have the right to teaching that is in accordance with their individual needs and qualifications. In addition, municipalities are required to provide biannual quality reports on the performance of their schools.

Student enrolment in public and private schools

Parents can choose private schools for their children, which provide education from pre-school to Year 10. Private schools do not have to accept all students, but can refuse to accept students if they wish. They decide the objectives for the education they provide, but have to offer an education that is equivalent to the *Folkeskole*. Private schools in Denmark are highly diverse, and both students with a weak and strong socio-economic background attend private schools. However, even though private schools and students in private schools are very heterogeneous, empirical studies find that students in private schools, on average, have a more advantaged socio-economic background than students in the *Folkeskole* (Houlberg et al., 2016).

Private schools constitute a significant part of compulsory education in Denmark. According to OECD statistics, the only European countries that have a larger share of students in private lower secondary schools than Denmark are the Netherlands and Spain (OECD, 2014a, Chart C7.1). Between 2008 and 2013, the share of students in private schools increased from just under 17% to over 19% (Figure 2.6).

Figure 2.6. **Trend in the number of students in public schools and in the share of students in private schools**

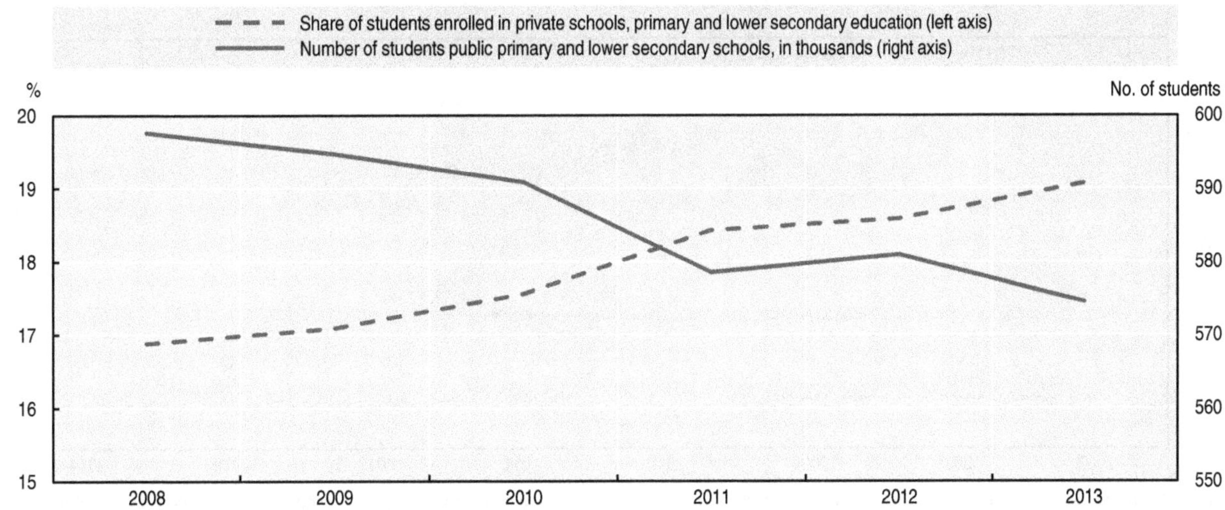

Note: Private schools include "continuation schools" (*Efterskole*).

Source: Houlberg, K. et al. (2016), *OECD Review of Policies to Improve the Effectiveness of Resource Use in Schools: Country Background Report for Denmark*, *www.oecd.org/edu/school/10932_OECD%20Country%20Background%20Report%20Denmark.pdf*, Table 2.2.

Private schools receive public grants. In 2013, the grant was equal to 71% of the average expenditure per student in the *Folkeskole*. The municipalities have to pay 89% of this grant, while the remaining 11% are paid for by the central government (Houlberg et al., 2016). From 2016 onwards, private schools have been receiving 73% of the average expenditure per student in the *Folkeskole*. Parents pay a fee that is determined by the individual private schools. The typical amount ranges from DKK 1 000 to 2 000 per month (Houlberg et al., 2016). This corresponds to 15%-30% of the average expenditure per student in the *Folkeskole*.

Since the public subsidy for private schools is relatively high, the share of private spending is low in Denmark despite the relatively high share of private schools. The OECD *Education at a Glance 2015* compares funding sources across countries, including primary education, all secondary education and post-secondary non-tertiary education as one group. The private school system in Denmark is similar for upper secondary education as for primary and lower secondary education. According to the OECD's data, only about 3% of spending on education at these educational levels comes from households (OECD, 2015, Chart B3.1).

The number of students in primary and lower secondary education has been stable in Denmark during the last years. Given the increasing share of students in private schools, this implies that the number of students in public schools has declined (Figure 2.6). The reduced number of students puts additional pressure on cost savings in public schools.

On average, public schools are twice as large as private schools. In addition, average school size has increased in recent years. From 2007 to 2014, the number of public regular schools declined by 17%, with the largest degree of consolidation in 2011 and 2012 (Figure 2.7). On the other hand, the increasing number of students in private schools has increased the number of private schools by 12%. School consolidation across Denmark has involved mainly the closure or merger of relatively small public schools. The total number of schools in Denmark has declined from 2 275 in 2007 to 2 043 in 2014.

Figure 2.7. **Trend in the number of schools**

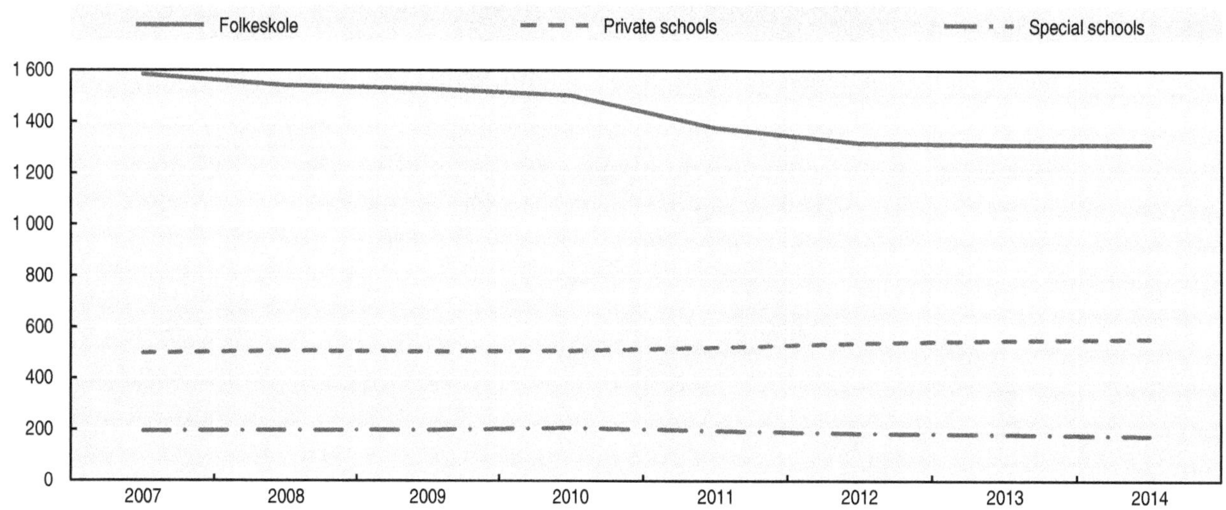

Source: Houlberg, K. et al. (2016), *OECD Review of Policies to Improve the Effectiveness of Resource Use in Schools: Country Background Report for Denmark*, *www.oecd.org/edu/school/10932_OECD%20Country%20Background%20Report%20Denmark.pdf*, Appendix 1, Table 2.

Since 2009, municipalities have reduced their service level by DKK 11 billion in real terms. As a result, unit costs in all service levels have been under pressure, including the *Folkeskole*. The school consolidation process has most likely contributed to a reduction in expenditure per student. The reduction in expenditure per student in real terms up to 2013 can also be observed by an increase in class size and a higher student-teacher ratio (Figure 2.8), even though it also has to be taken into account that pedagogues (a profession similar to early childhood and care staff in other countries, but supporting all stages of human development more broadly) have been working increasingly in schools since the 2014 *Folkeskole* reform. The student-teacher ratio is smaller than the class size as students have more hours in class than teachers and some students have extra teachers. On the other hand, increased travel time of students can also create new costs for municipalities. The municipalities are obliged to cover transportation costs for students living far away from the *Folkeskole* in which they are enrolled. For students in pre-school and Years 1-3,

Figure 2.8. **Teacher-student ratio, class size and school size**

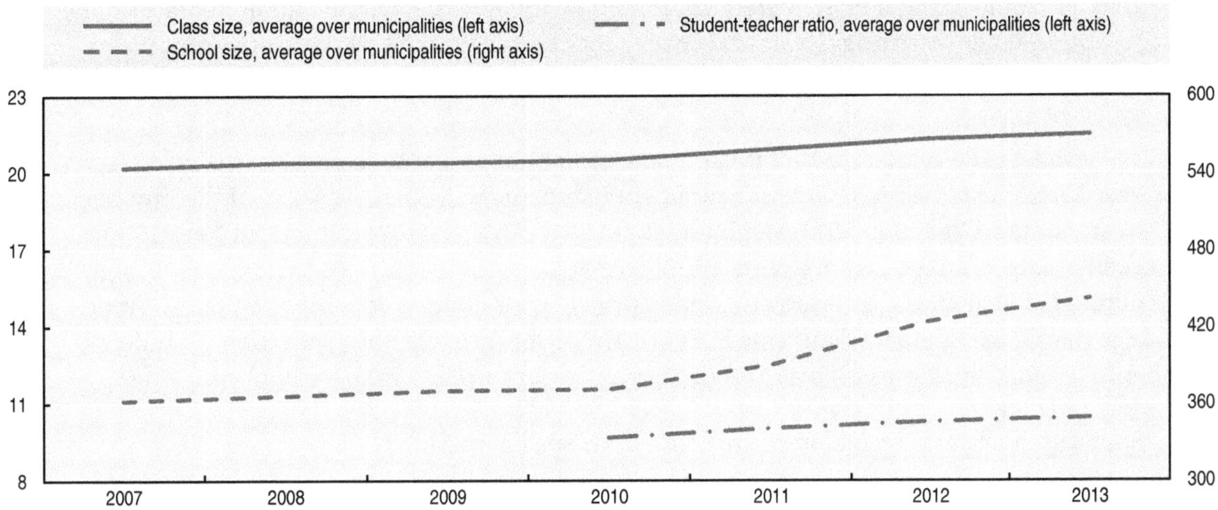

Source: Houlberg, K. et al. (2016), *OECD Review of Policies to Improve the Effectiveness of Resource Use in Schools: Country Background Report for Denmark, www.oecd.org/edu/school/10932_OECD%20Country%20Background%20Report%20Denmark.pdf*, Appendix 1, Tables 3, 4, and 10.

municipalities are obliged to pay for the transportation cost for students living more than 2.5 km away from their *Folkeskole*. For Years 4-6 it is 6 km, for Years 7-9 it is 7 km, and for Year 10 it is a distance of more than 9 km. If parents choose a private school, they lose the right to the free transportation of their child.

Student enrolment in Year 10

Students graduate from the *Folkeskole* after Year 9, typically the year they turn 16. Upper secondary education builds upon the qualifications that students have acquired in the *Folkeskole*. All young people in Denmark have the right to upper secondary education and thus must be offered such an education. This reflects the expectation that all children should complete and graduate from upper secondary education with only few exceptions.

When graduating from the *Folkeskole*, students are expected to have the necessary basic skills in order to complete upper secondary education successfully within the regular time. In between compulsory education and upper secondary education, however, students have the possibility to enrol in an optional Year 10 in the *Folkeskole* or a private continuation school (*Efterskole*). Continuation schools cover Years 8-10, comprise a broad range of school types, and specialise in different educational themes or specific youth groups. Typical examples are sports, outdoor activities and various creative arts productions. Continuation schools are typically boarding schools that are financially supported by the municipalities similar to other private schools. According to various groups interviewed by the OECD review team, one of the main rationales for Year 10 lies in some students needing more time to reach the qualifications necessary for enrolment in upper secondary education. According to the *Folkeskole* Act, Year 10 is an educational offer for young people who, after finishing basic education, are in need of additional qualifications and/or clarifications with regard to their further educational opportunities before entering upper secondary education. Students may, however, also enrol in an optional Year 10 for personal and social development, which is reflected in the wide range of available specialisations, particularly in private continuation schools.

Students have the right to enrol in Year 10 free of charge, which implies that the municipal authorities must have a pedagogical offer for Year 10 for all those that are interested. In reality, the pedagogical content varies largely between schools offering Year 10. Some schools offer merely repetition of the content of the earlier years in the *Folkeskole*, while others have a much broader set of goals. Year 10 consists of a compulsory part and an optional part. In private continuation schools, the optional part can be used in different ways.

Available data indicate that it is quite common for students to enrol in the voluntary Year 10. In the public *Folkeskole*, the number of students in Year 10 was 35% of the number of students in Year 9 in 2013 (Houlberg et al., 2016, Table 2.4). Enrolment in Year 10 has been stable over the last six years (Houlberg et al., 2016, Table 2.3). In addition, a high number of Year 10 students are enrolled in private continuation schools. Overall, counting also the a large number of students in Year 10 in private schools, the proportion of students enrolled in Year 10 is as high as 55% of the enrolment in Year 9 in the school year 2013/14.

Special schools and inclusion of students with special needs

Municipalities are responsible for the education of all children, including children with different kinds of special needs. Some municipalities have agreements that their students with special needs can attend a special school in another municipality and municipalities that do not themselves run a special needs school may draw on special needs schools run by the regions for a fee and according to specific framework agreements. It is a local choice whether to enrol a student in a regular school or in a special school, a decision taken in a process typically involving an assessment through an external visitation board and including parents and pedagogues in the municipality under general rules set by the individual municipalities. Following a recent legislative change, special needs education now includes children in special classes or special schools as well as children with special needs in regular classes with the need for instruction in a special class of more than nine teaching hours per week. Children who need less than nine teaching hours of special instruction per week can benefit from individualised teaching in regular classes, a temporary subdivision of classes, additional lessons and other types of professional support, two teachers in a class, teacher assistants, or individual support. The specific criteria used for enrolment in special schools, however, vary across municipalities, and this is also reflected in different degrees of inclusion of special needs students.

Denmark has followed a policy of greater inclusion of students with special needs in regular teaching situations as set out in the annual agreements between the central government and LGDK (see Chapter 1). As a result, the share of students in special schools has declined in the past few years, from 5.8% in 2010/11 to 4.8% in 2013/14 (Table 2.2). The national goal was to reduce the number of students in special schools to below 4% by 2015.

Table 2.2. **Percentage of students in the public *Folkeskole* enrolled in special schools**

	2010/11	2011/12	2012/13	2013/14
All students	5.8	5.4	5.3	4.8
Boys	8.0	7.5	7.2	..
Girls	3.4	3.2	3.0	..

..: Not available

Source: Houlberg, K. et al. (2016), *OECD Review of Policies to Improve the Effectiveness of Resource Use in Schools: Country Background Report for Denmark*, *www.oecd.org/edu/school/10932_OECD%20Country%20Background%20Report%20 Denmark.pdf*, Table 2.8.

Moving students with the least severe special educational needs previously enrolled in special schools to regular schools might reduce the overall expenditure per student in primary and lower secondary education. One motivation for the inclusion policy seems to be to teach these students more efficiently with less extra resources in regular schools than in special schools. For example, students with less sever special educational needs can participate in regular teaching without extra resources in some subjects, although not all subjects, with the same learning potential as in special schools. However, even though overall expenditure per student in the school system can be reduced by the inclusion policy, expenditure per student might nevertheless increase both in special schools and regular schools. Special schools are left with a student population with a higher level of special needs on average, which will increase expenditure per student. They will typically have to continue to cover the fixed costs of operating a school, but with fewer students. Houlberg et al. (2016, Appendix 1, Table 7) show that the expenditure per student in special schools has increased by 17% in the period 2010 to 2013. Figure 2.7 shows that the number of special schools has declined by 15% between 2010 and 2014.

At the same time, the movement of students to regular schools is likely to increase the expenditure per student also in regular schools as these schools need to make adequate arrangements to cater to an increasing number of students with some special needs. This effect is likely to be small considering the low share of the overall number of students being moved. In fact, increased inclusion in regular schools has occurred in a period of a general decline in expenditure per student. The overall cost saving is a result of fewer students in the costly special schools.

Distribution of teacher resources

Teacher employment conditions and salaries

Teacher quality is the main school-level factor affecting student achievement, and teachers are the main cost component in education (OECD, 2005). Thus, when analysing the resource situation in schools, teacher resources are of particular importance. There has been a reduction in the number of teachers in the *Folkeskole* in the last years following a decline in the number of students and an increase in the student-teacher ratio (Figures 2.7 and 2.8). While there were about 57 000 teachers (including pedagogues) in the *Folkeskole* in 2009, this number decreased to about 51 000 in 2014 (Houlberg et al., 2016). The low number of teachers in 2013 is related to the teacher lockout (Figure 2.9). However, as part of the 2014 *Folkeskole* reform, there has been an increase in the number of pedagogues working in the *Folkeskole* (see Chapter 4). According to data from the Ministry for Children, Education and Gender Equality, the number of pedagogues in the *Folkeskole* increased from 3 961 in 2010/11 to 5 785 in 2013/14 (Danish Ministry for Children, Education and Gender Equality, 2016b).

About 98% of the teachers in the *Folkeskole* are members of the Danish Union of Teachers (*Danmarks Lærerforening*, DLF). Private school teachers are organised in a separate union and do not a take part in the negotiations for teachers working in the *Folkeskole*. Historically, working conditions for teachers in the *Folkeskole* have been determined in negotiations between the teacher union and LGDK. Up until 2014, the central agreement resulting from these negotiations used to set a certain amount of preparation time for each lesson taught, independent of teacher experience, year and subject. The agreement also included compensation for a large range of different task in terms of reduction in number of lessons taught. Legislation passed in 2013 (Act no. 409 on teacher working time) set this agreement aside as of the school year 2014/15. Act no. 409 has given school leaders a higher degree of

Figure 2.9. **The number of teachers in the public *Folkeskole*, full-year equivalents**

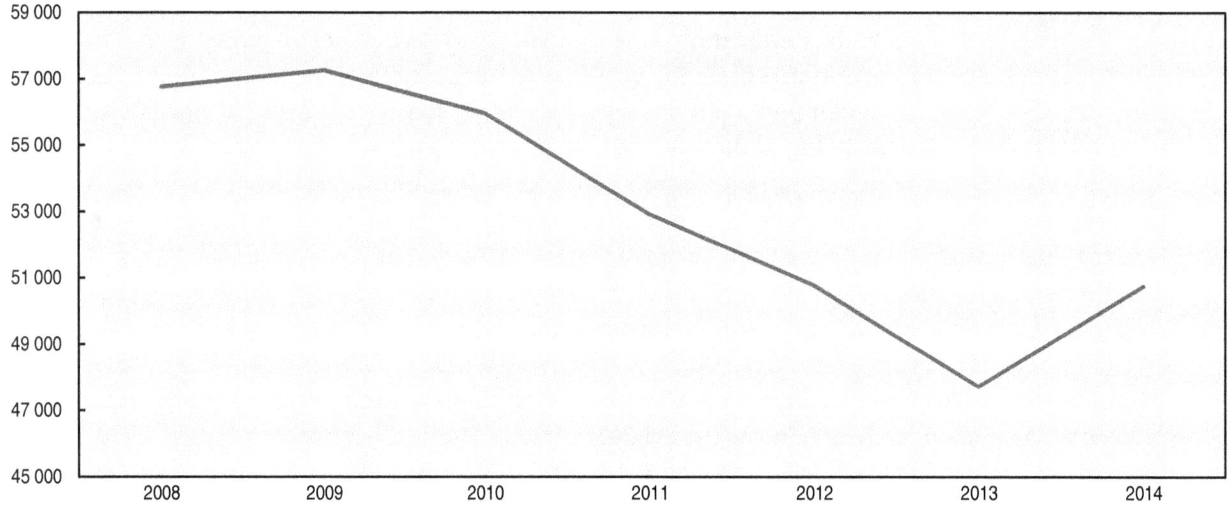

Note: Includes ordinary teachers, pedagogical leaders of pre-school classes, and substitute teachers.
Source: Houlberg, K. et al. (2016), *OECD Review of Policies to Improve the Effectiveness of Resource Use in Schools: Country Background Report for Denmark*, *www.oecd.org/edu/school/10932_OECD%20Country%20Background%20Report%20Denmark.pdf*, Table 4.1.

flexibility in the management of the teacher work force within the daily working time determined in the legislation (see also Chapters 1 and 4 for details).

The salaries of teachers in municipal schools are mainly determined in the central bargaining between the teacher union and LGDK. In the latest years, the bargaining parties have used most of their efforts on negotiating working conditions, while agreement on salary levels has been more easily reached. While the growth in teacher salaries is determined in the central bargaining process, there is some local flexibility for setting individual teachers' salaries. Local adjustments of teacher salaries are determined in bargaining processes between individual municipalities and their local teacher union. As a result of this process, salaries of teachers with the same experience differ somewhat across different municipalities.

The salaries of Danish teachers compared to the salaries for other tertiary educated workers are higher than the OECD average (OECD, 2015, Chart D3.1). The wage structure of Danish teachers is, however, much more compressed than in most other countries. This implies that the starting salary for teachers in Denmark is competitive compared to other countries, while the top salaries for senior teachers with the highest qualifications are low by international comparison (see Figure 2.10).

Teacher recruitment

Teachers are employed by the municipalities, but are attached to an individual school. School principals are in charge of the recruitment of new teachers, within national work and tariff regulations and municipal instructions. They determine the share of resources in the school budget that should be used on teacher salaries and recruit teachers accordingly. Before announcing a vacant position, school principals are responsible for determining the kinds of competencies that are required. The teacher recruitment situation varies across schools and municipalities. In the example of a rural municipality visited by the OECD review team, it was reported that they had fewer applicants to vacant positions than more urban areas. No national data on teacher supply and demand in different municipalities is

Figure 2.10. **Lower secondary teachers' salaries at different points in teachers' career, 2013**

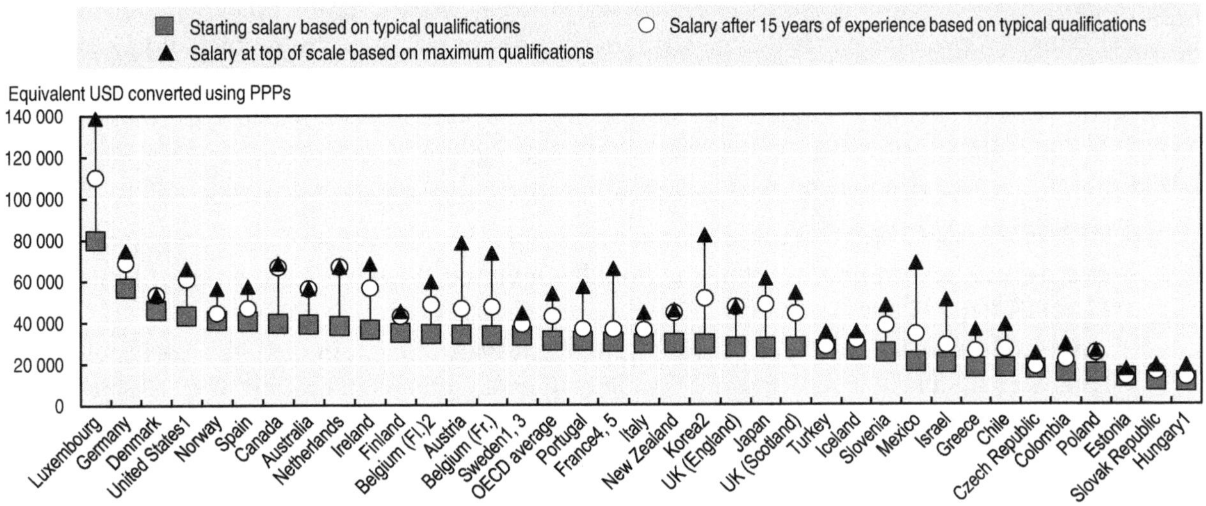

1. Actual base salaries.
2. Salaries at top of scale and typical qualifications, instead of maximum qualifications.
3. Salaries at top of scale and minimum qualifications, instead of maximum qualifications.
4. Includes average bonuses for overtime hours.
5. The typical qualification of starting teachers differs substantially from the typical qualification of all the current teachers.

Note: Countries are ranked in descending order of starting salaries for lower secondary teachers with typical qualifications. Annual statutory salaries in public schools measured in equivalent USD converted using PPPs for GDP.

Source: OECD (2015), *Education at a Glance 2015: OECD Indicators*, *http://dx.doi.org/10.1787/eag-2015-en*, Tables D3.1a and D3.6a.

available. A recent survey from January 2016 of the Danish Union of Teachers suggests an increasing challenge to recruit qualified teachers (DLF, 2016). The respondents were local union leaders in the municipalities. 75% of the local unions reported problems with recruiting qualified teachers in the previous year, and 33% considered this to be a problem of high degree. 74% of the respondents had the impression that the recruitment challenge had increased over the last years. In another survey carried out in autumn 2015, 11% of the municipalities reported challenges in recruiting qualified teachers to a high degree. 69% of the municipalities reported challenges to some degree. This is an increase in comparison to a similar survey conducted in the autumn of 2014. Challenges are especially reported with regards to recruiting teachers with teaching competencies in certain subjects and in certain geographical areas (LGDK, 2015b).

Most individuals with a teacher education actually work as teachers. According to data from the Ministry for Children, Education and Gender Equality, the Ministry of Higher Education and Science and Statistics Denmark, about 84% of qualified teachers in employment work in the education sector. The remaining individuals with teacher education work in different parts of the economy, including the private sector, social services and the cultural sector. The unemployment rate of teachers is about 2%, has been relatively stable over the last four to five years, and does not seem to have been influenced by the decrease in the number of teacher positions in the *Folkeskole* and the new legislation on working conditions (Danish Ministry of Children, Education and Gender Equality, 2016a).

It is too early to conclude whether the change in working conditions has reduced the attractiveness of the teaching profession. According to municipal payroll data 5 339 teachers (around 10%) left the public school sector between October 2013 and October 2014 and 5 315 between October 2014 and 2015. This is an increase in comparison to October 2012 and 2013 where only 4 261 teachers left the public school sector. However, in the years 2007-11 an average of 5 474 left the public school sector annually. Teachers leave public schools either for work in another sector, for work in private schools, into unemployment, or for retirement. Teachers' sick leave has also increased. According to the municipal payroll data, sick leave has increased by 12% after the reform in 2014 and is now at the same level as for other municipal employees (Kommunernes og regionernes Løndatakontor, 2016).

Strengths

Distribution of funding

Investment in education has been traditionally high and there has been a recent focus on the efficiency of spending

It is a clear goal of the Danish school system that every student in the *Folkeskole* should be prepared for further education and complete upper secondary education. The *Folkeskole* is the foundation for further education, such that the investment in basics skills in the *Folkeskole* must be seen in relation to the overall investment in education.

Historically, Denmark has allocated a high level of resources to education. Between 2009 and 2013, expenditure per student in the *Folkeskole* declined, but the proportion of overall municipal expenditure allocated to the *Folkeskole* remained unchanged. The overall decline in spending on the *Folkeskole* in this time period did not coincide with reduced ambitions for the performance of the *Folkeskole*. The expenditure per student has always been clearly above the average expenditure in the OECD and the EU, and relative expenditure increased markedly again in 2014 (Figures 2.1 to 2.4). Policies have expressed an increased ambition to improve educational performance and to strengthen the governance of the education sector. The central government acknowledges that the organisation of education and the support system for schools and teachers are crucial elements to improve performance.

Since the financial crisis, attention to the efficient use of resources in education has increased. In the process of preparing the 2014 *Folkeskole* reform, stakeholders acknowledged that better learning outcomes for all students should be possible without using more of society's resources on compulsory education. The present evidence does not indicate any reduction in student achievement since the introduction of the reform, but the full impact of the changes will need to be monitored over the years to come. The impression of the OECD review team is, however, that the Danish school system has been able to implement a reform with clear and high ambitions for improved student performance without a major increase in overall spending. The focus has been on improving school quality within the present resource situation. An important element has been a more flexible use of teachers' working hours, improving the utilisation of existing resources in schools. Previously, teachers' preparation time was bound in agreements. Under the new framework for the utilisation of teachers' working time it is the intention that teachers' work should be organised in a new and more flexible and collaborative way with discretion for school leaders to prioritise the teachers' tasks and teaching based on students' abilities and needs. As the new framework envisages, this should also give room for a more efficient organisation of teachers' preparatory work, so that more time can be dedicated directly to students. As another important element of the reform, the length of students' school day increased. This has been accomplished without hiring additional teachers. Instead, it has been possible to shift resources from after school programmes (*Skolefritidsordning og Fritidshjem*, SFO) to schools, enabling schools to employ more pedagogues, as students' time in after school programmes has decreased following the introduction of longer school days. Pedagogues are professionals trained in supporting all stages of human development from birth to old age, including early childhood education and care and leisure and youth education (see Chapter 4). In addition, the government has raised the block grant permanently with DKK 407 million, introduced a grant for competency development (DKK 1 billion from 2013-20), and allocated DKK 1.8 billion (2014-17) in order to facilitate the implementation of the reform.

However, as is discussed further below, the success of the reform will depend essentially on how teachers and school leaders are able to adjust to the new situation regarding the use of their time, and whether expectations for increased teaching time (in general two additional clock hours per week based on an agreement between the central government and LGDK, that is 18.3 hours compared to 16.3 hours previously) will influence teachers' engagement and time for other aspects of their work as teaching professionals (e.g. collaboration, mentoring, peer feedback etc.). For example, a recent research report on the school reform and new working conditions finds that teachers have experienced a reduction in their time for preparation and that this situation poses a challenge for their teaching (Bjørnholt et al., 2015, more on this below and in Chapter 4). The analysis also finds, however, that school principals consider that the mind-set and practices of teachers have remained unchanged.

In the Danish context of highly decentralised policy making, the goal of efficient school organisation has been taken on board at both the central and municipal level. Decentralised power in the school system can provide good conditions for efficiency and high performance (Barankay and Lockwood, 2007; Clark, 2009; Falch and Fischer, 2012; Hanushek et al., 2013). The Danish system is highly decentralised in the sense that the central government does not interfere in specific municipalities and schools, but governs the system mainly through general guidelines agreed in national negotiations. Central funding is related to national goals and targets as negotiated in the annual agreements between the central government and LGDK. A key central initiative to reduce spending following the financial crisis was the introduction of multi-annual expenditure ceilings for the central government, municipalities and regions by the Danish parliament.

A range of initiatives to increase the efficiency of spending in the education sector were implemented by individual municipalities without involvement of the national level. One example of the capability of the system to work on efficiency improvement is the school consolidation process. This process was led in a decentralised fashion by individual municipalities. Municipalities have sought to consolidate their school systems to both increase student achievement by improving the learning environment and to reduce expenditures in the *Folkeskole* by achieving economies of scale through larger school sizes.

The approach to funding entails explicit equalisation mechanisms

The funding system of the *Folkeskole* entails several equalisation mechanisms. The national system reduces financial differences across municipalities. Less advantaged municipalities in terms of private income and municipalities with a challenging socio-economic composition of the population get higher grants from the central government. There is an implicit tax sharing system as municipalities with rich inhabitants and consequently a high tax base receive small to no grants from the central government. In addition, this grant system takes detailed socio-economic measures into account. The equalisation system does not have the ambition to completely equalise the economic situation in all municipalities, conditional on socio-economic status, but to reduce major differences. Consequently, the differences in expenditure per student observed across municipalities are to a small extent related to differences in municipalities' financial bases. According to Houlberg et al. (2016) and Dalsgaard and Andersen (2016), differences in socio-economic characteristics explain more than half of the variation in expenditure per student across municipalities. In addition, the variation reflects differences in how municipalities prioritise the *Folkeskole* relative to other local public services. Notably, it is not the case that municipalities with a challenging student population and with low private income systematically use less resources on the *Folkeskole* compared to other municipalities. Rather, municipalities with a relatively disadvantaged socio-economic population spend more resources on education than other municipalities (Houlberg et al., 2016).

Within municipalities, mechanisms for school funding typically take socio-economic characteristics of the student body into account. Based on interviews conducted during the review visit, the OECD review team formed the impression that all municipalities use some sort of a funding formula known to schools when allocating financial resources. The specificities of the local systems vary considerably, but they typically take variations between schools into account. Municipalities with little variation across schools in the socio-economic background of students seem to put less weight on socio-economic conditions and to give relatively more importance to school size. Overall, these mechanisms result in a per student expenditure that is positively related to the share of students with a low socio-economic status at the school (Houlberg et al., 2016). The fact that students facing some kind of disadvantage need extra resources and follow-up is widely accepted. In addition, municipalities can apply to the central government for specific targeted funds for special needs education.

Students with special needs also receive additional resources. Special schools spend on average over eight times more per student than regular schools (Houlberg et al., 2016, Appendix 1), although this reflects to a large extent the costs of educating students with severe disabilities. Regular schools typically employ pedagogues with a specific relevant education to work with students with special needs. Additional resources are allocated to these students via support by teachers with the relevant competencies (see Chapter 4).

Organisation of the school offer

School structures provide good conditions for students from different backgrounds to succeed, even though equity concerns remain

Upper secondary education (youth education) is an important part of the education system, in which some students qualify for tertiary education while others choose a vocational path. Vocational programmes include apprentice training in close co-operation with employers. The goal that all students should be well prepared for upper secondary education in a comprehensive system implies strong demand for equalisation. This requires not only adequate funding to meet the needs of all students (see above), but also a school structure that offers extra support to those most in need.

Skill development at young ages is the most critical factor for equalising educational outcomes (Heckman, 2008). Compulsory education in Denmark starts the year a student turns six years of age. The first year in school (Year 0) differs from the other years in that much more time is used on play and non-formal learning. Schools typically use pedagogues for the youngest students and adapt the learning environment to their specific needs. Denmark has a well-developed system for early childhood education and care (ECEC). In 2013, 96% of children aged three participated in ECEC (OECD, 2015, Table C2.1). Schools can then build on the experience almost all students have from participation in ECEC, even if students with an immigrant background are less likely to participate in ECEC than their non-immigrant peers (see Chapter 1).

The *Folkeskole* offers its students an integrated and comprehensive education for the entire period of compulsory education and aims to differentiate teaching to meet individual student needs. As such, the structure of the *Folkeskole* avoids early tracking of students into different study programmes and keeps all educational options open for students until age 16. As described in Chapter 1, Denmark enjoys comparative success internationally in limiting the proportion of low performing students at the end of compulsory education. The between-school variation of performance in Denmark remains lower than the OECD average, which might indicate that the specific school a student attends has less of an impact on how the student performs than is the case internationally.

Despite these structural conditions that provide good conditions for students from different backgrounds to succeed, equity remains a concern in Denmark. Students' socio-economic background has a stronger impact on performance than in other Nordic countries and only a small proportion of students manages to overcome difficult socio-economic circumstances. Equity concerns are particularly strong for students with an immigrant background and more so than in many other OECD countries.

Various municipalities have been willing to adjust the school structure to demographic changes

In the past few years, the Danish *Folkeskole* has shown its ability to adjust the school structure to demographic changes. In particular at the start of the 2010s, there was a trend towards school consolidation in the context of declining student numbers in rural areas. Even though the past years have seen fewer changes, discussions regarding the organisation of the school offer appear to be a vivid part of local politics. Ares Abalde (2014) finds that there are several potential advantages to larger school size and school consolidation: larger schools are likely to be able to offer a larger curriculum, more specialised teachers and courses, a broader range of extracurricular activities and a higher share of administrative staff and para-professionals offering support to teachers and school leaders. On the other hand, potential negative effects on student wellbeing related to increased transportation time, reduced individual attention and fewer links to parents and the local community need to be taken into account.

Research from different countries indicates that expenditure per student is highest in small schools (Falch et al., 2008; Larsen et al., 2013) and that important economies of scale can be achieved up to a certain enrolment level. However, some studies also find that returns to scale diminish, and that, beyond a certain enrolment level, diseconomies of scale begin to emerge (Ares Abalde, 2014). The main scale effect when school size increases is most likely the potential to fill up classes towards the maximum allowed class size. According to Humlum and Smith (2015), school size affects a diverse set of outcomes such as student achievement and parental involvement, but in a non-consistent way. They conclude that the mixed evidence on the effects of school size on academic achievement suggests that optimal school size depends on the context, such as the country and student composition.

The infrastructure for learning (and other local public services) has characteristics of a local public good (Oates, 1972). Local knowledge is important for optimal decisions, and there are few externalities on other local governments. The infrastructure of schooling is clearly a local decision in Denmark. The national funding system is not related to actual decisions on school structure, and the central government does not take a standpoint on school structure. The consolidation process has been motivated by both effectiveness and efficiency arguments with the aim of enhancing learning as much as possible given limited resources available.

Private schools and school structure may support efficiency and innovation

Private schools have a long tradition in Denmark. From an efficiency point of view, the co-existence of public and private schools might be beneficial as it lays the ground for competition (Friedman, 1962). At the same time, there is evidence that the development and support of a large private school sector might go in line with threats to equity and risks of segregation, especially if the school choices of some families are inhibited by factors such as tuition fees, availability of and access to information, school transportation arrangements and admission practices. These points are addressed below in the section on Challenges.

Most proponents of school choice and the use of private providers in education make some combination of the following arguments as described in OECD (2010). First, competition between schools might improve schools' incentives because schools prefer to be attractive and will work to avoid losing students. In theory, competition and the threat that consumers can purchase goods and services from other providers create a strong incentive for supplying high quality products at low prices. Consumers "vote with their feet" and make their purchases elsewhere if dissatisfied (Hirschman, 1970). Regarding compulsory education, for example Figlio and Hart (2014) and Böhlmark and Lindahl (2015) find evidence for such an effect. Figlio and Hart use the introduction of a means-tested voucher programme in public schools in Florida in the United States to examine whether increased competitive pressure on public schools affects students' test marks. They find the greatest positive effect of the programme for students attending public schools located close to private schools. Böhlmark and Lindahl exploit the variation across municipalities of the expansion of independent schools (*Friskolor*) in Sweden in the 1990s, and find that an increase in the share of independent schools improves both student performance at the end of compulsory education and further educational attainment. They conclude that this is not because independent schools are of higher quality, and thus interpret their finding as a result of increased competition between schools.

A second argument for offering private schooling options suggests that with a wide variety of schools from which to choose and where each provides a different mix of services, customers will choose the mix of services that best meets their educational preferences. The result will be that schools cater to a relatively narrow range of educational preferences. Advocates of privatisation and school choice argue that such sorting by preferences will reduce the amount of time schools spend resolving conflicts among stakeholders, leaving them more time and energy to devote to developing and implementing education programmes (Chubb and Moe, 1990; Hill et al., 1997). Advocates of private providers in education also argue that the very act of choice will leave students, parents, and teachers disposed to work harder to support the schools they have chosen.

According to a third theoretical argument for privatisation, autonomous schools will develop innovations in curriculum, instruction and governance that should lead to improvements in outcomes. Traditional public schools could also improve by adopting the innovative practices that private or independent schools are expected to develop. Proponents also argue that privatisation is likely to bring a welcome dose of entrepreneurial spirit and a competitive ethos to public education.

Distribution of teacher resources

There seem to be no major difficulties for teacher recruitment

High quality schooling requires competent and motivated teachers. In order to recruit teachers of high quality in the *Folkeskole*, initial teacher education must be of high quality and be attractive for promising teacher candidates. The Danish initial teacher education system has been reformed over the last years with the aim of increasing teacher quality. The teacher education institutions themselves have actively taken part in changing the content and teaching methods to achieve this goal. In addition, the recent changes in Denmark reflect an increasing recognition that teacher competency and motivation need continuous development, with investments in further education and competency development for existing teachers (see Chapter 4).

The OECD review team formed the impression that the overall supply of teachers to the Danish school system was adequate. There is no observable shortage of formally qualified teachers. For the OECD 2013 Teaching and Learning International Survey (TALIS), only 14.8% of lower secondary teachers were in a school whose principal reported that a shortage of qualified and /or well-performing teachers hindered the school's capacity to offer quality instruction (OECD, 2014b, Table 2.19). Data from the OECD PISA 2012 paint a similar picture. School principals in Denmark were less likely to report a teacher shortage than in many other countries (OECD, 2013b, Figure IV.3.5, Table IV.3.11). Teacher education institutions seem properly scaled, and the large majority of individuals with teacher education choose to stay on in teaching. In addition, teachers are recruited by schools. This yields the best possibility to assess applicants to vacant teacher positions in relation to the specific needs of schools and promotes efficiency (Naper, 2010). The school leader can focus on the school's competency needs in the recruitment process.

Changes in the utilisation of the teachers' competencies increase the flexibility of schools to use their human resources according to their needs

Recent changes in the national rules on working conditions for teachers (Act no. 409) and the 2014 *Folkeskole* reform have increased schools' flexibility in using the time and competencies of their teachers. Under the new legislation, schools have the opportunity to let teachers better utilise their specific competencies. Schools can more easily focus on student learning as the key issue of school leadership (see Chapter 4 for a more detailed analysis and discussion).

The competencies of teachers need continuous development and updating (Jackson, 2012a). The system tries to combine professional development that is in the interest of the individual teacher, and, in addition, meets the needs of the school. The former is important to stimulate teacher motivation, while the latter is essential in order to develop the school in the desired direction. The establishment of a system with learning consultants is also an improvement of the system (also see Chapter 4 for greater detail).

Challenges

Distribution of funding

There are concerns related to the decentralised funding model

The national funding system implies that the resources available in each municipality to a large extent depend on national policies. The flexibility of municipalities to influence their own income is limited by the national steering of the income tax rate. At the same time, the central government's influence on expenditure on education is limited as education is only one of many local services the municipalities are responsible for and prioritise across.

The present system relies to some extent on the regulation of inputs, as illustrated by the maximum class size rule. Although the *Folkeskole* reform has changed the focus towards learning outcomes, the measurement of learning outcomes still has to develop and there are still challenges in moving from a teaching to a learning focus in practice (see Chapters 3 and 4). Further, there are at present no attempts to link expenditure decisions to realised outcomes. Expenditure per student clearly varies across municipalities. This indicates a situation where some municipalities prioritise spending on education more than others, but also a potential for efficiency savings. There is no information at the national level to which extent the different priorities set by the municipalities affect the quality and equity of learning outcomes. However, according to Houlberg et al. (2016) and Dalsgaard and Andersen (2016), more than half of the variations among municipalities can be explained by socio-economic conditions, with municipalities having more students from disadvantaged backgrounds spending higher amounts per student than other municipalities. There are hence variations in the expenditure level across the municipalities that can be explained either through differences in the decided level of service or through differences in productivity.

Research from different countries indicates that the relationship between expenditure per student and learning outcomes is context-dependent. There is some evidence for Denmark that smaller classes slightly increase student performance (Browning and Heinesen, 2007, Heinesen, 2010), but the findings in the international literature are mixed (Hanushek, 2003, 2006, Krueger, 2003, Fredriksson and Öckert, 2008, Leuven et al., 2008). Nevertheless, the variation in expenditure level across the municipalities indicates significant potential for efficiency savings in several municipalities. It is not the case that the reduction in average expenditure per student in Denmark during the period 2009-13 reflects spending cuts in the municipalities with the highest expenditures.

There is little system learning regarding effective school funding formulas

The funding of schools takes spending needs into account and intends to promote an equalisation of learning outcomes. Municipalities use different funding formulas for their schools. These formulas typically include parental background characteristics in addition to the number of students and the number of classes at the different year levels. However, the ways in which socio-economic differences are taken into account in the funding formulas vary greatly across municipalities. This suggests that the models vary not only as a result of deliberate decisions or different priorities. In one of the municipalities visited by the OECD review team, socio-economic measures were not considered in deciding on the distribution of funding across schools due to little variation in the socio-economic composition of the schools in the municipality.

There is a potential for municipalities to learn from each other from the diversity of approaches across municipalities, but it appears that there is no co-ordination or learning process across municipalities on how funding formulas can best contribute to equalise student performance. Each municipality develops its own formula based more or less on assumptions regarding school resource needs. The OECD review team saw examples of municipalities making efforts to identify student characteristics associated with learning difficulties and to direct resources to the relevant groups. The municipality of Copenhagen, for example, has worked together with the Danish Institute for Local and Regional Government Research (KORA) to develop a funding formula based on such analyses.

However, there appeared to be only weak mechanisms to share and spread such expertise and experience more broadly and systematically across municipalities. National measures on how much extra support specific groups of students receive on average could be of help for municipalities, without the intention to reduce local autonomy or the advantages of taking local contexts into account.

It is challenging to establish evidence on how extra resources towards specific groups of students or schools with a disadvantaged socio-economic composition will contribute to equalising performance (Costrell et al., 2008; Falch et al., 2008). Relationships between expenditures and some characteristics of students are not informative about the causal effect of a selective increase in expenditures. Extra resources directed to a large share of students from disadvantaged socio-economic backgrounds or students with special needs are likely to also benefit the other students in the school since such additional resources increase the possibility to cater to individual student needs more effectively and to reduce disruptions in classrooms.

There are reports about difficulties in the adjustment to the new framework for the utilisation of teachers' working hours

The 2014 *Folkeskole* reform has increased the length of the school day for students (see Chapter 1). Several cross-country studies indicate that increased instruction hours in a subject increase student achievement in this subject, but that the actual content of the additional hours is crucial for the effect on student achievement (Carlsson et al., 2015; Lavy, 2015; Gromada and Shewbridge, 2016). While it can be expected that the increased number of school hours for Danish students will have a positive effect on student achievement, the effect will depend on the quality of teaching and learning taking place during these extra hours. Act no. 409 changed teachers' working time arrangement, specifying the total number of working hours, but not the number of hours that teachers should be teaching in class or spend on other tasks and duties. As a result, schools have more flexibility in the use of teachers' working time (see Chapter 1 for a general description and above and Chapter 4 for an analysis of the potential benefits of this greater level of flexibility). The success of the reform will, thus, among other factors, also depend on how teachers and school leaders adjust to this new situation. Depending on how schools adapt to the new arrangement, it also carries some risks for the quality and equity of learning (also see Chapter 4).

Teachers' working time has remained unchanged, but, within regular working hours, teachers are expected to teach, on average, about two clock hours more per week than prior to the new arrangement (18.3 hours a week compared to 16.3 hours a week) (see Chapter 4 for an international comparison of teaching time based on the OECD *Education at a Glance* and the OECD TALIS). Some resources have been moved from after schools programmes (SFO) to schools (since students spend less time in SFO) and the central government has allocated some additional resources to the municipalities as a result of the reform and as a part of an agreement with LGDK. Nevertheless, schools reported to experience having fewer resources available overall, in particular, for other tasks as they have allocated more resources to teaching.

The OECD review team had the clear impression from its interviews and school visits that teachers used less time to prepare their lessons under the new legislation. This will, of course, differ across contexts and teachers and also depend on teachers' level of experience and the subjects a teacher teaches. A research report on the school reform and new working conditions, however, indeed finds that teachers experience a reduction in their time for preparation and that this situation poses a challenge for their teaching (Bjørnholt et al., 2015). Little international research evidence is available on this issue as the amount of time spent on preparation is typically a decision of individual teachers and it is challenging to disentangle the effect of teacher quality and teacher preparation time. However, if teachers do not have the right conditions for preparation, collaboration, mentoring, peer feedback and other important aspects of teacher professionalism, this carries a risk of adversely affecting the quality of their teaching. Teachers can initially rely to some extent on their preparation of previous years, but this opportunity may fade out over time and any possible negative effect of less preparation time on the quality of instruction is thus likely to increase if schools and teachers do not adjust well to the new situation. While the new flexible working time arrangements give school leaders the possibility to differentiate between beginning and experienced teachers, the average increase in teaching time may make the transition into teaching for beginning teachers more difficult if their school leaders do not use their new flexibility well. Unlike their more experienced peers, beginning teachers cannot rely on previous preparation to provide good teaching.

The new framework for the utilisation of teachers' working hours intends to bring about a change in the nature of teacher preparation, moving from individual preparation to more collaborative preparation made more efficient through joint planning, knowledge sharing and the use of digital learning resources. According to the abovementioned report, however, school principals found that teachers' mind-set and practices with respect to their preparation had remained unchanged (Bjørnholt et al., 2015). The local level thus seems to not have yet fully adjusted to less regulation in teaching hours and seems to need to develop greater knowledge on how to use their new flexibility in the best way. Through the implementation of Act no. 409, school leaders were given the same opportunities as other leaders in the public sector to manage and distribute work within their institution. Thus, school leaders can continuously assess how tasks are best solved, assigned and distributed. It also means that school principals can organise working arrangements so that teachers share materials and collaborate on preparation, for example. Working arrangements can theoretically better reflect differences in teacher competencies and experience (e.g. by giving new teachers a smaller teaching load than more experienced teachers as new teachers need more preparation time for each lesson in order to give lessons of the same quality or to differentiate the assignment of tasks depending on the subjects a teacher teaches).

There are concerns about the impact of recent reforms on equity and inclusion

The 2014 *Folkeskole* reform aims to change the system in the direction of achieving a better performance for all students. Several elements of the reform provide opportunities for improving equity. But if teachers get less prepared and collaborate less, the reform might come at the cost of vulnerable students if there are no specific policies at the municipal and school levels to mitigate such possible detrimental effects. In the case that school leaders and teachers do not adjust well to the new working time arrangements, there is a risk that the students most in need experience less teacher follow-up and feedback. At-risk students arguably need more teacher support and follow-up because they have fewer possibilities for such support at home than other students. If teachers experience reduced time for preparation and follow-up of individual students, it is likely to have negative effects mainly for students at risk of underperformance. This concern was expressed by stakeholders to the OECD review team. As part of the 2014 *Folkeskole* reform, the government intended to reduce the amount of homework and instead use some of the extra hours at school to cover material that used to be done at home. Schools thus need to find the right balance on the content of the extra teaching hours in schools. They need to use the new lessons to improve the competencies of the students that are highlighted in the 2014 *Folkeskole* reform. In addition, they need to strive for using the lessons such that homework contributes to student learning without having a negative effect on equity.[1]

Coinciding with the 2014 *Folkeskole* reform, Denmark is also working towards greater inclusion in schools. Fewer students are enrolled in special schools than only a few years ago. While there seems to be an expectation that some of the resources would be shifted from special needs schools to regular schools following students with special needs to facilitate their inclusion, there are no national rules on how the extra needs of these recently included students in regular schools should be translated into extra resources. In addition, the municipalities do generally not allocate specific resources for schools to be used for students with special needs or provide guidelines for how additional resources could be used to create inclusive learning environments (even though in some municipalities school can apply for funding for specific purposes specified by the municipality). Various interview partners during the OECD review visit thus expressed concerns about a lack of transparency and uncertainty if resources followed students with special needs that had moved to a regular school. They thus saw inclusion as carrying a risk that students with special needs do not receive adequate learning support in an inclusive setting in a regular school in comparison to a special school.

Nevertheless, it is important to recognise that the funding systems in the different municipalities allocate most resources to schools and students with a less favourable socio-economic background. Although it is difficult to provide research evidence on the effect of this policy on the equalisation of student performance as argued above, the system is based on a well-grounded belief that targeted funding contributes to equity in student performance. In addition, the increased focus on student performance may provide schools with an incentive to use resources for students with special needs, at least to the extent that students with special needs are included in the testing system related to the 2014 *Folkeskole* reform.

Organisation of the school offer

The growth of the private school sector might go in line with greater segregation

Private schools are an alternative for parents and students in Denmark. As described above, the share of students in private schools has been increasing, and there seems to be excess demand for admission in a number of private schools. One potential challenge in education systems relying on an extensive offer of private schools is increased segregation of students. All over the world, students in private schools are typically from relatively well-educated families with relatively high income. Available data indicate that this is the case on average also for Denmark (Rangvid, 2007, 2010), although the student population in private schools in Denmark is more heterogeneous than in some other countries.

Why do some parents prefer private schools? Understanding how schools are competing for students is important for judging whether competition contributes to improved performance of the school system. Is it competition based on student achievement or based on other factors? Increased competition in compulsory education often seems to have a limited effect on school performance (Böhlmark and Lindahl, 2015), as it does not by itself eliminate an information problem. Research indicates that while choice policies increase the level of information of all parents, the quantity and quality of information seems to be highly correlated with parents' level of education (Lacireno-Paquet, 2012; Hamilton and Guin, 2005; Bosetti, 2004; Schneider and Buckley, 2002; Schneider et al., 1998). It is, therefore, important that relevant, fair and comparable information on available school choices by the local community is easily accessible for all parents. Experience from different countries indicates that personal contact, at least in the initial stages, is key to ensuring that parents from different socio-economic backgrounds engage, understand the information and have the opportunity to seek clarification (Nusche, 2009).

There are significant information gaps in Denmark with respect to school quality. If students and parents are expected to make school choices in order to support their children's learning outcomes, they need reliable information about school quality and other school factors. If information on school quality is not available or not easily accessible, parents are likely to make their choices based on other criteria. If parents mainly care about extracurricular elements such as cultural activity, sports and the peer-composition of the students at the school, one should expect that schools also would compete along these dimensions. If parents care strongly about the peers of their children, this will work in the direction of segregation in the school system.

There is a risk that a lack of mechanisms to promote competition among schools based on quality, as for example exemplified by relevant and contextualised information on school quality and learning outcomes, might lead schools to compete on factors that enhance segregation. In order to be attractive for students and parents, schools might be inclined to focus on activities that do not contribute to the national goals of the 2014 *Folkeskole* reform. Such a focus can easily have a negative effect on student achievement in core subjects.

It is still too early to evaluate whether the new legislation on inclusion has contributed to the growing preference of parents for private schools. Some preliminary evidence on changes in the share of students enrolled in private schools from 2011 to 2012 indicates that there is no relationship between the inclusion policy and the demand for private schools (Houlberg et al., 2016), but this is an issue that needs to be monitored. Parents who experience that teachers devote less time and attention for their own children than for other students might be inclined to search for alternative schools for their children. During the OECD review visit to Denmark, several of our interlocutors voiced concerns that the inclusion policy could potentially lead more parents to consider choosing a private school for their children. In order to avoid flight of students to private schools under the new legislation, teachers and schools might prioritise the students most likely to shift to a private school. Given that these students tend to come from an advantaged socio-economic background, such behaviour will have a negative effect on equity. On the other hand, if teachers prioritise ongoing support for vulnerable students, this may result in an increasing demand for private schools.

It is unclear to what extent school consolidation policy has contributed to the establishment of new private schools, which may then undermine the gains of school consolidation efforts. During the OECD review visit, municipal leaders repeatedly reported that when closing public schools in certain rural areas with strong parental engagements, parents might respond by setting up a private school in the same location as a former public school.

Consolidation processes need to be managed locally

The consolidation of public schools requires local support. While there have been several successful consolidations in Denmark in the past, there are clearly different views on the optimal school structure. As Ares Abalde (2014) and Humlum and Smith (2015) point out, there are many factors that are important when making decisions about school size and consolidation. At least the effects on expenditure per student, the learning environment and students' travel time must be taken into account. The research literature cannot provide a "magic" number on the optimal size of schools. Rather, the optimal school size is context-dependent and varies according to local characteristics.

Combined with the decentralised nature of education in Denmark, this implies that the introduction of any national policy on school size and school consolidation is unwarranted. However, it needs to be emphasised that the issue of school structure is a very important part of local school policies. Ongoing changes in demography, settlement patterns, and learning technology imply that school structure should be a vivid part of local politics. It is a concern that the consolidation agenda sometimes seems to have been too strongly related to a cost saving strategy and less to improvements in school quality. A reduction in costs does not increase efficiency if student achievement falls substantially. Danish evidence indicates that achievement typically declines in the first few years after a school consolidation due to the disruption this implies, but that the performance of students increases in the longer term (Humlum and Smith, 2015).

High enrolment in Year 10 leads to delayed graduation

As analysed above, about half a cohort of students enrols in Year 10. One of the arguments for the public support of Year 10 rests on the possibility for students to improve their qualifications up to a level necessary for upper secondary education. If this is the real motivation for the main part of the students enrolling in Year 10, it reflects a serious defect of the educational system. Either the *Folkeskole* is not able to provide students with the necessary skills to succeed in upper secondary education, or the requirements in upper secondary education are too high compared with the quality of the *Folkeskole*.

If one of these reasons holds true, Year 10 can be seen as some form of year repetition. While year repetition in Denmark is below the OECD average – with 4.7% of 15-year-olds reporting that they have repeated a year – it is at a similar level as in Sweden and clearly above repetition rates in the other Nordic countries (OECD, 2014a), which do not offer their students a comparable Year 10. If enrolment in Year 10 is seen as a form of year repetition, it is highly questionable whether so much of the year repetition in the last year of compulsory education contributes most effectively to student learning. Year 10 is at an age where education no longer is compulsory, and remedial education is more efficient in early ages than towards the end of compulsory education (Heckman, 2008).

An alternative explanation for the high enrolment in Year 10 is that it provides some kind of "leisure" time and an opportunity for young people to enhance their wellbeing, to develop broader social and emotional skills and competencies, and to find out what to do later in life or which upper secondary track to choose. It is a year without much learning pressure on core subjects. The fact that most of the private continuation schools, which receive public funding, emphasise other objectives than basic skills and mainly enrol students from advantaged socio-economic backgrounds, indicates that a change in attitude among parents and students would be desirable. While there can be benefits (e.g. in terms of social competencies and clarity about future career choices), it is questionable whether a year without clear learning intentions for core subjects in school contributes to student performance in upper secondary education and labour market attachment for young adults. An additional year in education delays entry into the labour market and there is also a risk that children at this critical age start to prioritise leisure activities too highly, and downplay education as a life-long investment.

Distribution of teacher resources

There are concerns about the attractiveness of the teaching profession

A substantial body of research, mostly from the United States, finds a large variation in teaching quality across teachers (Hanushek, 2011; Jackson, 2012b; Chetty et al., 2013). It reflects that individual teacher competencies strongly matter for student learning. Thus, policies for the competency development of teachers and the recruitment of high-quality teachers must be a continuous effort.

It has turned out to be difficult to relate the variation in teacher quality to objectively measured characteristics of teachers. However, some empirical evidence suggests that students have better outcomes when their teachers have high test marks on achievement tests (Ehrenberg and Brewer, 1994; Goldhaber, 2007; Clotfelter et al., 2010; Grönqvist and Vlachos, 2014; Hanushek et al., 2014). A study for the Danish Productivity Commission investigated the relationship between teacher test marks and student test marks at the school level (Produktivitetskommissionen, 2014). This study finds that the average of the teachers' marks on their school leaving exams is positively related to the test marks of their students in lower secondary education.

The attractiveness of teacher education and the teacher profession is, therefore, crucial. Are high-achieving graduates from upper secondary education choosing to become teachers? Experience from different countries suggests a declining interest in the teacher profession in the last decades (Falch and Mang, 2015). In Denmark, there are indications that the teaching profession is not valued very highly. For the OECD TALIS 2013, only 18.4% of lower secondary teachers agreed or strongly agreed that the teaching profession is valued in society (TALIS average: 30.9%) (OECD, 2014b, Table 7.2). There are also concerns that teacher education is at present not particularly attractive for students with the best academic results in upper secondary education. It was reported to the OECD review team that several study programmes for initial teacher education are not able to fill the number of study places they have. Drop-out rates in teacher education are also relatively high. According to data from the Ministry of Higher Education and Science and Statistics Denmark's student register, 15.6% of students had dropped out during their first year of teacher education. Overall, 36% of students in teacher education programmes had dropped out in 2014. These dropout rates have remained relatively stable between 2010 and 2014.

Nevertheless, the number of study places offered by higher education institutions has not been adjusted to declining demand. As teacher education institutions are facing difficulties in attracting high-achieving graduates from upper secondary education, there is a risk that study places may be filled with students with relatively weak prior achievement. Given the Danish funding system for higher education based on student numbers (the "taximeter" system), higher education institutions seem to have a strong incentive to enrol a large number of students. However, in 2013 the new teacher education introduced stricter admission requirements. As a result, the general point average of the admitted students has risen between 2012 and 2015.

Teachers have limited career development opportunities

There are a number of challenges in organising schools in a way such that they offer attractive career pathways for teachers and give teachers the opportunity to take on different roles according to their strengths. In a context of strict working conditions, a highly compressed salary structure, no measurement of school quality and little external pressure on school performance, the incentives and motivations for innovations in teaching methods and teaching technology are limited. Productive innovations in the classroom require teachers that are willing and able to accomplish smart experimenting and adjustment of practice to respond to their students' needs. Act no. 409 has relaxed the rules on working conditions, for example by making it possible to give teachers specific roles such as being a "specialist" teacher with specific professional tasks for mentoring and peer support. This seems to be a change in the right direction (more on this in Chapter 4).

Compared to other professions, however, there are still limited possibilities for career development or salary increases within the teaching profession. The main channel for some kind of promotion is to become a leader or to enter the school administration. However, this kind of promotion seems to be only weakly related to the quality and competency as a teacher. If it was strongly related to teacher quality, it would be the case that the career system sorts the best teachers out of teaching, which would also be undesirable. In general, a career is more attractive for skilled and creative youngsters if they can expect to climb a career ladder to more recognised and better paid positions if successful. However, the principle of associating good professional performance to career progression is not in place in Denmark (Shewbridge et al., 2011).

Policy recommendations

Distribution of funding

Continue to pay attention to using resources efficiently

Developments in the *Folkeskole* over the last years have challenged the system in several ways. There has been a reduction in expenditure per student up to the 2014 *Folkeskole* reform, and the reform aims at a stronger focus on learning environments and student performance. The reform has increased the school day of students without a symmetric increase in the number of teachers. To the extent that the changes improve the student outcomes described in the reform package, these changes will clearly contribute to improved efficiency and effectiveness of the Danish school system.

Whether this can be achieved or not will, however, depend on the ability to use resources efficiently and on the way schools adjust to the new situation. When the average class size has increased and teachers need to teach more classes, it might be a challenge to maintain high quality teaching and learning. If teachers use less time for preparation and collaboration as they use more time on teaching, there can be a risk to both quality and equity in schooling. Therefore, future strategies to develop and allocate human resources effectively in schools will be crucial to the success of the reform. These strategies will be discussed in Chapter 4. It will also be key to ensure that all actors in the school system continue to work intensively on how resources can be used most effectively to improve student learning in relation to the national goals. Knowledge-sharing across schools and municipalities is of specific importance in light of the major systemic changes in the last years. Strategies related to the governance of school resource use will be discussed in Chapter 3.

Share experience about funding formulas across municipalities

As discussed above, the Danish municipalities use a plethora of different funding formulas for their schools, although it is unlikely that the need for adjustments with regard to the socio-economic status of students is very different across municipalities. The intention of such formulas is to give schools the same possibility to have similar learning environments. Except for school size, the main intention of the funding formulas is to have an equitable system in the sense that students with weaker initial competencies should receive more guidance and learning support from teachers than students with strong initial competencies.

There is a lot of potential for municipalities to learn from each other regarding the effective design of school funding formulas. For example, when a municipality develops a new funding system in collaboration with external researchers, the knowledge from the process and the new funding formula itself should be shared with other municipalities. It is unlikely that funding formulas that enhance equity the most are very different across municipalities. At the moment, it seems like many municipalities use a lot of effort on developing and maintaining funding formulas. Although local contexts and different local political prioritisations and decisions obviously need to be taken into account, the sharing of experiences should be encouraged and facilitated to create synergies and to avoid double efforts (for more details, see Chapter 3). LGDK and the association of municipal administrators responsible for culture, day care and education (*Børne- og Kulturchefforeningen* [BKF]) have the potential to play a key role here.

Pay attention to investing in early interventions for groups at risk of underperformance and ensure that the funding system incentivises high quality provision for students with special needs

Taking socio-economic measures into account in funding formulas by itself will not be sufficient to ensure equal opportunities for at-risk students across Denmark, and to reduce the impact of socio-economic background on student achievement in line with the equity goal of the *Folkeskole*. There should be particular attention to investing in early interventions for groups at risk of underperformance in pre-school and primary school. Research evidence clearly indicates that investment in early intervention strategies is more cost effective than remedial support later on in a student's lifecycle.

There is potential to improve competency building for students at risk in the Danish childcare system and throughout the *Folkeskole*, including Year 0 (see Chapter 3), although several initiatives already have been undertaken. One example is the development of clear goals for the instruction in Year 0 (the kindergarten class), which is intended to provide a clearer focus for evaluation, thus helping teachers identify children who are struggling to acquire basic competencies. Another example is the so-called "attention points" from the "Simplified Common Objectives". If a student is struggling to reach a minimum level of proficiency in Danish and mathematics, teachers must initiate a dialogue with the school leader regarding the efforts to be put in place to ensure the further academic development of the student. Further, the Ministry for Children, Education and Gender Equality has financed the development of a test designed to identify dyslexia in students from Year 3 and beyond. This test aims to ensure the identification of students with dyslexia and dyscalculia in order to help schools provide the needed assistance and interventions.

The policy of inclusion challenges the old way of thinking about funding students with special needs. When students with special needs are integrated in regular schools, or even regular classes, it is important that local contexts have the resources they need to ensure that all children can learn according to their individual needs. Adequate teaching and support most likely depends on the particular circumstances in the learning environment. On the other hand, there is a risk that the support for students with special needs will decline when funding is not targeted and this is a concern voiced by different stakeholders during the review visit. Introducing targeted funding for students with special needs and allocating resources to schools based on the number of students with special needs seems unwarranted as the diagnosis and declaration of students with special needs can be subject to manipulation and may set incentives for schools to seek the classification of students as having special needs to secure additional funding. Securing adequate resources and adequate teaching to every student in a context of inclusion, however, warrants close attention at the school, municipal and national levels. Greater transparency to the school community (e.g. through the school board) about the use of resources at the school level to facilitate inclusion and the way the use of resources translates into learning outcomes for students with special educational needs could help dispel concerns that students with special needs do not have the resources they need to succeed (see Chapter 3).

Organisation of the school offer

Consider reducing enrolment in Year 10

The OECD review team formed the impression that the goals of Year 10 are not clearly defined and that the large enrolment rate in Year 10 only weakly contributes to the educational outcomes in Denmark, even if there may other benefits (e.g. social and emotional skills). The review team recommends that public support for Year 10 should be more focused on those in real need to increase their skills. The obligation for municipalities to provide Year 10 to all students, including students from advantaged socio-economic backgrounds to spend a "leisure time" year, should be reconsidered. The target group for Year 10 could be better defined (e.g. it could be an offer targeted at students achieving below a specific skill level as measured by the final school results in Year 9) and students' right to enrolment could be linked to certain criteria. It appears highly inefficient that a large share of 16-17 year-old youth spend a year with low focus on improving basic or vocational skills. It should also be considered to implement stricter criteria in order for private schools to receive public financial support for Year 10 education.

For some students it seems necessary to improve their skills before they are ready to enrol in upper secondary education. For these students, Year 10 takes the form of year repetition. Considering that the empirical evidence clearly suggests that remedial education is more efficient the earlier it is introduced for students, the enhanced provision of targeted remedial education at an earlier stage in the *Folkeskole* should be a priority. The 2014 *Folkeskole* reform has the clear goal of improving the skills of students. This should reduce the need for Year 10 education as a means for skill upgrading, and contribute to more students transferring directly from the *Folkeskole* to upper secondary education. Denmark should consider establishing a national goal to gradually decrease enrolment in Year 10.

Develop a more strategic approach to school consolidation

It seems necessary to continue local considerations on school consolidation. The main uncertainty with school consolidation is how it will affect the learning environment and student performance. Further analyses of consequences of school consolidation and knowledge sharing across municipalities would be of help in the local political discourse on school structure. Continuous effort will be required to ensure that school structures respond to local and system needs in a context of demographic changes and lower municipal budgets compared to the period before the financial crisis.

Clear municipal leadership should help to highlight a key focus on learning environments, student achievement and school quality in any school consolidation process. It is necessary to communicate a vision of quality education to persuade others of the need for change instead of a narrow focus on cost savings. It is also important to provide access to schooling for younger children at a reasonable distance to home. School consolidation must go in line with visible improvements in the quality of the students' school. Otherwise some parents will transfer their children to the private school system based on a shorter commute instead of higher school quality.

Ensure that school competition can happen with regard to school quality not student composition

Information on school performance and school quality seems necessary in order for the relatively large share of private schools in Denmark to contribute to improved performance of the school system. For example, if parents choose schools based on the degree to which students perform relative to the national goals, there can be competition based on school quality. Without information on school quality, school choice will be based on other factors. If school choice is based primarily on peer composition in schools, the large degree of private schools will contribute to school segregation. In addition, parents are likely to be interested in a variety of other factors at schools, such as cultural and sport activities. In the present system, there is a risk that schools compete along these dimensions and that parents put larger weights on such issues than they ideally would prefer, simply because they have very limited information the learning environment and school quality. In this context, developing a shared vision of school quality, refining both external and internal evaluation of school quality and performance and improving parents' access to relevant information will be important to ensure that the large share of private schools can be used more strategically to improve performance and reach national goals (see Chapter 3). Equity concerns in the use of information about school quality, however, also need to be taken into account. As Blanchenay and Burns (2016) pointed out, in most countries, upper middle-class and middle-class families are those most aware of how to use the education system for their own interest and benefit and those more likely to use information about school achievement to place their child in the best performing schools.

Distribution of teacher resources

Make teaching a more attractive profession

A successful development of the *Folkeskole* over time requires that higher education institutions can attract talented secondary school graduates into teacher education. Various groups interviewed by the OECD review team share a concern about the limited ability of initial teacher education programmes to attract high-achieving students. In addition, overall drop-out rates from teacher education are very high. It is reasonable to believe that the high dropout rate is a result of relatively weak students being enrolled in the first place.

There are a range of ways in which the attractiveness of the teaching profession could be improved in Denmark by reconsidering pay, working conditions, career progression, and diversification of the role for teachers. While the starting salary for teachers in Denmark is relatively high by international comparison, possibilities for salary increases are limited, resulting in a relatively low lifetime income for teachers compared to other countries (see Figure 2.10). In addition, the workload of beginning teachers has traditionally been high as they have been expected to teach the same number of classes as experienced teachers (although school leaders now have greater flexibility to differentiate between their staff under the new working time regulations). Also, the recent disagreements and conflicts between the Danish Union of Teachers and LGDK could have a negative impact on the attractiveness of the profession.

As mentioned above, there are hardly any opportunities for formal promotion within schools (only out of teaching into school principal positions). This traditional approach does not convey the important message that the guiding principle for career advancement should be merit and it does not provide possibilities to reward teachers who choose to remain in the classroom. The lack of opportunities for promotion may reduce the attractiveness of the profession, possibly contributing to both attrition among young teachers and burn-out among older teachers (OECD, 2013b; OECD, 2005).

Research that can improve the understanding of the teacher labour market should be supported. The changes in the initial teacher education system in the last years should be subject to evaluations. In particular, better knowledge of the dropout rate from teacher education could contribute to a better understanding of factors that can make teacher education and the profession more attractive.

Make the incentives structure for teachers more flexible to ensure that the best teacher resources are directed towards the students most in need

Equity in education is particularly important at the level of early childhood and compulsory education, which lays the foundations for further education and skill development. Thus, it is important that students most in need of high teacher quality in order to develop adequate skills get support from experienced teachers with a good record. At present, the *Folkeskole* does not seem to have mechanisms in place to ensure that the best teachers work in the most challenging contexts and that the most vulnerable students thus receive high quality teaching.

The research literature from various countries suggests that teachers prefer schools with an advantageous student body composition (Falch and Strøm, 2005, for Norway; Barbieri et al., 2011, for Italy; Boyd et al., 2013 for the United States; Karbownik, 2014, for Sweden). Teachers might therefore select themselves into schools such that the vulnerable students do not get the best teachers. For Denmark, data from international surveys suggest a slightly mixed picture in this regard. The OECD TALIS 2013 suggests that teachers with five years or more of experience are more likely to teach in schools with more than 10% of students whose first language is different from the language of instruction and in schools with more than 10% of students with special needs. But they are less likely to work in schools with more than 30% of students from socio-economically disadvantaged homes (OECD, 2014b, Table 2.12.Web.1). Teacher shortages (as reported by school principals for the OECD PISA 2012) also seem to be more of a problem for instruction in socio-economically disadvantaged schools and in public schools. Principals in socio-economically advantaged and private schools were less likely to report that teacher shortages in different subjects hindered student learning "to some extent" or "a lot" (OECD, 2013b, Figure IV.3.5, Table IV.3.1). Schools with students from a low socio-economic background on average receive higher amounts of funding than other schools, but typically use extra funding to employ extra teachers, rather than to attract particular high performing teachers. If the school is not among the most attractive schools at the outset, the learning environment might thus improve only marginally by the extra funding.

A successful equalisation policy should include mechanisms to match the most adequate teachers and students at risk with the highest need of teacher support. Such mechanisms are weakly developed in the *Folkeskole*. School leaders could have more instruments to motivate teachers to work at a school that has challenges with recruitment of teachers and classes with students with special needs. In particular one should think of introducing salary allowances for working in difficult conditions or in areas of teacher shortages. Such policies have been found to have clear positive effects on teacher recruitment (Falch, 2010).

Create career pathways for teachers

There are challenges around the development of the teaching workforce and the longer run foundation for career development and innovation. Lack of career possibilities and remuneration flexibility for teachers and social educators might restrict the school leaders' opportunity to use incentives to promote pedagogical development and learning. Likewise, there are limited tools to attract teachers and social educators in cases of shortages, which seem to be of increasing concern.

It seems particularly important to develop a career structure within the teaching profession with a number of steps that recognises roles and responsibilities in the schools. Such a system of career pathways could introduce teaching standards describing the competencies needed for different career steps. Steps in the career should be associated with description of skills and competencies in professional standards. In a system with promotions, it is important that promotions are not mechanical related to for example experience, but related to professional skills and the teacher's contribution to the learning environment at the school.

A system with career pathways could also improve the possibility to allow for salary increases during the teaching career. The compressed wage structure in Denmark presently does not make it possibly to incentivise teachers by better salaries, in contrast to other professions. In addition, the possibility to develop according to specific career pathways during a lifetime position in the teaching profession would stimulate all teachers to continuously review their skills and improve their practice. This is important to stimulate training both at the school and externally, which is necessary to continuously develop the working skills in a changing environment. It would also stimulate systematic appraisal processes so that teachers in need of specific support can be identified and helped to improve skills and teaching practices.

The 2014 *Folkeskole* reform includes many new changes along with Act no. 409. Schools and municipalities are working on developing systems and mechanisms to get the best out of the teaching workforce under the new rules. The goal must be to let teachers with different interest take on different tasks, get a stronger relation between students' needs and the use of teachers, and to improve teacher motivation. The new regulations also make it easier to use the skills in the teaching workforce in accordance with the needs of schools and municipalities. Municipalities and schools are approaching the new legislation differently. This should be used to learn about the good governance of schools. Inspiration should, however, not only come from other schools, but also from other high-skilled professions.

Note

1. Although there is evidence indicating that homework may improve student achievement (Falch and Rønning, 2012), homework also has distributional effects, since students from a high socio-economic status typically receive more help with homework than students from a low socio-economic status. It may be particular challenging for immigrant parents to support their children with the homework. While homework is likely to have positive effects on students from more advantaged socio-economic backgrounds, who typically perform relatively well at the outset, they might have no effect on the learning of students from less advantaged backgrounds. In this regard, Falch and Rønning (2012) argue that the type of homework matters. Homework seems to have a larger positive effect when it has the form of repetition and serves a complement to in-class learning instead of being a substitute to in-school learning in the sense that topics supposed to be taught in school are given as homework.

References

Ares Abalde, M. (2014), "School Size Policies: A Literature Review", *OECD Education Working Papers*, No. 106, OECD Publishing, Paris, *http://dx.doi.org/10.1787/5jxt472ddkjl-en.*

Barankay, I. and B. Lockwood (2007), "Decentralization and the productive efficiency of government: Evidence from Swiss cantons", *Journal of Public Economics*, Vol. 91, Elsevier, Amsterdam, pp. 1197-1218.

Barbieri, G., C. Rossetti and P. Sestito (2011), "The determinants of teacher mobility: Evidence using Italian teachers' transfer applications", *Economics of Education Review*, Vol. 30, Elsevier, Amsterdam, pp. 1430-1444.

Bjørnholt, B. et al. (2015), *Pædagogiske Medarbejderes Oplevelser og Erfaringer i den Nye Folkeskole* [The Experience of Pedagogical Staff in the New *Folkeskole*], Det Nationale Institut for Kommuners og Regioners Analyse og Forskning (KORA) [Danish Institute for Local and Regional Government Research], Copenhagen, *www.uvm.dk/-/media/UVM/Filer/Udd/Folke/PDF15/Nov/151117-KORA-Paedagogiske-medarbejderes-oplevelser-og-erfaringer-i-den-nye-folkeskole.ashx.*

Blanchenay, P. and T. Burns (2016), "Policy experimentation in complex education systems", in T. Burns and F. Koester (eds.) (2016), *Governing Education in a Complex World*, OECD Publishing, Paris, *http://dx.doi.org/10.1787/9789264255364-10-en.*

Böhlmark, A. and M. Lindahl (2015), "Independent schools and long-run educational outcomes: Evidence from Sweden's large-scale voucher reform", *Economica*, Vol. 82, Wiley-Blackwell, Hoboken, NJ, pp. 508-551.

Bosetti, L. (2004), "Determinants of school choice: Understanding how parents choose elementary schools in Alberta", *Journal of Education Policy*, Vol. 19(4), Taylor and Francis, Oxford, pp. 387-405.

Boyd, D. et al. (2013), "Analyzing the determinants of the matching of public school teachers to jobs: Disentangling the preferences of teachers and employers", *Journal of Labor Economics*, Vol. 31, University of Chicago Press, Chicago, IL, pp. 83-117.

Browning, M. and E. Heinesen (2007), "Class size, teacher hours and educational attainment", *Scandinavian Journal of Economics*, Vol. 109, Wiley-Blackwell, Hoboken, NJ, pp. 415-438.

Carlsson, M. et al. (2015), "The effect of schooling on cognitive skills", *The Review of Economics and Statistics*, Vol. 97, MIT Press, Cambridge, MA, pp. 533-547.

Chetty, R., J.N. Friedman and J.E. Rockoff (2013), "Measuring the impacts of teachers II: Teacher value-added and student outcomes in adulthood", *American Economic Review*, Vol. 104, American Economic Association, Nashville, TN, pp. 2593-2632.

Chubb, J.E. and T.M. Moe (1999), *Politics, Markets and America's Schools*, Brookings Institution, Washington, DC.

Clark, D. (2009), "Politics, markets and schools: Quasi-experimental estimates of the impact of autonomy and competition from a truly revolutionary U.K. reform", *Journal of Political Economy*, Vol. 117, University of Chicago Press, Chicago, IL, pp. 745-783.

Clotfelter, C.T., H.F. Ladd and J.L. Vigdor (2010), "Teacher Credentials and Student Achievement in High School: A Cross-Subject Analysis with Student Fixed Effects", *Journal of Human Resources*, Vol. 45, University of Wisconsin Press, Madison, WI, pp. 655-681.

Costrell, R., E. Hanushek and S. Loeb (2008), "What Do Cost Functions Tell Us About the Cost of an Adequate Education?", *Peabody Journal of Education*, Vol. 83, Taylor and Francis, Oxford, pp. 198-22.

Dalsgaard, C.T. and M.M.Q. Andersen (2016), *Derfor er der Forskel På, Hvad Børnene Koster i Kommunerne – En Kvantitativ Analyse af Forskelle i Kommunale Enhedsudgifter til Skoler og Dagtilbud* [This is Why There is a Difference in What Children Cost the Municipalities – A Quantitative Analysis of the Differences in the Municipal Unit Cost of Schools and Day Care], *Det Nationale Institut for Kommuners og Regioners Analyse og Forskning* (KORA) [Danish Institute for Local and Regional Government Research], Copenhagen, *http://mit.kora.dk/media/4936303/10678_derfor-er-der-forskel-paa-hvad-boernene-koster-i-kommunerne.pdf.*

Danish Ministry for Children, Education and Gender Equality (2016a), *Database Befolkningens Uddannelse og Arbejdsmarked* (BUA) [Educational Attainment and Labour Market], *http://statweb.uni-c.dk/databanken/uvmDataWeb/MainCategories.aspx.*

Danish Ministry for Children, Education and Gender Equality (2016b), *Hold og Personale i Grundskolen* (HGS) [Staff in the *Folkeskole*] Database, *http://statweb.uni-c.dk/databanken/uvmDataWeb/MainCategories.aspx.*

Danish Ministry for Children, Education and Gender Equality (2016c), *Datavarehuset* [Datawarehouse], *www.uddannelsesstatistik.dk.*

DLF (2016), *Analysenotat. Undersøgelse af Lærermangel* [Analysis Brief. Investigating Teacher Shortage], The Danish Teacher Union, *www.dlf.org/media/8049237/analysenotat-laerermangel.pdf.*

Ehrenberg, R.G. and D.J. Brewer (1994), "Do school and teacher characteristics matter? Evidence from high school and beyond", *Economics of Education Review*, Vol. 13(1), Elsevier, Amsterdam, pp. 1-17.

Falch, T. (2010), "The elasticity of labour supply at the establishment level", *Journal of Labor Economics*, Vol. 28, University of Chicago Press, Chicago, IL, pp. 237-266.

Falch, T. and J.A.V. Fischer (2012), "Public sector decentralization and school performance: International evidence", *Economics Letters*, Vol. 114, Elsevier, Amsterdam, pp. 276-279.

Falch, T. and C. Mang (2015), "Policies to attract a high-quality and innovative teaching force", *EENEE policy Brief 4/2015*, European Expert Network on Economics of Education, Publications Office of the European Union, Luxembourg, *www.eenee.de/dms/EENEE/Policy_Briefs/PolicyBrief4-2015.pdf.*

Falch, T., M. Rønning and B. Strøm (2008), "A cost model of schools: School size, school structure and student composition", in N.C. Soguel and P. Jaccard (eds.), *Governance and Performance of Education Systems*, Springer, Netherlands.

Figlio, D. and C.M.D. Hart (2014), "Competitive effects of means-tested school vouchers", *American Economic Journal: Applied Economics*, Vol. 6, American Economic Association, Nashville, TN, pp. 133-156.

Fredriksson, P. and B. Öckert (2008), "Resources and student achievement – Evidence from a Swedish policy reform", *Scandinavian Journal of Economics*, Vol. 110, Wiley-Blackwell, Hoboken, NJ, pp. 277-296.

Friedman, M. (1962), *Capitalism and Freedom*, University of Chicago Press, Chicago.

Goldhaber, D. (2007), "Everyone's doing it, but what does teacher testing tell us about teacher effectiveness?", *Journal of Human Resources*, Vol. 42, University of Wisconsin Press, Madison, WI, pp. 765-794.

Gromada, A. and C. Shewbridge (2016), "Student Learning Time: A Literature Review", *OECD Education Working Papers*, No. 127, OECD Publishing, Paris, *http://dx.doi.org/10.1787/5jm409kqqkjh-en.*

Grönqvist, E. and J. Vlachos (2014), "One Size Fits All? The Effects of Teacher Cognitive and Non-Cognitive Abilities on Student Achievement", *IFAU and Stockholm University Working Paper*, Uppsala, *www.ifau.se/globalassets/pdf/se/2008/wp08-25.pdf.*

Hamilton, L.S. and K. Guin (2005), "Understanding how families choose schools", in J.R. Betts and T. Loveless (eds.), *Getting Choice Right: Ensuring Equity and Efficiency in Education Policy*, Brookings Institution Press, Washington, DC.

Hanushek, E.A. (2011), "The economic value of higher teacher quality", *Economics of Education Review*, Vol. 30, Elsevier, Amsterdam, pp. 466-479.

Hanushek, E.A. (2006), "School resources", in E.A. Hanushek and F. Welch (eds.), *Handbook of the Economics of Education, Vol. 2*, Elsevier, Amsterdam.

Hanushek, E.A. (2003), "The failure of input-based schooling policies", *The Economic Journal*, Vol. 113, Wiley-Blackwell, Hoboken, NJ, pp. F64-F98.

Hanushek, E.A., M. Piopiunik and S. Wiederhold (2014), "The value of smarter teachers: International evidence on teacher cognitive skills and student performance", *NBER Working Paper* No. 20727, National Bureau of Economic Research, Cambridge, MA, *www.nber.org/papers/w20727.pdf.*

Hanushek, E.A., S. Link and L. Wößmann (2013), "Does school autonomy make sense everywhere? Panel estimates from PISA", *Journal of Development Economics*, Vol. 104, Elsevier, Amsterdam, pp. 212-232.

Heckman, J.J. (2008), "Schools, Skills, and Synapses", *Economic Inquiry*, Vol. 46, Wiley-Blackwell, Hoboken, NJ, pp. 289-324.

Heinesen, E. (2010), "Estimating class-size effects using within-school variation in subject-specific classes", *Economic Journal*, Vol. 120, Wiley-Blackwell, Hoboken, NJ, pp. 737-760.

Hill, P., L.C. Pierce and J.W. Guthrie (1997), *Reinventing Public Education: How Contracting Can Transform America's Schools*, University of Chicago Press, Chicago.

Hirschman, A.O. (1970), *Exit, Voice and Loyalty: Responses to Decline in Firms, Organizations, and States*, Harvard University Press, Cambridge, MA.

Houlberg, K. et al. (2016), *OECD Review of Policies to Improve the Effectiveness of Resource Use in Schools: Country Background Report for Denmark, Det Nationale Institut for Kommuners og Regioners Analyse og Forskning* (KORA) [Danish Institute for Local and Regional Government Research], Copenhagen, *www.oecd.org/edu/school/10932_OECD%20Country%20Background%20Report%20Denmark.pdf*.

Humlum, M.K. and N. Smith (2015), "The impact of school size and school consolidations on quality and Equity in Education", *EENEE Analytical Report* No. 24, European Expert Network on Economics of Education, Publications Office of the European Union, Luxembourg, *www.eenee.de/dms/EENEE/Analytical_Reports/EENEE_AR24.pdf*.

Jackson, C.K. (2012a). "Recruiting, retaining, and creating quality teachers", *Nordic Economic Policy Review*, Nordic Council of Ministers, Copenhagen, pp. 61-104.

Jackson, C.K. (2012b). "Non-cognitive ability, test scores, and teacher quality: Evidence from 9th Grade teachers in North Carolina", *NBER Working Paper No. 18624*, National Bureau of Economic Research, Cambridge, MA, *www.nber.org/papers/w18624.pdf*.

Karbownik, K. (2014), "Do changes in student quality affect teacher mobility? Evidence from an admission reform", *IFAU Working Paper Series 2014:15, Institutet för Arbetsmarknads- och Utbildningspolitisk Utvärdering, IFAU* (Institute for Evaluation of Labour Market and Education Policy), Uppsala, *http://econpapers.repec.org/scripts/redir.pf?u=http%3A%2F%2Fwww.ifau.se%2FUpload%2Fpdf%2Fse%2F2014%2Fwp2014-15-Do-changes-in-student-quality-affect-teacher-mobility.pdf;h=repec:hhs:ifauwp:2014_015*.

Kommunernes og regionernes Løndatakontor (n.d.), Municipal Payroll Data, *Kommunernes og regionernes Løndatakontor* [Pay Data Department of the Municipalities and Regions], *www.krl.dk* (accessed 24 February 2016).

Krueger, A. (2003), "Economic considerations and class size", *The Economic Journal*, Vol. 113, pp. 34-63.

Lacireno-Paquet, N. (2012), "Who chooses schools, and why? The characteristics and motivations of families who actively choose school", in G. Miron et al. (eds.), *Exploring the School Choice Universe: Evidence and Recommendations*, Information Age Publishing Inc., Charlotte, NC.

Larsen, B.Ø., K. Houlberg and B.S. Rangvid (2013), *Metodenotat om Udgiftsanalyser på Folkeskoleområdet på Skoleniveau [Method Note on Cost Analyses of the Folkeskole at School Level], Det Nationale Institut for Kommuners og Regioners Analyse og Forskning* (KORA) [Danish Institute for Local and Regional Government Research], Copenhagen, *www.kora.dk/media/340370/metodenotat_om_udgiftsanalyser_paa_folkeskoleomraadet_paa_skoleniveau.pdf*.

Lavy, V. (2015), "Do differences in schools' instruction time explain international achievement gaps? Evidence from developed and developing countries", *The Economic Journal*, Vol. 125, Wiley-Blackwell, Hoboken, NJ, pp. F397-F424.

Leuven, E., H. Oosterbeek and M. Rønning (2008), "Quasi-experimental estimates of the effect of class size on achievement in Norway", *Scandinavian Journal of Economics*, Vol. 110, Wiley-Blackwell, Hoboken, NJ, pp. 663– 693.

Lotz, J., J. Blom-Hansen and S.H. Hede (2013), "The changing role of local income taxation in Denmark", in J. Kim, J. Lotz and N.J. Mau, *Interaction Between Local Expenditure Responsibilities and Local Tax Policy*, The Korea Institute of Public Finance, Seoul, and the Danish Ministry for Economic Affairs and the Interior, Copenhagen.

Ministry for Economic Affairs and the Interior (2014), *Municipalities and Regions – Tasks and Financing*, Ministry of Economic Affairs and the Interior, Copenhagen, *http://english.sim.dk/media/670682/municipalities_and_regions_-_tasks_and_financing__june_2014.pdf*.

Ministry of Social Affairs and the Interior (2016), *Key Figures*, *www.noegletal.dk* (accessed 24 February 2016).

Naper, L.R. (2010), "Teacher hiring practices and educational efficiency", *Economics of Education Review*, Vol. 29, Elsevier, Amsterdam, pp. 658-668.

Nusche, D. (2009), "What Works in Migrant Education?: A Review of Evidence and Policy Options", *OECD Education Working Papers*, No. 22, OECD Publishing, Paris, *http://dx.doi.org/10.1787/227131784531*.

Oates, W. (1972), *Fiscal Federalism*, Harcourt, Brace and Jovanovich, New York.

OECD (2015), *Education at a Glance 2015: OECD Indicators*, OECD Publishing, Paris, *http://dx.doi.org/10.1787/eag-2015-en*.

OECD (2014a), *Education at a Glance 2014: OECD Indicators*, OECD Publishing, Paris, *http://dx.doi.org/10.1787/eag-2014-en*.

OECD (2014b), *TALIS 2013 Results: An International Perspective on Teaching and Learning*, OECD Publishing, Paris, *http://dx.doi.org/10.1787/9789264196261-en*.

OECD (2013a), *Education at a Glance 2013: OECD Indicators*, OECD Publishing, Paris, *http://dx.doi.org/10.1787/eag-2013-en*.

OECD (2013b), *PISA 2012 Results: What Makes Schools Successful (Volume IV): Resources, Policies and Practices*, OECD Publishing, Paris, *http://dx.doi.org/10.1787/9789264201156-en*.

OECD (2012), *Education at a Glance 2012: OECD Indicators*, OECD Publishing, Paris, *http://dx.doi.org/10.1787/eag-2012-en*.

OECD (2011), *Education at a Glance 2011: OECD Indicators*, OECD Publishing, Paris, *http://dx.doi.org/10.1787/eag-2011-en*.

OECD (2010), *Education at a Glance 2010: OECD Indicators*, OECD Publishing, Paris, *http://dx.doi.org/10.1787/eag-2010-en*.

OECD (2009), *Education at a Glance 2009: OECD Indicators*, OECD Publishing, Paris, *http://dx.doi.org/10.1787/eag-2009-en*.

OECD (2008), *Education at a Glance 2008: OECD Indicators*, OECD Publishing, Paris, *http://dx.doi.org/10.1787/eag-2008-en*.

OECD (2005), *Teachers Matter: Attracting, Developing and Retaining Effective Teachers*, OECD Publishing, Paris, *http://dx.doi.org/10.1787/9789264018044-en*.

Produktivitetskommissionen (2014), *Utdannelse og Innovation. Analyserapport 4 [Education and Innovation Analysis report 4]*, *Produktivitetskommissionen* [Productivity Commission], Rosendahls, Copenhagen, *http://produktivitetskommissionen.dk/publikationer*.

Rangvid, B.S. (2010), "School choice, universal vouchers and native flight from local schools", *European Sociological Review*, Vol. 26, Oxford University Press, Oxford, pp. 319-335.

Rangvid, B.S. (2007), "Living and learning separately? Ethnic segregation of school children in Copenhagen", *Urban Studies*, Vol. 44, Sage Publications, Thousand Oaks, CA, pp. 1329-1354.

Schneider, M., and J. Buckley (2002), "What do parents want from schools? Evidence from the Internet", *Educational Evaluation and Policy Analysis*, 24(2), Sage Publications, Thousand Oaks, CA, pp. 133-144.

Schneider, M. et al. (1998), "Shopping for schools: In the land of the blind, the one-eyed parent may be enough", *American Journal of Political Science*, Vol. 42(3), Wiley-Blackwell, Hoboken, NJ, pp. 769-793.

Shewbridge, C. et al. (2011), *OECD Reviews of Evaluation and Assessment in Education: Denmark 2011*, OECD Publishing, Paris, *http://dx.doi.org/10.1787/9789264116597-en*.

Statistics Denmark (2016), StatBank Denmark, *http://statistikbanken.dk* (accessed 24 February 2016).

Chapter 3

Governance of school resource use in Denmark

Resource use can be viewed in terms of the architecture of the school system – how funding flows through different levels of the education administration and different resource categories – but also in terms of the outcomes of schooling. A critical scrutiny of the suitability, effectiveness and efficiency of the resourcing model depends on the availability of systematic knowledge of how well Danish schools work and for whom. The basic question addressed in this chapter is whether there is enough knowledge available to guide policy at a school, local and system level regarding the use of resources and the outcomes for different schools and student groups. The chapter first describes how educational goals are set and how goal achievement is being measured and reported. It then analyses how the use of resources in the pursuit of these educational goals is being governed, managed and evaluated. The chapter highlights the high level of consensus regarding the need for change, the clear targets that have been set to implement reforms, and the tools that have been put in place to monitor goal achievement and to follow up on the implementation of reform. At the same time, it discusses the tension between broad learning goals and narrow measures of learning, and the scope to strengthen both the monitoring of inputs and outcomes of different student groups and of promoting greater excellence among schools and students. The chapter points out the coherence and clarity in the distribution of responsibilities between the different levels of governance, but also the lack of transparency on the use of resources at a local level this implies. The chapter suggests a number of policy recommendations to improve the governance of school resource use.

The statistical data for Israel are supplied by and under the responsibility of the relevant Israeli authorities. The use of such data by the OECD is without prejudice to the status of the Golan Heights, East Jerusalem and Israeli settlements in the West Bank under the terms of international law.

Context and features

Educational goals and outcomes

Responsibilities for goal development and implementation

As described in Chapters 1 and 2, the Danish *Folkeskole* is embedded in a governance system of three layers – the central state, the municipalities, and schools – and a balance between central authority and local autonomy, between the implementation of national goals and regulations and their adaptation to local needs. The central level governs at a distance and sets central conditions and guidelines within which municipalities and schools exercise their autonomy.

The Ministry for Children, Education and Gender Equality sets the overall framework and objectives for schooling, monitors the quality of education, and ensures that municipalities and schools carry out the government's education policies. Within this central framework, the municipalities set local goals, develop their specific curricular plans and follow up on the results of their schools. Individual schools are responsible for providing education in line with the national aims for the *Folkeskole* and the requirements of their municipality.

Educational goals defined by the Folkeskole Act

The *Folkeskole* Act sets out the general goals of the *Folkeskole*. According to the Act, the *Folkeskole* should provide a broad education that fosters the holistic development of students as independent individuals and that develops students' awareness, imagination and confidence in their own abilities. In partnership with parents, the *Folkeskole* should provide students with the knowledge and skills that will prepare them for further education, training and learning, and for their role as citizens in a democratic society. Each school is responsible for ensuring the quality of education in accordance with the general goals of the *Folkeskole*, and students and parents are to work together with the school towards realising the aims of the *Folkeskole*.

The 'Common Objectives' for student learning

All public municipal primary and lower secondary schools share a set of binding learning progressions, achievement targets and curricular guidelines, the so-called Common Objectives. Common Objectives were introduced in 2003 and specify the purpose of the different subjects, the objectives to be met by the end of compulsory education in the Year 9 leaving examination, the objectives for different year levels, and a guiding curriculum for all subjects. Common Objectives specify the knowledge and skills of students that teaching should lead to. However, while the Common Objectives provide descriptions of how objectives can be reached, and while schools have to include learning and achievements targets in their curricula, there is no tight curriculum at the national level.

In 2014, the Common Objectives were reduced and simplified as part of the *Folkeskole* reform to ensure that learning objectives focus on learning outcomes rather than the content of instruction (see further below). This is intended to help school principals, teachers, parents, students and school boards to better understand the objectives so they can be an active partner in the learning process, and to assist schools and teachers to move towards a more goal-oriented approach to teaching and learning (Houlberg et al., 2016). In connection with this process, the curriculum document for Year 0 (the pre-school class) was also changed, setting explicit goals for students. This aims to further strengthen the development of crucial skills in Year 0 and improving their readiness for benefiting from the instruction in subjects from Year 1.

The change towards a clearer goal-orientation in the Common Objectives is also intended to provide a stronger and more precise basis for evaluation and assessment by teachers of their students' progression in relation to the learning goals. To further this intention, concrete guidance for evaluation in relation to all learning goals (including specific examples) were made available to teachers together with the Common Objectives at a web portal (*www.emu.dk*), which is to function as a "knowledge portal", providing guidance and inspiration for working with the Common Objectives. The portal also offers suggestions for concrete teaching modules and activities. These tools are intended to support a shared understanding of goal-oriented instruction and assessment, thus helping teachers to work with the Common Objectives in a more qualified way.

Goals set as part of the 2014 Folkeskole reform

Beyond the general goals of the education system set out in the *Folkeskole* Act, recent reforms established more specific goals and related measurable targets and objectives to monitor the performance of the education system. Most notably, as part of 2014 *Folkeskole* reform, the government set three national goals that should contribute to setting a clear direction and a high level of ambition for the development of the *Folkeskole* while ensuring a clear framework for a systematic and continuous evaluation:

- The *Folkeskole* must challenge all students to reach their full potential.
- The *Folkeskole* must lower the significance of social background on academic results.
- Trust in the *Folkeskole* and student wellbeing must be enhanced through respect for professional knowledge and practice in the *Folkeskole*.

These three national goals for the development of the *Folkeskole* are operationalised through a number of clear, simple and measurable targets:

- At least 80% of students must achieve "good" results (mark 3 or higher) at reading and mathematics in the national assessments. The baseline is the share of students achieving mark 3 or higher in the national assessments in 2012.[1]
- The number of high-performing students in Danish and mathematics must increase from year to year. The baseline is the percentage of students achieving the top mark 5 in the national assessments in 2012.[2]
- The number of low-performing students in reading and mathematics, independent of social background, must decrease from year to year. This target should focus on the percentage of students with parents with only compulsory or unknown education performing poorly in the national assessments.[3]
- The wellbeing of students as measured by a national survey must increase.[4]

The targets are measurable on national, municipal, school and class levels and are envisaged to become the basis for dialogue and follow-up regarding the development of students' academic performance and wellbeing at all levels. To fulfil the three national goals, the *Folkeskole* reform focuses broadly on three main areas of improvement, as described in Chapter 1: a longer and varied school day with more and improved teaching and learning; better professional development of teachers, pedagogical staff and school principals; and few and clear objectives and simplification of rules and regulations.

Goal-setting at the municipal and school level

Within the framework provided by national goals and the Common Objectives, municipalities define the goals and scope for the activities of their schools. The school leader is responsible, both administratively and pedagogically, for the school activities in relation to both the objectives and policies imposed by the municipal council and the principles set out by the school boards. Given the decentralised approach to schooling in Denmark, there are variations in the degree to which municipalities set local goals and hold their schools accountable for the achievement of these goals.

School leaders, in collaboration with the school boards, define the strategy for their school and may set more specific school-level goals. In a survey of Danish school leaders, Pedersen et al. (2011) found that most schools had developed goals or values for the wellbeing of their students (91%), the schools' educational performance (71%) and attainment targets for various subjects (74%). The study also found that larger schools typically devoted more attention to documentation and were working more intensely with written goals and evaluation and assessment of goal-achievement. Schools in more challenging socio-economic circumstances were more likely to develop their own performance goals that differed from national and municipal goals. These schools typically focused less on performance goals and more on other educational and social goals.

Wiedemann (2012) studied how Danish teachers responded to the Common Objectives. Based on focus group interviews at nine schools, the study finds a variation of teacher responses to the central steering through Common Objectives. While some teachers felt their professional identity reinforced through the visible demands for achievement set by the Common Objectives, others experienced the introduction of these central objectives as a form of de-professionalisation and de-valorisation of their professional judgments. Teachers who had participated in the implementation process had a more positive view of the Common Objectives. In a study on the effects of school autonomy in Denmark, Calmar Andersen and Winter (2011) found that school autonomy in goal-setting, and planning and choosing teaching methods in line with these goals, had beneficial effects for student performance.

The 2014 *Folkeskole* reform further emphasises the importance of goal-oriented teaching. In particular, a focus on setting "visible learning goals" had been very much taken on board in all the municipalities and schools visited by the OECD review team. Teachers reported paying more attention to sharing and co-constructing learning goals together with their students and making goals explicit, for example at the start of every lesson.

Processes to measure goal achievement

Over the last decade, and especially with the revisions of the *Folkeskole* Act in 2006 and in 2014, Denmark has implemented a range of measures to stimulate a culture of evaluation and assessment in the *Folkeskole* and to increase the collection and use of data at the different levels of the education system (also see Chapter 1). This includes the introduction of national student assessments, the establishment of a requirement for municipalities to produce quality reports, and the creation of national bodies to monitor and evaluate the quality of education (Shewbridge et al., 2011).

Measuring student learning outcomes

Traditionally, student assessment in Denmark has been the responsibility of schools and teachers, but a number of central measures have influenced assessment practice over the years. Since 1993, teachers have been required by law to ensure a continuous assessment of student learning. With the introduction of the Common Objectives in 2003, schools and teachers have had a common basis for their assessments through learning goals for the different years and subjects as well as the end of the *Folkeskole* in Year 9. Since 2006, schools and teachers are also required to develop individual student plans as a tool to systematically monitor and improve students' learning outcomes. Teachers have to establish a learning plan for each of their students, describing the student's current performance level and specifying areas on which the student, parents and the teacher will focus on over the coming months. Student learning plans need to be shared with parents at least once a year.

At the end of the *Folkeskole* in Year 9, students are required to sit a mandatory school leaving examination, and in Year 10, students can choose to take an optional examination. Municipalities and schools are required to publish results from the Year 9 school-leaving examinations by law through the Act on Transparency and Openness (Act no. 414 of 06/06/2002). The same act obliges schools to publish performance indicators such as average marks, transition frequencies to further education and results of evaluations conducted by the school. The publication of examination and assessment results has led to a public debate about the utility of such data as an indicator for school quality (Houlberg et al., 2016; Shewbridge et al., 2011).

In 2007, national assessments for different subjects in Years 2, 3, 4, 6, 7 and 8 were introduced to provide teachers with a better general assessment of students' learning progress and to follow up on students' attainment of the learning goals specified in the Common Objectives.[5] Since 2010, participation in national assessments has been compulsory for schools and teachers. The average results of Danish students in national assessments are published in the form of national profiles, but individual student results as well as the average results for schools and municipalities are confidential (for more information, see Box 3.1).

Box 3.1. **Availability of results of national assessments in Denmark: who has access to the results?**

Information on assessment results for individual students, groups of students, classes, schools and municipalities is to be kept confidential. Individual students, their parents and their teachers have access to information about individual student assessment result. Individual student assessment results are not shared with other teachers, except in specific cases such as join teaching. School principals have information about the average assessment results of their school in each assessment, the average results of each class and school data adjusted for socio-economic factors. Municipalities have information about the average mark of the schools in the municipality and the average results for each school as well as data for each school adjusted for socio-economic factors. At the national level, the national average test result for all schools together is published and available to the public.

Box 3.1. **Availability of results of national assessments in Denmark: who has access to the results?** *(cont.)*

This implies that different stakeholders can compare themselves against the national average, but benchmarking towards other schools or municipalities is not possible, i.e. municipalities cannot benchmark themselves against other municipalities, school principals cannot compare themselves to other schools and parents cannot compare different schools' average test results. Consequently, students, parents and teachers can use assessment results to follow an individual student's acquisition of knowledge and skills, and municipalities and schools can use the results to compare themselves against the national average and to aid decision-making, but results cannot be used as a basis for systematic benchmarking and sharing of best practice among different schools and municipalities or for ranking municipalities or schools (Houlberg et al., 2016).

This policy of confidentiality of assessment reflects the intended purpose of the national assessments. The national assessments were conceived i) to provide a pedagogical tool for teachers against testable areas of the Common Objectives; and ii) to provide a tool for monitoring national progress over time through a national performance profile showing national average test results and to enable municipalities to monitor their schools against this national profile. A previous OECD review of evaluation and assessment in education for Denmark analysed the question of transparency of the results from national assessments. It highlighted the importance of not compromising the reliability of the national assessments as a monitoring tool and the potential of the national assessments as a pedagogical tool. The OECD review encouraged Denmark to further support and promote the capacity of stakeholders to use national test results effectively in schools and municipalities. It also provided an analysis of the government's plans at the time of the review in 2010 to publish results the school level for greater accountability suggesting that such a step was premature at the time. It pointed out that private schools were allowed to opt out of national assessments, arguing that, if used for accountability purposes, private schools should be held accountable the same way – especially given the increase in the number of private schools offering compulsory education (Shewbridge et al., 2011).

Recent OECD work on governance and accountability in complex education systems and evaluation and assessment in education provide a broader context about the use of national assessment results for accountability. School performance accountability is a good tool for output steering as it enables central governments to monitor and control the quality of education, to steer schools and school governing boards based on their performance, and to make relatively objective and unambiguous comparisons between schools. The shift to school performance accountability has, therefore, been an important step in ensuring quality control and effective steering of decentralised systems and school performance accountability. The setting of national standards is now commonly used in a majority of OECD countries. However, school performance accountability is not a cure-all solution when it comes to securing the quality of education in a broad and comprehensive sense (Hooge, 2016). Indeed, analyses from the OECD PISA 2012 make it clear that simply making school achievement data public is not correlated with better student outcomes (Blanchenay and Burns, 2016).

School performance accountability systems entail a number of caveats. Essential elements of the quality of education are not so easy to measure, such as socialisation, general knowledge, integration, and personal development. Research has identified a number of unintended effects of school performance accountability: impoverishing the teaching and learning processes as a result of "teaching to the test"; narrowing the curriculum to focus on those elements that are tested emphasising failure instead of learning or improvement if

Box 3.1. **Availability of results of national assessments in Denmark: who has access to the results?** *(cont.)*

performance accountability lacks positive interventions designed to assist and support low-performing schools; and reducing the quality of staff in schools serving low-performing students. The higher the stakes are for school leaders and teachers, the more these unintended effects are likely to occur. Using results from national assessments for accountability purposes, then, requires transparency and fairness to mitigate the negative effects on teaching and learning and to reduce the misuse of results (Hooge, 2016; OECD, 2013b). The availability of performance data to a broader range of stakeholders for the purpose of transparency and accountability, furthermore, carries an underlying equity issue as different actors may be able to use the available data to different degrees. In most countries, middle-class parents are more likely than parents with lower socio-economic status to use school achievement and performance data to place their child in the best-performing schools and to lobby successfully for change in the system.

The availability of data per se then, is not a stand-alone solution to information asymmetries between stakeholders, and can in fact increase the complexity involved in their interactions (Blanchenay and Burns, 2016). While not a panacea itself and possibly leading to other unintended consequences, expanding school performance accountability to encompass a multiple school accountability approach can be a promising option for a central government searching for a holistic view of educational quality. Such an approach involves horizontal accountability to multiple stakeholders, including students, parents and the community, for multiple aspects of schooling based on various sources of information, including process-oriented measurements (Hooge, 2016).

Source: Blanchenay, P. and T. Burns (2016), "Policy experimentation in complex education systems", in *Governing Education in a Complex World*, *http://dx.doi.org/10.1787/9789264255364-10-en*; Hooge, E. (2016), "Making multiple school accountability work", in *Governing Education in a Complex World*, *http://dx.doi.org/10.1787/9789264255364-7-en*; Houlberg, K. et al. (2016), *OECD Review of Policies to Improve the Effectiveness of Resource Use in Schools: Country Background Report for Denmark*, *www.oecd.org/edu/school/10932_OECD%20Country%20Background%20Report%20Denmark.pdf*; OECD (2013b), *Synergies for Better Learning: An International Perspective on Evaluation and Assessment*, *http://dx.doi.org/10.1787/9789264190658-en*; Shewbridge, C. et al. (2011), *OECD Reviews of Evaluation and Assessment in Education: Denmark 2011*, *http://dx.doi.org/10.1787/9789264116597-en*.

Evaluation of municipalities and schools

In 2006, Denmark introduced the requirement for municipalities to produce annual quality reports. Since the 2014 *Folkeskole* reform, these reports have been required on a biannual basis. Quality reports seek to further the co-operation between local politicians, local authorities and schools and aim to contribute to transparency as they are made public. In their quality reports, municipalities must describe their schools' quality of education, the measures the municipal board has taken to evaluate the quality of education, and the steps the municipal board has taken in response to the previous quality report. As part of the 2014 *Folkeskole* reform, special emphasis was put on ensuring that quality reports focus less on input factors and more on outcome information. Quality reports should be based on data available from a national data warehouse (more on this below) and refer to a number of indicators such as the number of teachers with teaching competencies in the subjects they teach, results regarding academic performance and wellbeing in relation to the indicators set in the 2014 *Folkeskole* reform, average marks correlated for socio-economic background, transition rates to upper secondary education and inclusion rates for students with special educational needs. In line with the policy of keeping results from national student assessments confidential at the level of municipalities and schools, the quality reports do not make available results from national assessments. For monitoring purposes, the quality reports can, however, disclose information whether the municipality or individual schools meet their performance targets and how performance develops over time.

The external evaluation of public schools is the responsibility of the municipalities, and practices vary across Denmark. The six municipalities visited by the OECD review team all reported having procedures in place to ensure the quality control of their schools. This typically involves annual meetings with school leaders to discuss student results, based on national and municipal assessments and surveys of students and/or school staff. Some municipalities reported to employ specialists working with schools around assessment data or experts in the core subjects to help school leaders devise strategies for improvement. One of the municipalities conducted regular quality visits at its schools involving the observation and review of teachers' classroom practices, followed by the development of a capacity development plan for the school. While all the municipalities and schools visited by the OECD review team affirmed having a lot of data at their disposal, they expressed facing challenges in using this data to formulate strategies and improve results (more on this below). The OECD 2012 Programme for International Student Assessment (PISA) provides some information about the use of assessment data at administrative levels as reported by school principals. According to these data, 69.9% of students were in a school whose principal reported that an administrative authority tracked achievement data over time (OECD average: 72.1%) (OECD, 2013a).

School boards also play a role in evaluating school quality and holding school leaders accountable for results. School boards typically comprise five to seven parent representatives, two teacher representatives and two student representatives elected by their peers. It is part of the school boards' role to set principles and long-term goals for the school and to follow up on school budgets, policies and results. The Danish national parents' organisation supports school boards in these tasks and has received dedicated funding for this type of support with the 2014 *Folkeskole* reform. However, the degree to which school boards confront school leaders and get involved with monitoring school results varies across schools. Some of the school board representatives interviewed by the OECD review team reported that they had become more involved with monitoring school results since the 2014 *Folkeskole* reform.

The national level also monitors school quality from a distance. In April 2015, the Agency for Education and Quality (*Styrelsen for Undervisning og Kvalitet*) was created to replace the former Quality and Supervision Agency (*Kvalitets- og Tilsynsstyrelsen*). The new agency is responsible for the quality supervision for the *Folkeskole*. This includes supporting quality and capacity development activities in areas such as the new learning consultant corps, including consultants working with inclusion and bilingual children as well as international supervisors, and the development and operation of assessments and examinations. National supervision comprises a regular monitoring of the data available in the data warehouse (see below) and further screening and follow-up with those schools that are considered "at risk" based on these indicators. If there is evidence of consistent underperformance in a particular school or municipality over several years, the national level can oblige the municipality to work with the national learning consultants in order to develop improvement strategies.

Evaluation at the system level

For evaluation of compulsory education as a whole, Denmark has traditionally been reliant on information provided via international assessments such as the OECD PISA. But results from such external surveys have led to increased demands for national information on the school system. Since 2006, significant efforts have been made to produce such information, most notably through the publication of results from the mandatory school-leaving examinations in Year 9 by schools and municipalities, as well as the publication of "national profiles" showing average results from the national assessments designed to measure progress over time (Shewbridge et al., 2011). National information on student performance is typically contextualised with information about the performance of Danish students in international assessments.

Following the introduction of national performance targets as part of the *Folkeskole* reform in 2014, which include a target related to student wellbeing, a national survey on student wellbeing (*National måling af elevers trivsel*) has been developed and implemented for the first time in March 2015. This constitutes a major step in going beyond the measurement of basic academic skills and ensuring that broader aims of the *Folkeskole* related to the wellbeing of students are monitored. Results are intended to inform municipalities, schools, principals, teachers, parents and students and to provide a basis for discussions and initiatives enhancing students' wellbeing (see Box 3.2).

Box 3.2. **The Danish national survey on student wellbeing**

While individual student results are confidential, teachers, school management, the school board, and the municipality have access to all class results so they can collectively support further work on wellbeing. For anonymity, answer distributions for classes with fewer than five students are not available. For schools, the results of the wellbeing survey form the basis for developing a systematic approach to students' wellbeing at school as a whole and in each class. Teachers present results to the students in their class and teachers or principals present results to parents. For municipalities, the results must be part of the quality reports, i.e. what is the state of student wellbeing in the schools of the municipality and what does the municipality do to follow up on results and promote wellbeing. For more information in Danish, see *www.uvm.dk/Den-nye-Folkeskole/En-laengere-og-mere-varieret-skoledag/Trivsel-og-undervisningsmiljoe/National-maaling-af-elevers-trivsel.*

Source: Danish Ministry for Children, Education and Gender Equality (2016b), *Trivselsmåling* [National Wellbeing Survey], *www.uvm.dk/Uddannelser/Folkeskolen/Elevplaner-nationale-test-og-trivselsmaaling/Trivselsmaaling.*

Denmark also makes use of special thematic evaluations or studies to bring more information at the system level. The school council decides on national large-scale evaluations to be conducted in compulsory education. These include major evaluations of national initiatives that are conducted by the Danish Evaluation Institute (EVA) and other partners.

The data warehouse

As part of the 2014 *Folkeskole* reform, growing emphasis has been placed on data collection, analysis and evaluation. A new data warehouse (*www.uddannelsesstatistik.dk*) has been gradually developed since 2013 by the National Agency for IT and Learning of the Ministry for Children, Education and Gender Equality to monitor key aspects of basic education. This data warehouse is envisaged to fully replace the previous public database of education statistics (*Databanken*). Key purposes of this system are to promote data-driven approaches at the level of schools, municipalities and the Ministry for Children, Education and Gender Equality and to allow the analysis of data in relation to the national goals of the

Folkeskole reform. The information in the data warehouse is also available to the public with the exception of confidential data on results from national assessments at the level of individual schools and municipalities.

At the time of the OECD review visit in April 2015, the data warehouse included information on the *Folkeskole* sector, but it was foreseen to integrate information on private basic education as well. By the time of drafting the report, the system had been extended to youth education and adult education. The intention is to bring together data from different sources in a single location to allow policymakers and stakeholders at different levels of the system to access information easily for evaluation and planning purposes. Municipalities and schools are required to enter specific information into the data warehouse.

At the time of the OECD review visit, the data warehouse encompassed 35 indicators to monitor basic education. These included: examination results, national test results, results from student wellbeing surveys and transition rates to youth education. Since the results from the national tests are confidential, schools and municipalities have to log in to see their own results on these tests. The data warehouse also provides information on inclusion (number of students in special schools or classes), student absences, and annual expenditure per student. With respect to human resources, it includes information on teacher competencies, based on information entered by teachers regarding their formal education. There are plans to further broaden the information on human resources in schools and to also include information on the number of lessons received by students.

It is mandatory for municipalities to draw on the data included in the data warehouse to prepare their biannual quality reports. The data warehouse system appears to be particularly useful for smaller municipalities which may have little capacity to organise their own data collection and analysis. The system includes a function for schools to generate a statistical and quality report based on data for their own school. School leaders and teachers are encouraged to use the information from the data warehouse, for example in quality discussions with their municipal educational administration. The data warehouse is complemented by an online knowledge portal (*www.emu.dk*), which provides more qualitative information for schools. It describes the Common Objectives and reform goals and makes available examples of teaching and learning materials that can be helpful for stakeholders in reaching the goals (see above).

Management and monitoring of school resources

In Denmark's decentralised school system, most financial and personnel management decisions are taken at the local and school level. Figure 3.1 presents results from data collected across OECD countries in 2011 on decision making at the lower secondary level of education. In Denmark, the school level made 54% of resource management decisions and the local level made the remaining 46% of such decisions. This domain of decision-making includes the allocation and use of resources for teaching staff, non-teaching staff, capital and operating expenditure, and professional development of principals and teachers. With respect to personnel management, 25% of the decisions were made at the central level, 42% were made at the local level and 33% were made at the school level. This domain of decision-making includes the hiring and dismissal of principals, teaching and non-teaching staff; duties and conditions of service of staff; salary scales of staff; and influence over the careers of staff (OECD, 2012).

Figure 3.1. **Decisions taken at each level of government in public lower secondary education, 2011**

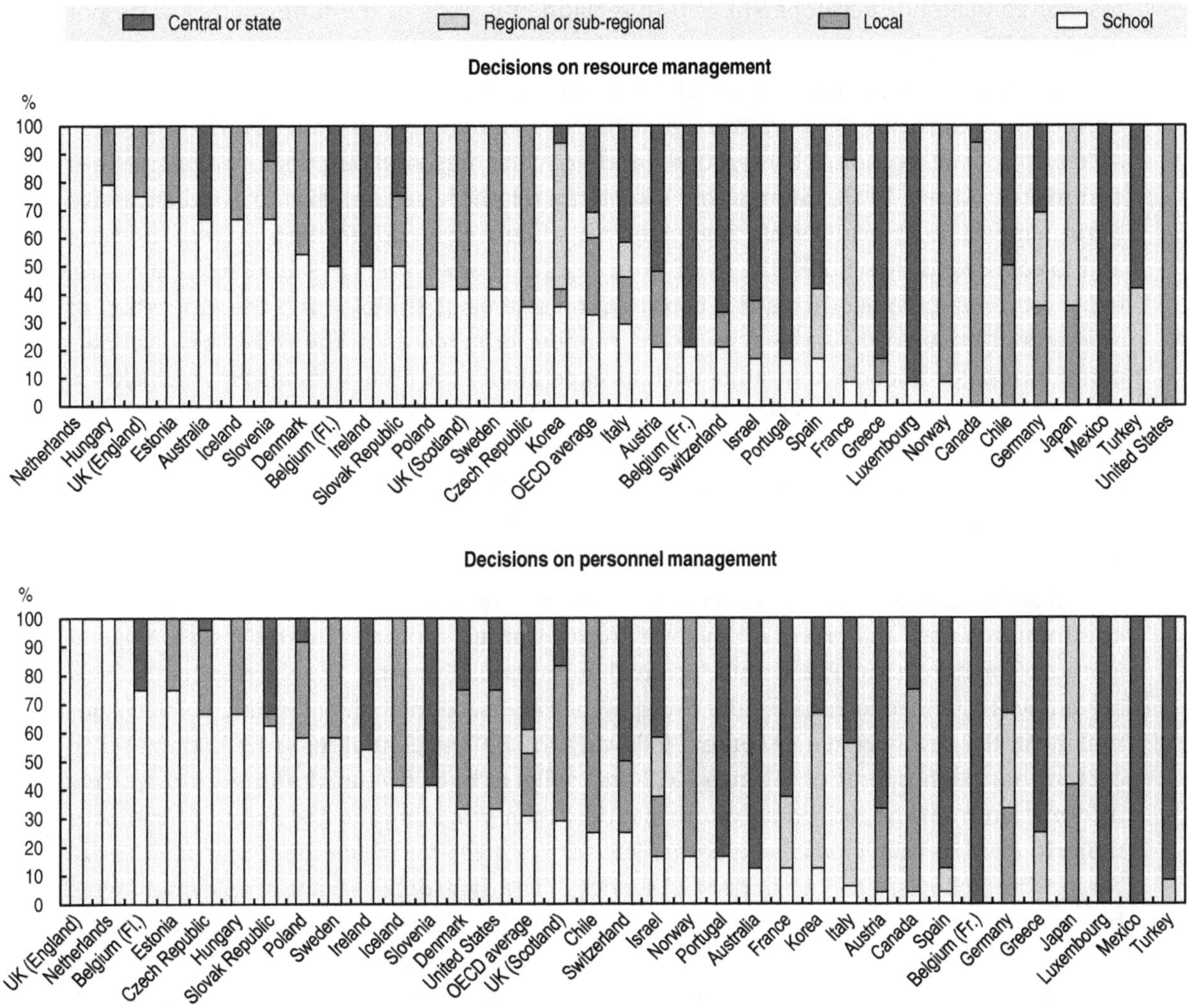

Note: For each domain, countries are ranked in descending order of the percentage of decisions taken at the school level.
Source: OECD (2012), *Education at a Glance 2012: OECD Indicators, http://dx.doi.org/10.1787/eag-2012-en*, Table D6.2a and D6.2b.

Resource management, accountability and reporting at the local level

As described in Chapters 1 and 2, the municipalities provide most of the services of the welfare state including compulsory education. The *Folkeskole* is almost exclusively financed by the unconditional block grant from the central government in addition to local taxes. There are very few earmarked grants to the *Folkeskole* and they typically concern relatively small amounts compared to the overall spending level in schools. The intended utilisation of such specific grants is laid down in annual agreements between Local Government Denmark (KL/LGDK) and the central government. As long as national framework laws are respected, the Ministry for Children, Education and Gender Equality does not get involved in monitoring municipality budgets.

With the 2014 *Folkeskole* reform, however, there has been a deliberate emphasis on monitoring the use of specific grants by the municipalities. For example, the utilisation of earmarked funding for teacher competency development is managed at the municipal level, but municipalities are required to report in an accounting system their levels of spending on formal teacher education. In 2020, the Ministry for Children, Education and Gender Equality plans to evaluate how municipalities have spent the funding destined for teacher competency development and to reclaim any parts of the funding that were not used for this purpose.

The Ministry of Social Affairs and the Interior manages a system for monitoring municipal performance (*Nøgletal* [Key figures]). The system makes available data that describe social conditions, economic background, local financial data, and outputs for municipalities and regions (Mizell, 2008). Information is kept at a relatively general level to avoid excessive bureaucratisation. It includes information on per student expenditure, the number of primary and lower secondary schools, the number of regular classes, average school and class size, expenditure on private schools and continuation schools (*Efterskole*), and the proportion of students in private schools relative to the number of students in the *Folkeskole*. It allows comparing basic financial indicators such as expenditure per student across municipalities, but, as reported during the review team's interviews, comparisons based on this system are not always easy to make as there are differences across municipalities in how expenditure is reported. For example, some staff categories are counted as local level employees in some municipalities and as school employees in others. The Ministry of Finance may also prepare ad hoc analyses to benchmark municipalities on certain areas of spending.

In addition, since the 2007 structural reform, the municipalities have been developing a common business management system for all Danish municipalities (*Fælleskommunal ledelsesinformationsystem*, FLIS [Joint Municipal Information System]). The development of this system was intended to enhance the transparency and accountability of municipal decision-making in the new governance context following the 2007 structural reform (Chapter 1). The system has been operational since 2013 and collects both financial and administrative information from the individual municipalities, thus providing the possibility to compare indicators across municipalities. It covers key service areas for which the municipalities are responsible (schools, eldercare and social services). The data for health and employment were being implemented in the system at the time of drafting the report. Regarding the school sector, the system includes information on aspects such as: spending per student, school size, class size, teachers' age, teachers' salaries, inclusion, and student characteristics (such as age, gender and ethnic background). The data can be viewed for individual municipalities.

While the system provides information on key input variables, it does not include outcome information from the national tests. Representatives from LGDK reported that the intention is to further develop the system into a data hub, which would allow making connections between national goals and local leadership decisions. This would help LGDK and/or individual municipalities in conducting their own analyses and evaluations of relationships between inputs and outcomes. The data are not accessible to the general public or the Ministry for Children, Education and Gender Equality. LGDK uses and selectively publishes the data for political dialogue and for conferences, such as the national conferences for mayors and economic committees of the municipalities organised by LGDK on a regular basis.

Resource management, accountability and reporting at the school level

As described in Chapter 2, the municipalities have different funding formulas to calculate the amount of funding allocated to each of their schools. Schools are typically informed of the budget for the next year several months in advance and they can start planning the budget for the next school year at the beginning of the calendar year. As student numbers influence the school budget, there may be variations from year to year due to fluctuations in student numbers. In one municipality, it was reported that in case of an unexpected decline in student numbers, schools had the possibility to apply for flexible funding from the municipalities' social services. School boards may meet with local politicians and comment on local budget proposals.

In most schools, the school leader prepares the school budget with input from the teaching staff and presents it to the school board. By law, it is the role of the school board to hold the school leader accountable and make the final decision on the school budget. However, according to the national parents' organisation, school boards are not always well informed of their rights and their involvement in determining the school budget varies across schools. In all schools visited by the OECD review team, the school boards were informed of the budget, but there were variations in the degree to which they felt in a position to question and influence the budget and strategy of the school. As part of the 2014 *Folkeskole* reform, the national parents' association received DKK 12 million to raise the competencies and professionalism of the school boards to strengthen democratic involvement of stakeholders and horizontal accountability at the school level.

School leaders, in consultation with their school boards, have wide-reaching autonomy in the use of the resources they receive. In their decisions on the allocation of funding, they are mainly restricted by national regulations about class size, hours to be taught by subject and students' right to receive teaching in accordance with their needs. School leaders need to recruit teaching staff with the relevant competencies and specialisations to fulfil these aims and the largest part of school budgets is dedicated to salaries for staff. School leaders interviewed by the OECD review team reported that they were facing increased reporting obligations since the 2014 *Folkeskole* reform, as there was increased national monitoring of their compliance with national regulations, such as the number of lessons students receive in Danish and mathematics, the number of lessons cancelled, the background of substitute teachers and the degree to which teachers are specialised in the subjects they teach.

Based on the interviews conducted during the review visit, the OECD review team formed the impression that, in line with the Danish focus on school autonomy, municipalities do not monitor the allocation of funding to different budget lines by the school leaders. However, they appeared to monitor closely that schools operate within their allocated budget and follow up with school leaders in case of financial problems. Municipalities may also offer accounting support to their schools, so that school leaders can focus on the less technical and more strategic aspects of budgeting. In one of the municipalities visited by the OECD review team, there was an approach by which all school leaders were jointly following the budgets for all schools in the municipality. There was a regular dialogue between municipal staff and all school leaders on their spending, which also made it easier for the municipality to shift resources between schools when necessary.

According to Houlberg et al. (2016), little information is available at a system level regarding the capacity for effective resource management at the local and school level and there are no central initiatives to build up a knowledge base and disseminate good practice in this area among schools and municipalities. This is linked to the decentralised approach to resource management in Denmark that leaves the responsibility for developing and implementing approaches to budgeting and accounting to the municipalities and schools.

Strengths

There is a high level of consensus regarding the need for change

High performing school systems typically set clear objectives for their education system, ensure that there are the right institutions to deliver, engage stakeholders in the process, and find the right balance between central and local direction, while at the same time ensuring that financial, material and human resources are aligned to the objectives (OECD, 2015). Successful governance hinges on stakeholders having adequate knowledge of educational policy goals and their consequences, on their ownership and willingness to effect change, and the tools to implement a reform as planned (Burns and Cerna, 2016). As will be discussed in more detail below, with the implementation of the 2014 *Folkeskole* reform, Denmark has been able to realise many of these elements of successful educational governance and steering. This is supported by the broad agreement of all the major political parties on the reform, the annual negotiations between the government and the municipalities, annual discussions in the individual municipal councils and the involvement of key stakeholder groups in designing, implementing and monitoring the reform.

The OECD review team was impressed by the ability of the Danish school system to build consensus around the need for change and to implement a wide-reaching reform of the school system, supported by a broad partnership involving several ministries at the central level and the representative organisations of municipalities, school leaders, parents and students. Although the individual teachers and the teachers' representative organisations interviewed by the OECD review team voiced strong concerns about the introduction of a new framework for the utilisation of teachers' working hours (Act no. 409) which preceded the reform of the *Folkeskole*, they also expressed their support for the overall aims and principles of the *Folkeskole* reform itself. It should be noted that the Danish school system is witnessing a period of major change, characterised not only by the 2014 *Folkeskole* reform but also by parallel ongoing changes related to the inclusion of students with special educational needs and the initial education of teachers. Despite the challenges all actors are confronted with in such a major change process, there appeared to be wide agreement among the main groups in the system that these changes were necessary to work towards the improvement of the education system.

There are clear national targets for the school system to guide decentralised spending

In a school system relying on decentralised management of resources, establishing a small number of clear, prioritised and measurable goals that can drive the system is key to guiding education policy improvement (OECD, 2015). In recent years, Denmark has put a major emphasis on ensuring that reforms are introduced along with clear goals and targets. This outcome-oriented approach to designing and implementing reforms was described by policy makers and stakeholders as a new way of educational steering in Denmark, which has the potential to create greater transparency and a sense of common purpose within a highly decentralised school system. There is a clear intention to make sure that the central goals for reform implementation are also translated into concrete targets at the local and school level. In line with this intention, evaluation and reporting mechanisms have been introduced to monitor progress towards these goals at the central, municipal and school level (see next sub-section).

The most notable example of this goal-oriented approach is the 2014 *Folkeskole* reform with its three core objectives for student achievement, equity and wellbeing, which are broken down into a range of measurable indicators. These indicators are monitored for every school and the relevant progress information is provided to each municipality. Based on the interviews conducted in Denmark, the OECD review team formed the impression that these goals were well understood and supported by all stakeholder groups. Similarly, the 2012 inclusion reform set the clear target of an overall inclusion rate of 96% by 2015. This target provided a common objective for actors at all levels and appeared to have been taken on board by municipalities and schools for their local educational planning.

Another noteworthy example is the government's policy for teacher competency development and specialisation, which is part of the 2014 *Folkeskole* reform. The government formulated the quantitative target that 95% of teachers in Denmark should be certified in all the subjects that they teach by 2020. As mid-term objectives, this certification goal should be achieved for 85% of teachers in 2016 and for 90% of teachers by 2018. To facilitate goal achievement, the Ministry for Children, Education and Gender Equality has made available additional funding of DKK 1 billion for teacher competency development along with evidence-based recommendations on how this funding could be spent. Municipalities applying for this funding are required to develop a plan for the use of this funding and to report back on their progress. By 2020, any unspent money from this fund will have to be repaid by the municipalities to the Ministry for Children, Education and Gender Equality.

Denmark has developed a range of tools to monitor goal achievement and follow up on reform implementation

As described above, Denmark has made available an increasing range of tools in order to monitor goal achievement and measure the impact of changes in policy and practice. Key instruments include the national tests, the calculation of "expected" exam grades for all students, the national wellbeing survey, and the recently developed survey to monitor the effect of inclusion on wellbeing (following 10 000 students in "included" classrooms). The use of the results from these measurements is being facilitated by increasingly user friendly mechanisms for actors at all levels to access the data. In particular, the new data warehouse is a key tool facilitating the follow-up of initiatives and providing access to steering and performance data for schools and municipalities. According to Simola et al. (2011), the increasing circulation of data in the Danish education system helps provide a shared agenda through which stakeholders with different interests are brought together to discuss and interpret the information communicated to them.

In addition, a number of arrangements have been made to monitor the implementation of the 2014 *Folkeskole* reform on an ongoing basis. There is a steering group composed of different parties including the Ministry for Children, Education and Gender Equality, the Ministry of Finance and LGDK, which used to initially meet every six weeks and was meeting three times a year at the time of drafting the report to follow up on the implementation of the reform. In addition, a research and evaluation programme regarding the reform has been set up with the aim to: provide a basis for actors at all levels of the management chain to learn from experiences and results (how the reform is implemented and what works best); document the implementation and effect of the reform overall and of its most important initiatives; and strengthen the empirical research on school leadership, teaching and learning. LGDK conduct surveys on the implementation among municipalities twice a year. Finally, results of the reform are also documented in a yearly status report prepared by the Ministry for Children, Education and Gender Equality and in the digitally supported quality reports of the municipalities. These steering and monitoring functions were built into the reform from the outset to allow further analyses and adequate responses in case the set targets are not met.

There are also a range of initiatives developed by stakeholder groups to evaluate the impact of the reform on their members and identify any potential negative effects. For example, the Danish Union of Teachers (DLF) reported to the OECD review team that it was monitoring the reform's implementation through information collected from their school representatives and local branches, as well as through questionnaires and national surveys. The Danish Union of Early Childhood and Youth Educators (BUPL) also developed a survey for their members regarding the impact of the reform. This also responds to concerns among its members that the national evaluation of the reform may not sufficiently evaluate the wellbeing of the professionals working in schools, an important aspect of measuring the success of the reform.

There is coherence and clarity in terms of the respective responsibilities for the central and local level

The Danish approach to resource management reflects a system based on trust, local autonomy and horizontal accountability, where the respective responsibilities of each level are clearly defined.

School autonomy provides good conditions for effective management of resources

Governance arrangements in Denmark combine a focus on clear central goals and targets with financial decentralisation and autonomy. Resource allocation decisions are based on principles of autonomy and devolution of decision-making to schools. The fact that the largest part of school funding is not earmarked gives municipalities and schools the necessary flexibility to use funding to fit their own needs. It allows schools to make critical decisions that they are best placed to meet, for example regarding the recruitment of teachers, the organisation of the curriculum and the planning of extracurricular activities. The school leaders' responsibility for budget development is likely to promote their ownership of the budget and provides scope to set local priorities in budget decisions.

There is local accountability and support for schools in resource management

At the same time, there are mechanisms to ensure that Danish school leaders do not make resource management decisions in isolation. As described above, there is involvement of local stakeholders in budget decisions via the work of the school boards. Although their level of involvement varies across schools, school boards have a formal role in monitoring results and approving school budgets, thereby offering a degree of horizontal accountability to school-based resource management. The 2014 *Folkeskole* reform provided DKK 12 million for the national parents' association to raise the competencies and professionalism of the school boards. In addition, the municipal education offices provide their school leaders with various degrees of help with the more technical aspects of school budgeting such as accounting and bookkeeping, allowing school leaders to focus more on strategic and pedagogical organisation of the school. The municipalities also play an important role in the delivery of services and can help their schools achieve scale economies, for example by buying materials and services for several schools at the same time.

Supervision and support for the municipalities is available

As described above, the quality reports prepared by the municipalities provide a tool for goal-oriented management of the local school systems, horizontal accountability and central supervision of schools. As part of the 2014 *Folkeskole* reform there has been a new approach to the central supervision of municipalities, with a clear ambition to reduce bureaucracy and paperwork: municipal quality reports are now only required on a biannual basis and they should rely primarily on data that are available in the data warehouse. Based on these data, the central level monitors progress towards the reform goals and follows up in cases of underperformance. Central follow-up focuses more on support than on pressure. While there are no ways to reward or sanction municipalities, the central level will intervene if there is evidence that laws are not respected or that individual schools are consistently underperforming. In such cases, it is possible for the central level to recommend municipalities and schools to work with the central learning consultants to achieve improvement of processes and outcomes.

The central level plays a knowledge management function

The central level has also been taking on an increasing role in collecting and disseminating knowledge of good practice, for example through the creation of a specific division for knowledge mobilisation in the Ministry for Children, Education and Gender Equality. The ministry's "resource centre for the *Folkeskole*" plays a key role in overseeing the central learning consultants and bringing together both evidence from research and practical knowledge from the field. In the OECD review team's interviews it appeared that the central learning consultants had come to be well accepted within municipalities and schools. Central knowledge management based on research evidence was seen as complementary to local level expertise. This acceptance indicates good levels of trust and co-operation between the central and local level in the effort towards making educational practice more evidence-based.

Challenges

Challenges for maintaining a focus on broad learning goals

Danish education pursues a broad set of learning goals for all-rounded student development. As emphasised in the *Folkeskole* Act, Danish students are to acquire not only subject-specific knowledge but also cross-curricular learning goals such as imagination, confidence, collaboration and citizenship skills. The Common Objectives provide a fairly broad curricular frame and the 2014 *Folkeskole* reform again emphasises the importance of cross-curricular learning and the acquisition of competencies relying on a complex integration of knowledge, skills, attitudes and action. According to Houlberg et al. (2016), research in Denmark indicates that Danish teachers are motivated in their work primarily by the broader aims and purposes of the *Folkeskole*.

However, as in many other countries, there appears to be some lack of alignment in Denmark between these broad goals for student learning and relatively narrow measurements of learning. Although Danish teachers use a wide range of student assessment methods in the classroom (Shewbridge et al., 2011), there was a strong perception among teachers and school leaders interviewed by the OECD review team that schools were held accountable primarily based on the results of students on the national tests. This impression is reinforced by the fact that the main benchmarks for monitoring the

2014 *Folkeskole* reform are based primarily on the national test results. At the same time, official information on the national tests clearly repeats the message that the national tests only measure a discrete area of student knowledge and skills – providing a snapshot of student achievement in select learning targets – and that supplementary assessments are necessary to fully gauge student process.

If stated learning goals and measures of goal achievement are not well-aligned, there is a risk that the learning process itself will be impacted negatively. Research from different countries indicates that while assessment is primarily intended to measure the progress and outcomes of learning, it also has effects on the learning process itself (Somerset, 1996). Several authors have described this influence of assessment on teaching and learning as the "backwash effect" of student assessment (Alderson and Wall, 1993; Baartman et al., 2006; Somerset, 1996). This close interrelationship makes assessment an important tool to signal and clarify the key goals that students are expected to achieve. However, if assessment only covers a small fraction of the valued curriculum goals, then the impact of assessment on teaching and learning can be restrictive (Harlen, 2007).

There are some indications of this being the case in Denmark. Danish research indicates that the national goals seem to be implemented only to a limited degree at the school level (Normann Andersen and Strømbæk Pedersen, 2012; Skolens Rejsehold, 2010). Moos et al. (2013) observe a shift in focus within schools towards curriculum subject areas, resulting in less attention on cross-curricular activities. Research based on case studies published in 2008 found that a trend could be observed towards a more uniform, low-trust model between the school authorities (central and local) and schools, related to detailed standards for student achievement and a strict testing system. The studies also indicated that successful school leaders were able to challenge the narrow focus of assessment on basic academic skills and to point to the tension between such a focus and the general purpose of the *Folkeskole* regarding all-rounded student development and inclusiveness (Moos et al., 2008). Nevertheless, it also needs to be recognised that there are inevitable trade-offs between different goals in school systems, and that the focus on one goal may lead to a smaller focus on other goals.

There is limited attention to monitoring inputs and outcomes for different student groups

The OECD review team commends Denmark for its traditional focus on supporting equity and its ambition to offer needs-based and differentiated instruction to all student groups within a comprehensive compulsory school system (Chapter 2). The 2014 *Folkeskole* reform restates this focus on equity in education by placing among its three main goals that "the *Folkeskole* must lower the significance of social background on academic results". Attention to equity is also reflected in municipal funding strategies. Available expenditure data clearly indicate that schools enrolling higher proportions of students from disadvantaged socio-economic backgrounds typically have considerably higher resource profiles than other schools (Houlberg et al., 2016).

Yet, although Denmark invests highly in schools enrolling students from socio-economically disadvantaged backgrounds, there is little evaluation of how this additional funding is used and in how far it contributes to improving learning opportunities for these student groups. Funding allocated for students from disadvantaged socio-economic backgrounds is not earmarked or tracked by municipalities. As a result, there is no empirical picture of expenditure outputs. In other words, we do not know what different student groups get out of the use of school resource and how effectively such funding is used to address their learning needs. The review team also noted that the 2014 *Folkeskole* reform does not include an explicit vision or targeted measures to impact particularly on student groups at risk of underperformance. Hence, it is unclear how the goal of lowering the impact of student background variables on student learning is to be brought about. There is no public central pool or clearinghouse to bring together evaluations by schools or municipalities of the use of funding to support the learning of student groups at risk of underperformance.

In addition, the OECD review team formed the impression that only limited attention was paid in the evaluation and assessment framework to monitoring the equity outcomes of the system. The 2014 *Folkeskole* reform does not set specific targets or benchmarks for reducing educational disadvantage for particular groups, such as those students from lower income families, with a disability or with an immigrant background. In the monitoring of educational quality at the school, local and central level, student assessment results are not systematically disaggregated for student groups from different backgrounds, and there appeared to be little differential analysis on how the reform initiatives impact on different student groups. Except for the reference to socio-economic background in the reporting of final examination grades, information on student outcomes reported in the data warehouse is not systematically broken down for different student groups, such as by socio-economic background, gender, language spoken at home, place of birth, or special educational needs. As a result, system evaluation does not include measures to assess whether or not equity objectives are being achieved.

Similarly, at the level of municipalities and schools, while there is increasing focus on analysing student assessment results to formulate improvement strategies, it did not appear to be common practice to analyse results separately for different groups at risk of underperformance. Although for the national assessments teachers can specify particular groups of students and see an overview of their results, in the schools visited by the OECD review it was not common practice to analyse data separately for students from different backgrounds in order to develop targeted teaching and learning strategies. However, such differentiated analysis appears necessary in order to understand whether certain interventions may have differential effects on students from different groups and in order to design adequate strategies to meet specific learning needs (OECD, 2013b).

There is room to strengthen the focus of evaluation and assessment on the quality of learning for students with special educational needs

In the context of the current inclusion policy, stakeholder groups expressed concerns about the quality of learning for students with special educational needs (SEN). As part of the inclusion process, the government and LGDK had set themselves the target of achieving a 96% inclusion rate until 2015, but had paid less attention to measures to evaluate the quality of learning for SEN students.[6] Stakeholders expressed such concerns both for students in inclusive settings and in separate special schools.

Denmark is aware of the importance of monitoring outcomes for SEN students and has taken some steps to adapt evaluation and assessment to their needs. There is a focus on the inclusion of SEN students in the national tests and these tests observe current international guidelines for accessibility (WCAG 2.0) for students with functional impairment at Level A. The Ministry for Children, Education and Gender Equality has prepared and continuously updated test performance instructions for teachers of students with functional impairment. The executive order on national tests establishes that if students are exempted from tests, alternative forms of evaluation should replace national tests to ensure that all students are assessed.

Despite these national arrangements and guidelines, however, many schools appear to struggle with providing adequate learning and assessment opportunities for their students with SEN. Teachers working with SEN students interviewed by the OECD review team indicated that it was not clear to them how the national learning goals could be used and adapted for their students. Although teachers are required to draw up individual learning plans for each of their students, these plans were reported to be more content/activity-oriented than learning goal-oriented for students with SEN. While teachers and school leaders were keen to work with assessment and measurement to monitor the progress of their students towards learning goals, they felt that they had not been adequately prepared with knowledge and skills on how to do so.

This is in line with findings from international and national surveys. According to the OECD Teaching and Learning International Survey (TALIS) 2013, Danish lower secondary teachers expressed a high level of need for professional development in teaching students with SEN (more on this in Chapter 4). According to a survey from the Danish School of Education (DPU) and the Danish National Centre for Social Research (SFI) conducted in 2015, 40.9% of teachers taking part in the survey reported feeling professionally equipped to handle the challenges of inclusion they meet in their everyday life "to some degree" and 39% of teachers reported to feel professionally equipped "to a lesser degree". Only 9.8% of teachers reported to feel professionally equipped to handle the challenges of inclusion "to a high degree". According to another survey for 2016, 58% of participating teachers reported feeling competent to teach specific SEN students "to some degree". 27% of teachers reported feeling competent "to a high degree", while 14% of teachers reported not feeling competent to do so. Teachers interviewed in a Copenhagen special school further mentioned that there was no in-depth initial teacher education to prepare special educational needs teachers, and that schools typically needed to set up their own training to prepare new staff, although training offers did also exist at the level of some municipalities.

A stronger focus on excellence might be needed as well

With a view to achieving the goal of the 2014 *Folkeskole* reform to "challenge all students to reach their full potential", the Danish school system would also benefit from a stronger focus on monitoring continuous improvement and excellence. By international comparison, Denmark has a relatively low proportion of top performing students and there is concern that highly talented students may not be receiving adequate levels of challenge and support to fully realise their academic potential in the *Folkeskole*. Evidence from the OECD PISA assessments has repeatedly shown a comparatively low proportion of Danish students able to perform the most demanding assessment tasks (Chapter 1).

In a study on the development of quality assurance and evaluation in Denmark, Normann Andersen et al. (2009) find that one of the most important functions of quality assurance and evaluation in Denmark has been to direct attention to what appears to be low performance. In line with this finding, Nielsen (2014) reports that school leaders give priority to educational goals on which their school is currently performing below expectations. In other words, low performance in particular areas is most likely to trigger school leaders' analysis of performance data and increase their incentives to use such data for future planning and development. This is probably linked to the fact that current arrangements for central supervision focus mostly on detecting and addressing serious cases of underperformance. The work of central learning consultants also has its main emphasis on helping struggling schools improve. While this attention to ensuring good education for all students is commendable, there is also room for the Danish school system to simultaneously pay attention to moving more schools "from good to great" by promoting excellence in school practices and outcomes.

There is a lack of transparency in the use of resources at the level of schools and municipalities

If the first step in evaluating resource use is to measure student outcomes in relation to national goals, the second is to measure expenditure outputs. The expenditure output is the real cost of educating a student. This is distinct from the spending priorities set at a national and even local level. The difference between inputs and expenditure outputs lies in the policies set at the municipal and school level.

Given Denmark's decentralised approach to school funding, it is difficult to monitor how resources are being distributed and used at the local and school levels. As Hooge's (2016) work on multiple school accountability in OECD countries highlights, when the national level is increasingly held accountable for the outcomes of the education system, while goals are set and decisions are made at the local level, making accountability work at lower levels of governance within the overall accountability framework becomes a critical topic. In Denmark, the Ministry of Social Affairs and the Interior manages a system for monitoring municipal performance that includes information on public spending by municipalities. But due to different accounting practices across the municipalities and different ways of organising the local school systems, it can be difficult to compare municipal spending data. Accounting data are available to the public, but the variation in the use of the account plan by different municipalities makes these data difficult to analyse in terms of monitoring the impact of funding. The municipal performance monitoring system does, furthermore, not include information on the outcomes of the education system, such as transition rates to youth education or results from national examinations. At the school level, too, there is a lack of fiscal transparency. Schools, as autonomous entities, receive a budget, but the real cost of running different programmes and services is not reported. Hence, there is little knowledge at the local and system level on how resources are used, whether resources are spent efficiently, and how inputs translate into outcomes. Municipalities often take little interest in monitoring the spending choices of their schools.

Although new laws are typically accompanied by central funding for the municipalities to achieve the law's purpose, municipalities are autonomous in their spending decisions and the central level will only follow up if there is evidence that laws are not respected. In other words, there is no guarantee that funding allocated for specific purposes is in fact used for these purposes.

The development of the common business management system (FLIS) by the municipalities (see above) is commendable as it can support municipalities, and particularly those with weaker capacity, in their decision-making and analysis of resource use decisions. What is more, it has the potential to create greater transparency regarding school resources between municipalities and to allow municipalities to compare and benchmark themselves against other municipalities in selected key indicators. However, like the system run by the Ministry of Social Affairs and the Interior, FLIS does not yet include data on outcomes and it does not yet allow municipalities to analyse the effectiveness of their spending levels and priorities. The lack of availability of more disaggregate results of national assessments is, of course, linked to the overall policy of confidentiality (see Box 3.1). Further, there does not yet seem to be much reflection how data systems developed at the central and local levels complement each other.

Available data could be used more effectively

As discussed in the previous sections, the availability of relevant data on both inputs and outcomes of schooling is a precondition for analysing the effectiveness of resource use and adapting strategies so as to work for further improvement. However, the availability of data alone will have little impact on the quality and equity of the school system – it is the use that is made of such data by professionals at all levels of the system that matters for the continuous improvement of teaching and learning.

Research published in 2008 noted that the publication of student outcome information was more in line with a broad concern for "openness and the right to know" rather than having a strict focus on accountability or measurement of effects. In addition, the key end users of the information (schools and parents) were not expressing any strong interest in the data (Normann Andersen et al., 2009). The groups of policy makers, stakeholders and researchers interviewed by the OECD review team reported that important progress had been made since 2008 both in the availability of relevant data and the focus of professionals on the assessment of outcomes. However, they were also consistent in reporting that further progress needed to be made in using this data effectively for accountability and improvement purposes.

As researchers from the Danish Evaluation Institute (EVA) reported to the OECD review team from their research on the use of data in Danish schools, data analysis for improvement planning is still not common practice in Denmark. Schools tend to focus more on practical aspects of school organisation and to analyse student behaviour more than student performance and progress. While some individual teachers seem to work effectively with the national tests, others seem to still be sceptical about the usefulness of these tests as a pedagogical tool and the extent to which the test results could help them inform future teaching and learning strategies. Shewbridge et al. (2011) noted that teachers still struggled with adapting their instructional strategies after diagnosis of student learning status and that school leaders had limited capacity to use data to best effect for whole-school evaluation and improvement. At the level of municipalities, while the awareness of information on student achievement is growing, different studies indicate that many municipalities still do not fully utilise the potential of evaluation and assessments and the data that these tools generate in order to follow up on the performance of individual schools (Houlberg et al., 2016; Shewbridge et al., 2011).

Policy recommendations

Ensure that all learning goals are given attention in the evaluation and assessment framework

A key challenge in monitoring the quality and progress of education systems is to develop indicators and measures of system performance that permit a good understanding of how well the education system is achieving its objectives. While national education goals are typically comprehensive and broad, monitoring systems may be rather limited in the information they can offer. This runs the risk of policy being driven primarily in areas where there are measures available (OECD, 2013b). For education monitoring to be meaningful, it must be well-aligned to the type of learning that is valued. In this context, as recommended by Shewbridge et al. (2011), it would be beneficial for Denmark to consider introducing broader national measures of student learning to monitor the school system's progress in stimulating students to excellence in higher-order thinking and development of complex competencies.

A great deal of assessment research in recent years has focused on innovative and "authentic" forms of assessment that would be able to capture the type of learning that is valued in today's societies. These alternative forms of assessment are most commonly referred to as performance-based assessment. They may include open-ended tasks such as oral presentations, essays, experiments, projects, presentations, collaborative tasks, real-life cases, problem-solving assignments and portfolios. The main characteristic of performance assessments is that they assess a range of integrated knowledge and skills by asking students to perform a task rather than to provide a correct answer. As such, they are more effective at capturing more complex achievements than closed-ended formats (Looney, 2011). They are, however, more costly to implement on a large scale than closed-ended test formats.

One option for Denmark would be to consider introducing a light monitoring sample survey to supplement the current national monitoring system with information on broader competency goals. Such sample surveys can provide stable trend information and monitor a broader range of student knowledge and skills at a lower cost compared to a full cohort test. For an example from New Zealand, see Box 3.3.

Box 3.3. **New Zealand's National Education Monitoring Project**

In New Zealand, the National Education Monitoring Project (NEMP), conducted between 1995 and 2010, was designed to assess students in primary education in two different year groups (Years 4 and 8) and followed a set four-year survey cycle. In this way the NEMP was conducted each year, but assessed a different set of disciplines each time, with each discipline being tested only every four years. This allowed monitoring of a broad coverage of the national curriculum.

NEMP was designed to be as well aligned as possible with the curriculum by incorporating competency and value elements. The national curriculum encourages the development of values and key competencies, in addition to learning areas that students should master. Many of the NEMP assessment tasks were performance-based, requiring students to transfer learning to authentic close-to-real life situations. There were different assessment situations including one-to-one interviews, work stations and teamwork. As the assessment did not carry high stakes for students it was particularly important that tasks were meaningful and enjoyable to them. The assessment provided rich information on the processes used by students to solve problems or conduct experiments. Most assessment tasks were carried out orally so as to analyse what students can do without the interference of reading and writing skills. Some of the tasks were videotaped to allow for an in-depth analysis of student responses and interaction with teachers. NEMP also assessed students' cross-curricular skills, and attitudes towards the learning areas being assessed.

Another strength of NEMP was the high involvement of practicing teachers in all aspects of the assessment. Teachers participated in the development, trialling and implementation of NEMP. About 100 practicing teachers were freed from their teaching responsibilities each year to conduct the assessments. The teachers received one week of training and then administered the tasks over a period of five weeks. The intention was to ground the assessment

Box 3.3. **New Zealand's National Education Monitoring Project** *(cont.)*

practice in sound teaching practice and to build and strengthen teachers' assessment capacities. While NEMP was designed for system monitoring, examples of previous assessment tasks were available for teachers and could be used in the classroom. This could help teachers estimate how their own group of students compares to national assessment results. The project was replaced in 2010 by the National Monitoring Study of Student Achievement (for more information, see *http://nemp.otago.ac.nz*).

Source: Nusche, D. et al. (2012), *OECD Reviews of Evaluation and Assessment in Education: New Zealand, http://dx.doi.org/10.1787/9789264116917-en.*

System-level attention to broader learning goals can help communicate to municipalities and schools a shared focus on the broader aims of the *Folkeskole*. In addition, the central level should continue communicating to schools the importance of supplementing standardised national assessment tools with a range of other assessments to obtain relevant information on student learning across the curriculum and to use this information to design differentiated teaching strategies. As recommended by Shewbridge et al. (2011), it is important to continue to develop teachers' assessment capacities and to support data-driven professional learning communities that work with assessment data in non-threatening ways. To be able to assess students' progress in developing complex competencies, it is important that teachers learn to select and/or develop a variety of assessment approaches and understand different aspects of validity, including what different assessments can and cannot reveal about student learning (OECD, 2013b) (for more detail, see Chapter 4).

Pay special attention to monitoring the learning outcomes of students at risk of underperformance

While Denmark has comparatively fewer weak performers than other OECD countries international student assessments, there is evidence of significant performance disadvantage for some students. In particular, Denmark is well aware of the challenge of increasing the academic performance of bilingual students (Shewbridge et al., 2011). There is room to give more prominence to the monitoring of inequities in learning outcomes between specific student groups. For example, education system targets could pay attention to the achievement of different student groups to monitor the equity of outcomes of, for example, students not speaking Danish at home, students with a less advantaged socio-economic background, or students with a disability. It would be important to review how more targeted indicators for the achievement of equity goals could be included in the monitoring strategy for the 2014 *Folkeskole* reform.

The monitoring of results and goal achievement at the system level holds a strong potential to pay attention to equity issues and to inform policies on how to address these and to target support more effectively. Analyses from international and national research have proven the strong influence that socio-economic and other contextual factors have on student performance. Therefore, when comparing performance measures across municipalities and schools, it is imperative to make comparisons meaningful in light of different contexts. National research into how student background characteristics and school contextual characteristics are associated with student performance can identify the type of information that is most pertinent to collect systematically. Typically, information on the student socio-economic background may include a mix of the following factors:

immigrant/cultural/linguistic background, parental level of education, occupation and income level (OECD, 2013b).

Ensuring that key performance indicators in the data warehouse are systematically disaggregated for different groups at risk of underperformance would be helpful for monitoring the equity goals of the Danish school system at all levels of the system, including municipalities and schools. It would be of interest to provide national assessment data broken down by specific student groups at risk of underperformance in order to monitor trends and analyse whether certain groups face particular challenges with some tasks. Overall, the value of annual monitoring reports could be further enhanced by regularly reporting information on student learning outcomes for groups where there is evidence of systematic underperformance. This would allow tracking the education system's progress in responding to the needs of diverse groups. Feeding such disaggregated information back to municipalities and schools should also enhance their focus on equity outcomes and strategies in their own self-evaluations and development and improvement planning.

In addition, given the high investment of the Danish school system in schools enrolling students from socio-economically disadvantaged backgrounds and students with special educational needs, it would be important to monitor specifically how such funding is used at the school level and how resource use decisions in schools translate into performance for students at risk of underperformance (even if monitoring also requires regulations and implies costs). Analysing the relationship between investments in particular initiatives and student outcomes is a key step to understanding what works to improve equity in education and progressing towards the equity objective of the 2014 *Folkeskole* reform. To provide an example for the monitoring of resources at the school level, in England (United Kingdom), schools receive a per pupil premium for each deprived or otherwise disadvantaged student. Schools are free to spend this additional funding at their own discretion, but they are held accountable for how these additional funds translate into student achievement. External school evaluators (Office for Standards in Education Children's Services and Skills, Ofsted) identify schools in which disadvantaged students do very badly as requiring improvement and the spending of the pupil premium in these schools will be more closely monitored (Chowdry and Sibieta, 2011; Carpenter et al., 2013). In the case of Denmark, it would be the role of municipalities to collect data, track resources spent on different student groups and monitor how these resources support teaching and learning for students at risk of underperformance in schools. At the school level, it would be the role of school boards to discuss the use of resources and the achievement levels for different student groups with their school management.

Another option would be for the central level to commission thematic studies on the use of resources for equity and inclusion in Danish schools. In the Flemish Community of Belgium, for example, two in-depth studies on the use of schools' operational funding were published in 2015. The Belgian Court of Audit (2015) relied on a direct analysis of school accounts and addressed three main points: allocation mechanisms for school operating budgets, supervision of school budgeting and schools' use of budgets and objectives. A second study commissioned by the Flemish government to a group of researchers (Groenez et al., 2015) relied on a mix of qualitative interviews in 20 schools, a survey of school principals and a survey of municipalities to address the distribution of operating grants to schools and the use and management of operating grants by schools. The findings of these studies are directly useful for different levels of the education system in reviewing the efficiency of the funding model and making adjustments where necessary.

For example, the Court's audit of school operating budgets criticised that supervision of schools did not comprise a risk assessment procedure and that the Flemish authorities did not have the means to acquire a global view on the use of operating grants. It also found that there was little difference between the expenditure patterns of schools with high and low numbers of disadvantaged students, with the most disadvantaged schools having little resource margin to invest into specific pedagogical measures to enhance equal educational opportunities (for more information, see Nusche et al., 2015).

Further enhance goal orientation and quality assurance for students with special educational needs

As discussed above, there are concerns in Denmark – similar to other OECD countries – that the evaluation and assessment framework does not provide adequate mechanisms to monitor the quality of learning for SEN students. In the context of special education and inclusion, there is a risk that curricula and assessment frameworks may define achievement and progress too narrowly to capture many valuable areas of learning for SEN students. This makes it difficult to monitor quality for these students at a system level. At the school level, teachers may not always have the awareness and competencies to ensure adequate and innovative assessment of students with diverse needs and to report accordingly to parents. Research indicates that the quality of school leadership is fundamental to the quality of schools' inclusion (OECD, 2013b). This points to the need of providing focused professional learning opportunities in this area not only to teachers, but also to school leaders.

In Denmark, improving the quality of learning and the wellbeing of students with SEN is an important focus area for the central learning consultant corps. In addition to their work with municipalities and schools to plan and carry out improvements in the quality of inclusion, learning consultants also work with the quality of instruction in segregated SEN schools. This includes supporting the schools in improving the academic proficiency of students through working with goal-oriented teaching and the Common Objectives, for example through a series of professional development activities for teachers in SEN schools.

Going further, it would be important to synthesise the available evidence from both research and practice in Denmark regarding successful inclusive practices and goal-oriented teaching for students with SEN. A first step would be to conduct a thematic review or study of promising practices currently developed in Danish schools. Such a study could be commissioned by the Ministry for Children, Education and Gender Equality to the Danish Evaluation Institute (EVA) or other partners. Based on the findings of such a review, it is important that dimensions of inclusive assessment are further included and developed in both initial education and professional development for teachers.

In New Zealand, for example, a thematic review on Including Students with High Needs was conducted by the Education Review Office (ERO, 2010). The study found that of 229 reviewed schools, approximately 50% had mostly inclusive practices, while 30% had some inclusive practices and 20% had only few inclusive practices. Among the schools with few inclusive practices, weaknesses included poor assessment of student progress and insufficient monitoring of the teaching provided for students with high needs. The review identified a set of good practices related to the assessment of students with high needs which are likely to be relevant for Danish schools also (Nusche et al., 2012):

- Good reporting and communication with parents, which helps support students both at home and at school. In inclusive schools, parents were included in the development of the Individual Education Programme (IEP) for their child and they also received less formal reports about their child's day to day progress.

- Good use of information on student achievement, interests, strengths, medical conditions, behaviour and parental expectations to inform the Individual Education Programme (IEP) given to individual students with high needs. The IEP is "a living document" that should guide the education programme for an individual student for a defined period and be reviewed at least twice a year. It should bring together the school, parents, student and possibly other agencies around the basic processes of assessing, objective setting, teaching, monitoring, evaluating, re-assessing and further planning to support the learning of the student. It should identify individual learning goals and define the time in which these goals should be achieved.
- SMART (specific, measurable, attributable, realistic and time-bound) objectives for the students' development, including academic, social and extracurricular development.
- Inclusion of the student's voice where possible and a focus on identified strengths and interests of the students rather than just on areas of difficulties.
- School-wide systems to monitor the effectiveness of initiatives for all students with special educational needs. This helped schools review and improve their performance in this area.

The New Zealand Ministry for Children, Education and Gender Equality is also supporting innovative approaches to assessment and reporting for diverse students and has launched a project on Assessment for Learners with Special Education Needs, which includes development of "narrative assessment" exemplars, guidance, and resources. Two key resource documents Narrative Assessment: A Guide for Teachers and The New Zealand Curriculum Exemplars for Learners with Special Education Needs are available to support teachers in maximising learning opportunities and pathways for children with special educational needs (Nusche et al., 2012). The development of such tools to support schools, teachers and school leaders to monitor the learning outcomes of students with special needs is also an option for Denmark.

Further support schools in striving towards excellence

As part of the 2014 *Folkeskole* reform, the Danish government aims to challenge all students to reach their full potential and to increase the number of high-performing students from year to year. A policy focused on increasing the number of high performers and supporting schools in achieving excellent results must set high standards for achievement, which not everyone can reach, or at least not at the same speed. In this context, using differentiated approaches to teaching, assessment and evaluation can help to take contextual differences into account and provide the right level of support and challenge to individual students, professionals and schools as organisations.

At the level of individual students, excellence could be supported through further attention to monitoring student progress and providing differentiated feedback for improvement. At the level of professionals and schools, Denmark could consider introducing differentiated supervision mechanisms. This would involve maintaining close attention to helping underperforming schools improve, but at the same time focussing also on schools that are already achieving average or good results so as to raise ambitions and move towards excellence. Box 3.4 provides examples of experiences in the Netherlands, where the government has made achieving excellence a key goal for the school system.

Box 3.4. **The strive towards excellence in Dutch schools**

There are a range of recent evaluation and assessment initiatives in the Netherlands that can be described as pursuing excellence through differentiation.

At the level of individual students, recent educational policy-making in the Netherlands has had a strong focus on stimulating differentiated instruction through "results-oriented work" at the school level. Results-oriented work involves helping schools to more fully exploit student monitoring assessments and, by analysing the information generated, to design appropriate teaching and learning strategies. Teachers are expected to explicitly define learning targets, regularly assess student performance, adapt teaching and learning to student needs, and intervene rapidly to help those who are falling behind in relation to set targets. Such approaches are to be stimulated and monitored by the Inspectorate. Recent laws require primary schools to use student monitoring systems for results-oriented work in schools, although schools retain the freedom to choose the provider and the frequency of test administration. There are three comprehensive student monitoring systems available to schools for this purpose, but virtually all primary schools participate in the Student Monitoring System (LVS) developed by the Central Institute for Test Development (Cito). The formative/diagnostic function of this assessment system is accomplished through provision of interpretive materials together with the results, as well as suggestions for relevant pedagogical strategies.

At the level of professionals in schools, the Dutch Ministry for Children, Education and Gender Equality, Culture and Science has implemented a prize for excellent school practices, as part of a system of national competition and quality awards. Such an award can become a powerful incentive for already "good" schools to make further efforts to improve their internal quality management practices. These practices can be significantly influenced by the selection criteria for the quality award.

At the level of schools as organisations, the Dutch Inspectorate is developing a differentiated inspection approach with the intention of helping schools that already provide basic quality education to further improve towards excellence. In the past few years, the Inspectorate had focused mainly on risk-based inspection where schools considered "at risk" have received a full quality inspection while "schools to be trusted" have been visited less frequently for a more basic Inspection. While risk-based inspection remains an important aspect of school evaluation in the Netherlands, the Inspectorate is developing new forms of inspection which are extended to a wider group of schools with the aim of encouraging their excellence. Inspectors will, in the future, make a distinction not only between the categories of basic, weak or unsatisfactory schools, but additional categories of "moderate", "average" and "good" are also to be used. This extension of attention from weak to good schools in order to help them move towards excellence is a key feature of the current government policy and fits with the government's ambitions for achieving excellence both at the student and the school level.

Source: Nusche, D. et al. (2014), *OECD Reviews of Evaluation and Assessment in Education: Netherlands 2014, http://dx.doi.org/10.1787/9789264211940-en.*

Enhancing school evaluation practice would be key to continuously challenge all schools to improve. While Denmark does not have a system of regular national inspections of every school, the national level could play a stronger role in stimulating more effective self-evaluation at the school and local level. Mourshed et al. (2010) suggest that, whilst frequent high-stakes inspections of every individual school may be an appropriate strategy for systems seeking to raise themselves up from a relatively poor level of performance, systems that are seeking to move from good levels of performance to achieve yet higher levels should focus their national support and external intervention on driving more effective self-evaluation.

The EC-funded Effective School Self-Evaluation project which analysed how 14 European countries or regions were promoting and supporting the development of self-evaluation in their schools concluded that self-evaluation will not develop effectively without some key elements of national infrastructure to support it, including an element of external review (SICI, 2003). The Danish Ministry for Children, Education and Gender Equality could take a stronger direct role in establishing and managing a national sample programme of external reviews of schools. This could be done working in partnership with LGDK and individual municipalities across Denmark, and involving the learning consultant corps. Cross-fertilisation through involving a wide range of school leaders in reviews of other schools in their local area would help maximise the positive impact of this programme as well as helping to ensure the validity and usefulness of its products. The focus of such a programme should be very strongly on capacity building and strengthening self-evaluation practice across the country.

In addition or alternatively to such a programme, it would be useful to centrally develop evaluation frameworks and criteria and to model good practice (Shewbridge et al., 2011). The central level (e.g. through the Agency for Education and Quality [*Styrelsen for Undervisning og Kvalitet*]) could consider creating a package of resources designed to support school leaders and municipal education offices with a practical toolkit for structuring any or all aspects of school evaluation. The development of a comprehensive national toolkit for school evaluation does not necessarily preclude the possibility that individual schools or whole municipalities might elect to use their own alternative approaches, or perhaps adapt and customise the national approach to suit their own circumstances. Experience from Scotland can provide some examples (Box 3.5).

Box 3.5. **Scotland's "Journey to Excellence"**

The Scottish education inspectorate (HM Inspectorate of Education) has developed a national web-based resource which provides schools and school managers with a comprehensive set of tools which they can use to structure effective school-level evaluation. This resource, known as Journey to Excellence has grown and developed over two decades and can be traced back to the publication of *How Good is our School?* in the late 1980s.

The complete Journey to Excellence package now includes the following parts:

- Part 1: *Aiming for Excellence*; explores the concept of excellence, what is meant by "learning" and "barriers to learning" and introduces ten dimensions of excellence.
- Part 2: *Exploring Excellence*; explores the ten dimensions in detail, giving practical examples from real schools which show the journey from "good" to "great".
- Part 3: *How Good is our School?* and *The Child at the Centre* present sets of quality indicators for use in the self-evaluation of schools and pre-school centres respectively, along with guidance on their use.
- Part 4: *Planning for Excellence* provides a guide for improvement planning in schools and pre-school centres.
- Part 5: *Exploring Excellence in Scottish Schools* consists of an online digital resource for professional development containing multimedia clips exemplifying aspects of excellence across a wide range of educational sectors and partner agencies. It also contains short videos from international education experts and researchers.

Box 3.5. **Scotland's "Journey to Excellence"** *(cont.)*

Plans are underway to enhance the resource further with new resources to support schools in the process of developing long-term strategic thinking and managing major change in a school context.

The package is very widely used by schools across the country and by all Scotland's 32 local authorities and most independent schools. The framework of quality indicators at the heart of the package are also used by inspectors for external review of schools. They were built on the criteria inspectors developed for their inspections and they are regularly refreshed and updated on the basis of developing understanding of the characteristics of effective practice.

Source: Education Scotland (2016), The Journey to Excellence, *www.journeytoexcellence.org.uk* (accessed 24 February 2016).

Strengthen public reporting about the performance of the system and analyse the effectiveness of resource use in municipalities and schools

To move the school system towards excellence while further narrowing equity gaps requires strong public consensus regarding fiscal effort and inclusiveness. The Ministry for Children, Education and Gender Equality has already undertaken considerable steps to make data from its monitoring system available for use by different stakeholders, and municipalities and schools in particular. The development of a data warehouse has been an important step in this regard. To build and sustain the overall consensus for investments in the *Folkeskole*, Denmark should consider strengthening its reporting about the performance of the school system also to the public at large at all levels of the system. Data on inputs and outcomes should be easily publicly available, e.g. through the data warehouse developed by the Ministry for Children, Education and Gender Equality and the system for monitoring municipal service performance of the Ministry of Social Affairs and the Interior. While it is difficult to evaluate the impact of indicator systems on changes to efficiency and effectiveness, well-designed indicator systems are information tools that can enhance the quality of decision making by reducing information asymmetries, and promote the accountability of public services to national, subnational, and citizens' priorities (Mizell, 2008).

The system of the Ministry of Social Affairs and the Interior to monitor municipal service performance could be extended to include information on different outcomes of the school system. Systems in other countries that provide information for sub-national benchmarking and for evaluating the efficiency of sub-central spending could provide inspiration for doing so. Both, the Australian Review of Government Service Provision (*www.pc.gov.au/research/ongoing/report-on-government-services*) and Norway's KOSTRA (Municipality-State-Reporting) system (*www.ssb.no/en/offentlig-sektor/kostra*), for example, monitor the extent to which services achieve equity, efficiency, and effectiveness goals. Both indicator and reporting systems include information on student learning outcomes (by state or territory in the case of Australia and by region in the case of Norway). The level of disaggregation of data on student assessments results in Denmark will depend on the overall policy of confidentiality.

Denmark could strengthen its reporting to the public further by developing a system-wide reporting framework that brings a broader range of financial indicators and outcome indicators together. The central and local authorities could collaborate in the development of such a reporting framework and in reporting the respective data to increase the relevance and usefulness of the framework (Mizell, 2008). The reporting framework could form the basis for the periodic publication of key national analytical reports in addition to the digital publication of the data (e.g. in the ministry's data warehouse). While one needs to weigh the costs involved, the quality of the available budgeting and accounting information should be improved in the long run through the development of common reporting standards to ensure that data are comparable across municipalities. It could also be considered to extend the breadth of the available data on local inputs (e.g. by making available information on the teacher salary costs as a percentage of total expenditure, current expenditure on educational material per student, etc.).

New Zealand and Norway provide two examples for the development of a reporting framework to communicate information about the performance of the system, including on resources and outcomes. New Zealand has developed an Education Indicators Framework that helps decision makers analyse the state of the education system and monitor trends over time. The indicators described in this framework relate to six priority domains: education and learning outcomes; effective teaching; student engagement and participation; family and community engagement; quality education providers; and resources. For each of these six indicator domains, there are specific measures to determine the extent to which certain aspects of a result have been achieved. The Indicator Framework also includes contextual information to help the interpretation of results. The performance of the education system is assessed against these indicators and the data are available on line at the Education Counts website (*www.educationcounts.govt.nz*) (Nusche et al., 2012). In Norway, the Directorate for Education and Training reports its results from the national monitoring system through two major vehicles, the Education Mirror (*Utdanningsspeilet*), the Directorate's annual report on education in Norway (*http://utdanningsspeilet.udir.no*), and the web-based School Portal (*Skoleporten*) (*https://skoleporten.udir.no*). Both respect a common structure: learning outcomes; learning environment; completion rates in upper secondary education; resources; and school facts. Each edition of the Education Mirror presents a different selection of results in each area depending on the analytical interest and also includes both a special introductory chapter providing examples of schools participating in national initiatives and a final chapter on quality development providing information on national research and initiatives to promote better local monitoring of quality (Nusche et al., 2011).

Municipalities and schools should make efforts to bring together and analyse data on the use of resources and outcomes. LGDK should pursue its plans to develop the municipalities' common business management system (FLIS) into a data hub that brings together information on resources and outcomes. Individual municipalities should be encouraged to consider both financial and pedagogical dimensions in their biannual quality reports and to use data with a greater focus on the effective use of resources to meet the goals of the education system and the 2014 *Folkeskole* reform. At the school level, transparency could be enhanced by introducing a school-level reporting framework which enables schools to examine the fiscal impact of their resource and curriculum decisions. This is important as school professionals are key decision-makers on resource use in Denmark's decentralised school system. Such a reporting framework should be developed in consultation with schools, but the preparation of reports should be undertaken at a higher level of the administration, using existing budgeting and accounting data and not imposing more paperwork on schools. This should help making more transparent the costs of delivery of school strategies and the budget impact of strategic decisions. Schools should also be encouraged by their municipalities to consider the impact of their resource use decisions as part of their self-evaluations.

Promote the better use of data at all levels

In many education systems, there is more data available from system-level indicators, evaluations and assessments than previously. Information, however, can only lead to school improvement if it is relevant, available in adequate quantity, and properly interpreted. These are all aspects to bear in mind when promoting the better use of data. At the same time, it is important for all actors of the system to be aware that the availability of large amounts of data must not be confounded with having a full understanding of any given situation. Current data collections omit important (and potentially explanatory) variables on issues as diverse as the role of non-cognitive skills in student achievement and motivation, teacher expectations, and a whole range of system-level variables. In complex environments these kinds of information can be as or more important in understanding interpersonal and institutional interactions than standard indicators on student achievement and teacher practice. Furthermore, even for standard measures, important information might be collected only partially or not systematically (for example, reasons underlying student dropout or issues with teacher retention (Blanchenay and Burns, 2016; Burns and Cerna, 2016).

As the Danish school system is highly decentralised and relies on resource management and evaluation competencies of all its agents, it is of key importance to increase the capacity at all levels to ensure the effective use of available information in order to inform and improve future practices and resource decisions, and particularly at the level of schools and municipalities. Such capacity building must respond to the diverse needs of different stakeholders in the school system and consider equity issues inherent in the use of data and information. Some municipalities and schools may be more likely than others to fully use the available data – perhaps those that care more about education quality or those that have better capacity to analyse and interpret the available data.

For municipal staff, this means developing the capacity to understand, interpret and make decisions based on evaluation and assessment data collected from schools and drawn from the central data warehouse together with their own data on resource inputs, and to engage in meaningful discussions with their schools and school leaders on the basis of these data. This capacity needs to be sustained over time and ongoing resources should be set apart to make sure municipalities can play their supervision role to their full extent. Research on the use of education data at the local level from the United States provides some further insights into the challenges that local authorities can face and where they may need particular support. The major challenge that school districts reported for this report was to link the multiple data systems that had developed over time to better support decision making and in particular to better link student data to instructional practice. Less than half the school districts could link outcomes to processes in order to monitor and promote continuous improvement. For example, only 42% of school districts could link student performance to participation in particular programmes (U.S. Department of Education, 2010).

For school principals and teachers, it means developing the capacity to collect and report data on school budgets and student outcomes to students, parents, school boards and municipalities in effective ways without oversimplifying the complex issues involved in student learning. In other words, school leaders and educators need to be able to interpret data and transform data into knowledge that meets their own needs and those of their different stakeholders. Earl and Katz (2002; 2006, cited in Hooge, 2016), point to three capacities that school leaders need to work in a data-rich world. First, school leaders need to develop an inquiry habit of mind. Leaders need to reserve judgment and have a tolerance for ambiguity, to value deep understanding, take a range of perspectives and systematically pose increasingly focused questions. Second, they need to become data literate. Leaders must to be aware of how different data are needed for different purposes; they need to be able to evaluate data, recognising sound and unsound data, to be knowledgeable about statistical and measurement concepts, to recognise other kinds of data (not only numbers, but also opinions, anecdotes, observations), to make interpretation paramount (instead of using data for quick fixes), and to pay attention to reporting to different audiences. And third, school leaders need to be able to create a culture of inquiry. Leaders need to involve others in interpreting and engaging with the data, to stimulate an internal sense of urgency (refocusing the agenda), to make time for data interpretation and for coming to collective meaning and commitment, and to use critical friends. Exemplars of good practice in data interpretation, analysis, reporting and communication should be provided nationally to schools and municipalities to make sure some minimum requirements are met. Municipalities should, furthermore, support their schools to use the available data. Examples of support provided by school districts in the United States include: technical expertise to schools, "data coaches" available to schools, creating easy-to-read data "dashboards" to make information more accessible to teachers, and developing benchmark and formative assessments providing teachers with more timely data on student progress (U.S. Department of Education, 2010).

School professionals need to develop not only the capacity to use, interpret, follow up on, and communicate results obtained from nationally provided evaluation and assessment tools, but also to develop valid and reliable tools themselves which meet their own specific local needs. They need to be able to properly self-evaluate to obtain real insights into the quality and the processes of their school (Hooge, 2016). The ability to develop valid and reliable assessments is especially pertinent in curricular areas that are not covered in national assessments and in areas in which the school results are particularly problematic and where more information is needed on sub-groups of students. The central level (Ministry for Children, Education and Gender Equality, University Faculties of Education, the Danish Teachers' Union) could consider developing a unique set of teachers' competencies in assessment and evaluation, whether it has to do with assessment of student learning, teachers' self-assessment of their professional development needs, the aggregation and interpretation of school results or the evaluation of the effectiveness of particular intervention strategies. Such a list of teachers' competencies could be used to set clear targets for agreeing university programmes and country-wide graduating standards to be used by teacher educators. It could also be used to set priorities for mentoring beginning teachers and providing in-service teachers with continuous professional development (also see Chapter 4).

National expertise in this area could also be further developed. As Burns and Cerna (2016) noted, even though the focus is often placed on the local level in discussions of capacity, systemic weaknesses may be observed on every level of governance, especially in the ability to use data and research evidence for policy-making. In parallel to the spread of an emerging culture of assessment and evaluation among schools, it has, furthermore, become increasingly important to invest in higher education and research to increase the number of experts capable to anticipate and respond to future needs, offering the best advice available from scientific knowledge and scholarly work. For example, Danish researchers interviewed by the OECD review team reported that relatively little research evidence was available in Denmark regarding the relationship between inputs and outputs, and the causal links between interventions and outcomes in the school system. Both the Ministry for Children, Education and Gender Equality and LGDK have an important role to play in the management and dissemination of such knowledge and the data required to undertake such analyses. They can facilitate interconnections within the system to increase the coherence of the evaluation and assessment framework and to properly align efforts and resources on priorities. Two types of connections are required:

- **Horizontal connections.** In a highly decentralised system, horizontal connections allow schools and municipalities to share expertise among them thus reducing duplications and helping the dissemination of transfers of good practice. Developing more deliberate improvement networks among practitioners can be a powerful organisational tool that embeds reform in interactions of different stakeholders, shares and disperses responsibility, and builds capacity through the production of new knowledge and mutual learning that can feed back into policy and practice (Katz et al., 2009; Chapman and Aspin, 2003). The central authorities and LGDK can contribute to creating an ambition-friendly and innovation-friendly environment by providing funding and support for schools and networks of schools to accelerate their work, and to provide regional and national forums where they can showcase their efforts to a broader audience (for an example from Norway, see Box 3.6). Municipalities also have an important role to play in facilitating learning and collaboration between their schools. They could use the available data on performance and context to link schools with similar profiles and challenges to share experiences and work together to improve the outcomes of all students (also see Chapter 4 and Box 4.3 on the London Challenge and City Challenge and the Ontario Focused Intervention Partnership).
- **Vertical connections.** Some local issues in students' achievement may be overwhelming for small schools and municipalities. Issues such as special needs education, second language literacy and impact assessment of resource strategies require levels of expertise and the mustering of resources that are beyond the scope of a local school or a small municipality. Here, the Ministry for Children, Education and Gender Equality can play a key role in connecting schools and municipalities to regional centres of expertise, universities, central learning consultants and other bodies offering support. Connecting schools, school leaders and teachers with researchers and engaging them in the use of research and knowledge through networks that are supported structurally (e.g. through universities) constitutes a promising avenue to build professionalism that is informed by evidence (Cordingley, 2016).

Box 3.6. **Norway's local and regional networks for school efficiency and quality improvement**

Policy making in Norway is characterised by a high level of respect for local ownership and school autonomy. In such a decentralised system, it is essential that different actors co-operate to share and spread good practice and thereby facilitate system learning and improvement. Networking is a common form of organisation among municipalities in Norway and there are a range of good examples where networks and partnerships have been established between different actors as a means to take collective responsibility for quality evaluation and improvement.

Box 3.6. **Norway's local and regional networks for school efficiency and quality improvement** *(cont.)*

Municipal networks for efficiency and improvement: In 2002, the Norwegian Association of Local and Regional Authorities (KS), the Ministry of Labour and Government Administration and the Ministry of Local Government and Regional Development set up "municipal networks for efficiency and improvement" that offer quality monitoring tools for local use and provide a platform for school owners to share experience, compare data and evaluate different ways of service delivery in different sectors. For the education sector, an agreement has been established between KS and the Directorate for Education and Training to allow the networks to use results from the national user surveys that are part of the national evaluation and assessment framework. The networks bring together municipal staff and school leaders to discuss school evaluation and assessment issues and engage in benchmarking exercises. Each network meets four or five times and then the opportunity is offered to another group of municipalities.

Regional groups working on external school evaluation: The Norwegian national school improvement project Knowledge Promotion – From Word to Deed (2006-10) was launched by the Directorate for Education and Training to strengthen the sector's ability to evaluate its own results and plan improvement in line with the objectives in the Knowledge Promotion reform. One of the outcomes of the project was the establishment of 11 regional groups to continue to work on school evaluation. These groups received training in the programme's methodology for external school evaluation and have begun to establish local systems for external evaluation of schools.

Guidance Corps for school improvement: The Norwegian Directorate for Education and Training has also established a "Guidance Corps" of exemplary school leaders who make themselves available to work together with school owners that have been targeted as needing help with capacity development.

Source: Nusche, D. et al. (2011), *OECD Reviews of Evaluation and Assessment in Education: Norway 2011, http://dx.doi.org/10.1787/9789264117006-en.*

The establishment of a central group of learning consultants that work with municipalities and schools is a promising initiative to develop local capacity and to promote the use of data in schools and municipalities (also see Chapter 4). This initiative should be sustained and further developed. Ontario, Canada, created a Literacy and Numeracy Secretariat (LNS) in 2004 as part of its Literacy and Numeracy Strategy. Through the LNS, highly skilled and experienced educators (known as student achievement officers) work directly with schools and school boards across the province to build capacity and implement strategies to improve students' skills in reading, writing and mathematics. An evaluation of the impact of initiatives introduced by the LNS concludes that they have had "a major, and primarily highly positive, impact on Ontario's education system" strengthening the use of evidence, research, evaluation and data throughout the system (Canadian Language and Literacy Research Network, 2009).

A further area in which efforts are needed is to ensure schools and local education authorities are provided with useful information for their own management. For example, it is important to enable schools to compare their own data with indicators aggregated to meaningful benchmark groupings (e.g. the similar pedagogical philosophy, etc.) (OECD, 2013b). The development of a data warehouse by the Ministry for Children, Education and Gender Equality that facilitates easy access to the data that are available, therefore, constitutes an important tool to facilitate and encourage the use of data at a local level. As Blanchenay and Burns (2016) highlighted, too much information can obscure information pertinent to decision-making and/or render it unusable by its sheer magnitude. The abundance of information may even be counterproductive, as "teachers and schools may metaphorically and literally close the door on new information, shutting out the noise" (O'Day, 2002 cited in Blanchenay and Burns, 2016). There is, then, the question how all the information that is available can be gathered and maintained in a way that can be used by different parties. The data warehouse initiative should be developed further in collaboration with municipalities, schools and the broader public to ensure the system meets the needs of different stakeholders.

Notes

1. In 2013/14, 74% of students in Year 2, 71% of students in Year 4, 72% of students in Year 6 and 76% of students in Year 8 achieved good results in Danish; in mathematics 64% of students in Year 3 and 69% of students in Year 6 achieved good results. In 2011/12, 73% of students in Year 2, 66% of students in Year 4, 69% of students in Year 6 and 74% of students in Year 8 achieved good results in Danish; in mathematics, 63% of students in Year 3 and 66% of students in Year 6 achieved good results (Danish Ministry for Children, Education and Gender Equality, 2016a).
2. In Danish, the share of high-performing students in Year 2 increased from 7% in 2011/12 to 8% in 2012/13, but remained stable in 2013/14. In Year 4, the share of high-performing students increased from 6% in 2011/12 to 7% in 2012/13 and to 8% in 2013/14. In Year 6, the share of high-performing students increased from 6% in 2011/12 to 7% in 2012/13 and remained stable in 2013/14. In Year 8, the share of high-performing students increased from 8% in 2011/12 to 9% in 2012/13 and to 11% in 2013/14. In mathematics, the share of high-performing students in Year 3 remained stable at 4% between 2011/12 and 2012/13 and increased to 5% in 2013/14. In Year 6, the share of high-performing students increased from 4% in 2011/12 to 6% in 2012/13 and remained stable in 2013/14 (Danish Ministry for Children, Education and Gender Equality, 2016a).
3. In Danish, the share of poor-performing students in Year 2 decreased from 11% in 2011/12 to 10% in 2012/13 and remained stable in 2013/14. In Year 4, the share of poor-performing students decreased from 14% in 2011/12 to 12% in 2012/13 and remained stable in 2013/14. In Year 6, the share of poor-performing students decreased from 12% in 2011/12 to 11% in 2012/13 and remained stable in 2013/14. In Year 8, the share of low-performing students decreased from 10% in 2011/12 to 9% in 2012/13 and remained stable in 2013/14. In mathematics, the share of poor-performing students in Year 3 remained stable at 15% between 2011/12 and 2013/14. In Year 6, the share of poor-performing students decreased from 17% in 2011/12 to 16% in 2012/13 and remained stable in 2013/14 (Danish Ministry for Children, Education and Gender Equality, 2016a).
4. The first wellbeing survey was carried out in 2014/15. Results are available on the data warehouse of the Danish Ministry for Children, Education and Gender Equality (2016).
5. Students must participate in the following assessments:
   - Danish, with a focus on reading in Years 2, 4, 6 and 8
   - English in Year 7
   - mathematics in Years 3 and 6
   - geography, biology and physics or chemistry in Year 8.

   Assessments are computer-based and adaptive, i.e. if a student answers a question incorrectly, students are given an easier question; if students answer correctly, they are given a more difficult question. Assessments are one pedagogical tool for teachers to evaluate, develop and plan their teaching and for schools to plan their programme of education. Assessment results can guide students and help strengthen collaboration with parents by providing information about students' learning progress.
6. In June 2016, the Danish government and LGDK agreed to focus more on the individual child and that the creation of inclusive learning environments should be based on consideration of the individual child rather than an overall inclusion target of 96%.

References

Alderson, C. and D. Wall (1993), "Does washback exist?", *Applied Linguistics*, Vol. 14, Oxford University Press, Oxford, pp. 115-129.

Baartman, L.K.J. et al. (2006), "The wheel of competency assessment: Presenting quality criteria for competency assessment programs", *Studies in Educational Evaluation*, Vol. 32, Oxford University Press, Oxford, pp. 153-170.

Belgian Court of Audit (2015), *Werkingsbudgetten voor het Gewoon Basisen Secundair Onderwijs Toekenning en Aanwending* [Operating Grants for Mainstream Elementary and Secondary Education, Allocation and Utilisation], Verslag van het Rekenhof aan het Vlaams Parlement, Brussels, *http://ebl.vlaanderen.be/publications/documents/80761*.

Blanchenay, P. and T. Burns (2016), "Policy experimentation in complex education systems", in *Governing Education in a Complex World*, OECD Publishing, Paris, *http://dx.doi.org/10.1787/9789264255364-10-en*.

Burns, T. and L. Cerna (2016), "Enhancing effective education governance", in *Governing Education in a Complex World*, OECD Publishing, Paris, *http://dx.doi.org/10.1787/9789264255364-13-en*.

Calmar Andersen, S. and S.C. Winter (eds.) (2011), *Ledelse, læring og trivsel i folkesko-lerne (Rapport 11:47)* [Leadership, Learning and Wellbeing in Schools (Report 11:47)], SFI – *Det Nationale Forskningscenter for Velfærd* [SFI – The National Centre for Social Research], Copenhagen, *https://pure.sfi.dk/ws/files/254638/1147_Ledelse_laering_trivsel.pdf*.

Canadian Language and Literacy Research Network (2009), *Evaluation Report: The Impact of the Literacy and Numeracy Secretariat: Changes in Ontario's Education System*, Canadian Language and Literacy Research Network, *www.edu.gov.on.ca/eng/document/reports/OME_Report09_EN.pdf*.

Carpenter, H. et al. (2013), *Evaluation of Pupil Premium Research Report*, Department for Education, London, *www.gov.uk/government/uploads/system/uploads/attachment_data/file/243919/DFE-RR282.pdf*.

Chapman, J. and D. Aspin (2003), "Networks of learning: A new construct for educational provision and a new strategy for reform", in B. Davies and J. West-Burnham (eds.), *Handbook of Educational Leadership and Management*, Pearson, London, pp. 653-659.

Chowdry, H. and L. Sibieta (2011), "Trends in education and schools spending", *IFS Briefing Note*, BN121, Institute for Fiscal Studies, London, *www.ifs.org.uk/bns/bn121.pdf*.

Cordingley, P. (2016), "Knowledge and research use in local capacity building", in *Governing Education in a Complex World*, OECD Publishing, Paris, *http://dx.doi.org/10.1787/9789264255364-9-en*.

Danish Ministry for Children, Education and Gender Equality (2016a), *Datavarehuset* [Datawarehouse], *www.uddannelsesstatistik.dk* (accessed 4 February 2016).

Danish Ministry for Children, Education and Gender Equality (2016b), *Trivselsmåling* [National Wellbeing Survey], *www.uvm.dk/Uddannelser/Folkeskolen/Elevplaner-nationale-test-og-trivselsmaaling/Trivselsmaaling*.

Education Scotland (2016), *The Journey to Excellence*, *www.journeytoexcellence.org.uk* (accessed 24 February 2016).

ERO (2010), *Including Students with High Needs*, New Zealand Education Review Office, Wellington, *www.ero.govt.nz/assets/Uploads/Including-Students-with-High-Needs-2010-pdf-with-cover.pdf*.

Groenez S. et al. (2015), *Analyse van het Nieuwe Financieringsmechanisme voor de Werkingsmiddelen van Scholen, Evaluatie van het Financieringsdecreet van 2008: Eindrapport* [Analysis of the New Financing Mechanism for School Operating Grants, Evaluation of the 2008 Decree on School Funding: Final Report], *www.ond.vlaanderen.be/obpwo/rapporten/Analyse_nieuwe_financieringsmechanisme_werkingsmiddelen_scholen_DEFINITIEF_RAPPORT_HIVA.pdf*.

Harlen, W. (2007), "Criteria for evaluating systems of student assessment", *Studies in Educational Evaluation*, Vol. 33, Elsevier, Amsterdam, pp. 15-28.

Hooge, E. (2016), "Making multiple school accountability work", in *Governing Education in a Complex World*, OECD Publishing, Paris, *http://dx.doi.org/10.1787/9789264255364-7-en*.

Houlberg, K. et al. (2016), *OECD Review of Policies to Improve the Effectiveness of Resource Use in Schools: Country Background Report for Denmark*, *Det Nationale Institut for Kommuners og Regioners Analyse og Forskning* (KORA) [Danish Institute for Local and Regional Government Research], Copenhagen, *www.oecd.org/edu/school/10932_OECD%20Country%20Background%20Report%20Denmark.pdf*.

Katz, S., L.M. Earl and S. Ben Jaafar (2009), *Building and Connecting Learning Communities: The Power of Networks for School Improvement*, Corwin, Thousand Oaks, CA.

Looney, J. (2011), "Alignment in Complex Systems: Achieving Balance and Coherence", *OECD Education Working Papers*, No. 64, OECD Publishing, Paris, *http://dx.doi.org/10.1787/5kg3vg5lx8r8-en.*

Mizell, L. (2008), "Promoting Performance – Using Indicators to Enhance the Effectiveness of Sub-Central Spending", *OECD Working Papers on Fiscal Federalism*, No. 5, OECD Publishing, Paris, *http://dx.doi.org/10.1787/5k97b11g190r-en.*

Moos, L., O. Johansson and G. Skedsmo (2013), "Successful Nordic school leadership", in L. Moos (ed.), *Transnational Influences on Values and Practices in Nordic Educational Leadership* (Studies in Educational Leadership, 19), Springer, Amsterdam, pp. 159-172.

Moos, L., J. Krejsler and K.K. Kofod (2008), "Successful principals: telling or selling? On the importance of context for school leadership", *International Journal of Leadership in Education*, Vol. 11 (4), Taylor and Francis, Oxford, pp. 341-352.

Mourshed, M., C. Chijioke and M. Barber (2010), *How the World's Most Improved School Systems Keep Getting Better*, McKinsey & Company, New York.

Nielsen, P.A. (2014), "Learning from performance feedback: performance information, aspiration levels, and managerial priorities", *Public Administration*, Vol. 92(1), Wiley-Blackwell, Hoboken, NJ, pp. 142-160.

Normann Andersen, V., P. Dahler-Larsen and C.S. Pedersen (2009), "Quality assurance and evaluation in Denmark", *Journal of Education Policy*, Vol. 24(2), Taylor and Francis, Oxford, pp. 135-147.

Normann Andersen, V. and C.S. Pedersen (2012), "Evaluering af (og i) den danske offentlige grundskole" [Evaluation of (and in) the Danish public *Folkeskole*], *Nordiske Organisasjonsstudier*, [Nordic Organisation Studies], Vol. 14(1), Fagbokforlaget, Bergen, pp. 3-27.

Nusche, D. et al. (2015), *OECD Reviews of School Resources: Flemish Community of Belgium*, OECD Publishing, Paris, *http://dx.doi.org/10.1787/9789264247598-en.*

Nusche, D. et al. (2014), *OECD Reviews of Evaluation and Assessment in Education: Netherlands 2014*, OECD Publishing, Paris, *http://dx.doi.org/10.1787/9789264211940-en.*

Nusche, D. et al. (2012), *OECD Reviews of Evaluation and Assessment in Education: New Zealand*, OECD Publishing, Paris, *http://dx.doi.org/10.1787/9789264116917-en.*

Nusche, D. et al. (2011), *OECD Reviews of Evaluation and Assessment in Education: Norway 2011*, OECD Publishing, Paris, *http://dx.doi.org/10.1787/9789264117006-en.*

OECD (2015), *Education Policy Outlook 2015: Making Reforms Happen*, OECD Publishing, Paris, *http://dx.doi.org/10.1787/9789264225442-en.*

OECD (2013a), *PISA 2012 Results: What Makes Schools Successful (Volume IV): Resources, Policies and Practices*, OECD Publishing, Paris, *http://dx.doi.org/10.1787/9789264201156-en.*

OECD (2013b), *Synergies for Better Learning: An International Perspective on Evaluation and Assessment*, OECD Publishing, Paris, *http://dx.doi.org/10.1787/9789264190658-en.*

OECD (2012), *Education at a Glance 2012: OECD Indicators*, OECD Publishing, Paris, *http://dx.doi.org/10.1787/eag-2012-en.*

Pedersen, M.J. et al. (2011), *Ledelse af Folkeskolerne. Vilkår og Former for Skoleledelse [Management of Public Schools. Terms and Forms of School Leadership]*, SFI – Det Nationale Forskningscenter for Velfærd [SFI – The National Centre for Social Research], Copenhagen, *https://pure.sfi.dk/ws/files/254548/1139_Ledelse_af_folkeskolerne.pdf.*

Shewbridge, C. et al. (2011), *OECD Reviews of Evaluation and Assessment in Education: Denmark 2011*, OECD Publishing, Paris, *http://dx.doi.org/10.1787/9789264116597-en.*

SICI (2003), *Effective School Self-Evaluation*, Standing International Conference of Central and General Inspectorates of Education (SICI), Brussels.

Simola, H. et al. (2011), "Governing by numbers: The rise of data in education" in J. Ozga et al. (eds.), *Fabricating Quality in Education: Data and Governance in Europe*, Routledge, London, pp. 96-106.

Skolens Rejsehold (2010), *Baggrundsrapport til Fremtidens Folkeskole – én af Verdens Bedste. Anbefalinger fra Skolens Rejsehold. Rapport B* [Backgroundreport for the Future Folkeskole – One of the World's Best Recommendations from the School Journey Team B Report], *Styrelsen for Evaluering og Kvalitetsudvikling af Folkeskolen (Skolestyrelsen)* [Agency for the Evaluation and Quality Improvement of the *Folkeskole* (School Council)], Copenhagen.

Somerset, A. (1996), "Examinations and educational quality", in A. Little and A. Wolf (eds.), *Assessment in Transition, Learning Monitoring and Selection in International Perspective*, Pergamon, Elsevier Science Ltd., Oxford.

U.S. Department of Education (2010), *Use of Education Data at the Local Level – From Accountability to Instructional Improvement*, U.S. Department of Education, Office of Planning, Evaluation and Policy Development, Washington, DC, *www2.ed.gov/rschstat/eval/tech/use-of-education-data/use-of-education-data.pdf*.

Wiedemann, F. (2012), "Styring af styringsværktøjer? Om folkeskolelærernes erfaringer med 'Fælles mål'" [Control of management tools? On the experience of *Folkeskole* teachers with the "Common Objectives"], in K. Hjort et al. (eds.), *Der Styres for Vildt: Om Paradokser i Styring af Pædagogik* [Managing the Game: About the Paradoxes of Managing Education], Klim, Aarhus, pp. 123-139.

Chapter 4

Management of the teaching workforce in Denmark

This chapter discusses the initial training, distribution, professional development, working conditions, and support for and leadership of the teaching workforce across the public Danish public school system. It also discusses the use of other staff to support student learning as well as the use of data, evaluation and assessment in schools to support improvements in student performance and attainment levels. It highlights the positive changes Denmark has implemented to strengthen initial teacher education and the availability of central funding for the competency development of in-service teachers. It identifies a desire for and instances of collaborative work at all levels of the system as well as a growing focus on pedagogy and goal-oriented teaching. But it also analyses the challenges in moving from a teaching to a learning focus. This includes, in particular, the potential to strengthen teacher professionalism and pedagogical school leadership. The chapter analyses the potential benefits of the new framework for the utilisation of teachers' working time for the organisation of teaching and learning in schools, but also discusses stakeholders' concerns about the new arrangements and challenges for adapting to this change. In addition, the chapter discusses the policy of inclusion of children with special educational needs in regular education. The chapter concludes in suggesting a number of policy recommendations to address these issues.

The statistical data for Israel are supplied by and under the responsibility of the relevant Israeli authorities. The use of such data by the OECD is without prejudice to the status of the Golan Heights, East Jerusalem and Israeli settlements in the West Bank under the terms of international law.

Context and features

Initial education and professional development of teachers

The current initial teacher education model in Denmark is based on a four-year professional bachelor's degree which was introduced in the early 2000s. As of 2015, there were 16 degree programmes for initial teacher education offered at seven university colleges across the country which may also develop a certain specialisation (e.g. in science education). Previous teacher education programmes involved a relatively detailed regulation of the content and structure of initial teacher education. This was especially the case following a reform introduced in 2006. Based on a four-year evaluation process by a mandated group of experts, however, a number of significant changes were again proposed in 2012 (Følgegruppen for ny læreruddannelse, 2012). These recommendations were followed up by a comprehensive reform of initial teacher education that same year. Changes to initial teacher education that were implemented in 2013 involved a significant deregulation process. A ministerial order describes competency profiles, that is the professional competencies expected of future teachers for each subject, as well as the overarching structure of initial teacher education. The precise organisation and content of individual degree programmes is left to university colleges themselves. In addition, this reform changed initial teacher education to be slightly less oriented towards teaching subjects and more towards general pedagogical content. The 2012 evaluation had concluded that pedagogical content had been somewhat neglected in favour of subject content. As a result, a system of modules with competency examinations focusing on subject didactics as well as subject content was introduced. On average, a teacher student is expected to graduate with teaching competencies in three main subjects, but it is possible to graduate with just two main subjects. The 2012 reform of initial teacher education also made special needs education and Danish as a second language obligatory for all teacher students.

While the priority for teacher education institutions used to be to produce enough candidates to fill all teacher positions in schools, the focus has recently shifted towards the quality of candidates. Entry into teacher education used to be strictly based on marks obtained in upper secondary education, but the dropout rates of students entering this programme used to be very high (as much as 41% in 2005 according to data from the Ministry of Higher Education and Science and Statistics Denmark) and needed to be reduced. As a result, admission requirements have become stricter and there are now specific requirements in terms of performance in upper secondary education. Entry is now a two-tier process. Those with the highest marks are granted direct admission, but anyone else wishing to enrol has to take an examination including an interview both of which are scored to determine entry. As initial impressions of the Ministry of Higher Education and Science suggest, the dropout rate has already been somewhat reduced with the introduction of these new admission requirements (15.6% among first year students and 36% among all teacher students in 2014 according to data from the Ministry of Higher Education and Science and Statistics Denmark).

Professional development for Danish teachers is not regulated by law and there is no minimum requirement. Decisions about teachers' participation in professional development rest fully with the school management, which may plan teachers' professional development activities in the context of school development priorities. Costs for participation in professional development are partially subsidised or covered by the government. Participation in professional development activities has only a limited direct effect on teachers' pay levels or career progression (e.g. promotion is not conditional upon having taken part in professional development activities, but teachers can receive a supplementary salary for some professional development activities). Professional development is primarily organised by the Danish School of Education, university colleges and municipalities. Specialised training institutions, teachers' associations and the Ministry for Children, Education and Gender Equality also offer in-service training activities. Regional committees for teacher in-service training have been established to align municipal and school training needs with the supply of programmes by professional development providers (OECD, 2014a; Shewbridge et al., 2011).

As part of the 2014 *Folkeskole* Reform, the Danish government has set 2020 as the year in which 95% of the subject-divided lessons should be given by teachers who have either obtained main subject qualifications from their initial teacher education within the subjects they teach, or who have obtained corresponding academic qualifications through continued professional development. Milestones on the way to the target have been set at 85% in 2016 and 90% in 2018. Experienced teachers can take courses at teacher education institutions and sit competency exams to obtain corresponding academic qualifications in the subjects they teach. This has resulted in schools examining what competencies they need and requires schools to sponsor teachers to take courses to fulfil the school's needs. The Danish government has allocated earmarked resources for municipalities to develop the competencies of teachers and school leaders. These available resources amount to DKK 1 billion. Other areas that municipalities should use the extra resources for besides the qualification in subjects teachers teach include the inclusion of students with special needs, classroom management, and other specialised areas such as ICT (Information and Communication Technologies). These changes in initial teacher education and professional development for experienced teachers are part of a move to professionalise teaching in Denmark.

Data from the OECD 2013 Teaching and Learning International Survey (TALIS) indicate that Danish teachers participate to a similar extent in professional development as teachers in other countries, but that they tend to spend less time on professional development overall than in other countries. 86.4% of lower secondary teachers reported having undertaken some professional development activities in the previous 12 months, only slightly below the TALIS average of 88.4%. While 72.9% of lower secondary teachers in Denmark reported having participated in courses or workshops over the past 12 months (TALIS average: 70.9%), they spent fewer days on average on such activities than teachers in other countries. On average across TALIS countries, teachers spent 8.5 days on courses and workshops. Teachers in Denmark spent only four days on these professional development activities. Also, only 10.2% of teachers in Denmark reported having taken part in a qualification programme during the last year, compared to 17.9% of teachers on average across TALIS countries. Observation visits to other schools were less common among teachers in Denmark (5.7%) than the average for all TALIS countries (19.0%), but those teachers in Denmark who did visit other schools spent more time on this activity (4.6 days on average) than the average across other countries (three days) (OECD, 2014b).

Teacher working conditions

The working conditions of teachers in the *Folkeskole* are determined in negotiations between teachers and municipalities through their respective stakeholder organisations, the Danish Union of Teachers and Local Government Denmark (KL/LGDK) (see Box 4.1 for an overview of teacher working time arrangements in Europe based on a 2015 Eurydice report). The agreement resulting from these negotiations used to define the annual number of working hours, which included teaching and preparation time and time for other tasks. Preparation time was fixed proportionally in relation to teaching time with a factor 1 to 1 and teachers had to teach the same amount of time irrespective of their subject and required preparation time (Eurydice, 2016). In 2013, national legislation (Act no. 409) revised the agreement that was then in place to give schools and school leaders greater flexibility in the management of their teaching workforce, while leaving teachers' total working hours unchanged (also see Chapters 1 and 2). Unlike previous agreements, the new regulations do not stipulate the amount of time to be used for different purposes, such as teaching and preparation. Decisions about the use of teachers' time and place of work now rest with the school leadership and teachers are expected to work differently.

Box 4.1. **Organisation of teachers' working time in Europe, 2013/14**

A 2015 Eurydice report provided an overview of the organisation of teachers' working time in Europe and teachers' contractual obligations in terms of their teaching time, availability at school, and their total working time.

In most countries, teachers' employment contracts specify the number of hours they are required to teach. In 35 systems, teaching time is contractually specified. Only five education systems – Estonia, Sweden, and the United Kingdom (England, Northern Ireland and Wales) – do not contractually specify a number of teaching hours, while two (Belgium and Italy) regulate only teaching time. The weekly total varies considerably among countries, ranging from a minimum of 14 hours in Croatia, Finland, Poland and Turkey, to a maximum of 28 hours in Germany.

As regards total working time and time of availability at school, three scenarios are possible. A country's regulations can specify: i) requirements pertaining to both (as is the case in 10 education systems); ii) requirements applicable to one or the other (the situation in the majority of countries); or iii) no requirements with regard to either (as in Belgium and Italy). The great majority of countries also centrally regulate the total working time of teachers, which averages 39 hours a week. On average, teaching time constitutes 44% of a teacher's total working time. In 18 education systems, teachers' obligatory time of availability at school is contractually specified either in addition to or instead of teachers' teaching time and/or working time. Nine education systems refer specifically to working time, teaching time and time available at school, while the remainder cite them in different combinations. Among those countries that regulate both total working time and obligatory availability at school, the gap between the two (in hours) varies greatly.

Source: European Commission/EACEA/Eurydice (2015), *The Teaching Profession in Europe: Practices, Perceptions, and Policies*, *https://webgate.ec.europa.eu/fpfis/mwikis/eurydice/index.php/Publications:The_Teaching_Profession_in_Europe:_Practices,_Perceptions,_and_Policies.*

With the 2014 *Folkeskole* reform, a longer school day was introduced. Teachers are, thus, on average expected to spend a higher proportion of their total working time teaching in the classroom and to be present for a greater amount of time at school. Under Act no. 409, on average, teachers teach about two clock hours more per week within regular working hours (18.3 hours compared to 16.3 hours prior to the new working time arrangements). The new working time regulations came into force in the school year 2014/15. The 2014 *Folkeskole* reform in general has also affected expectations for teachers in terms of the organisation of their working time. The reform changed the length of the school day for students; provided for more lessons in Danish and mathematics, earlier foreign language learning, daily exercise and homework assistance while at school; and sought to promote greater collaboration between teachers and staff at school.

As reported for the OECD *Education at a Glance*, in 2013, the latest year for which comparable data are available and the year prior to the introduction of the new framework for the utilisation of working hours, the total statutory working time for primary and lower secondary education amounted to 1 680 hours over the school year. This was slightly higher than the OECD average of 1 600 hours for primary and 1 618 hours for lower secondary education. Net teaching time amounted to 662 hours per school year, which was less than in many other OECD countries (OECD average: 772 hours for primary and 694 hours for lower secondary education) (see Figure 4.1, OECD, 2015a).[1] With the implementation of the 2014 *Folkeskole* reform, it is expected that teachers on average teach 80 hours more during a school year. A school year is usually 40 weeks in Denmark.

Figure 4.1. **Number of teaching hours per year and share of working time spent teaching, 2013**

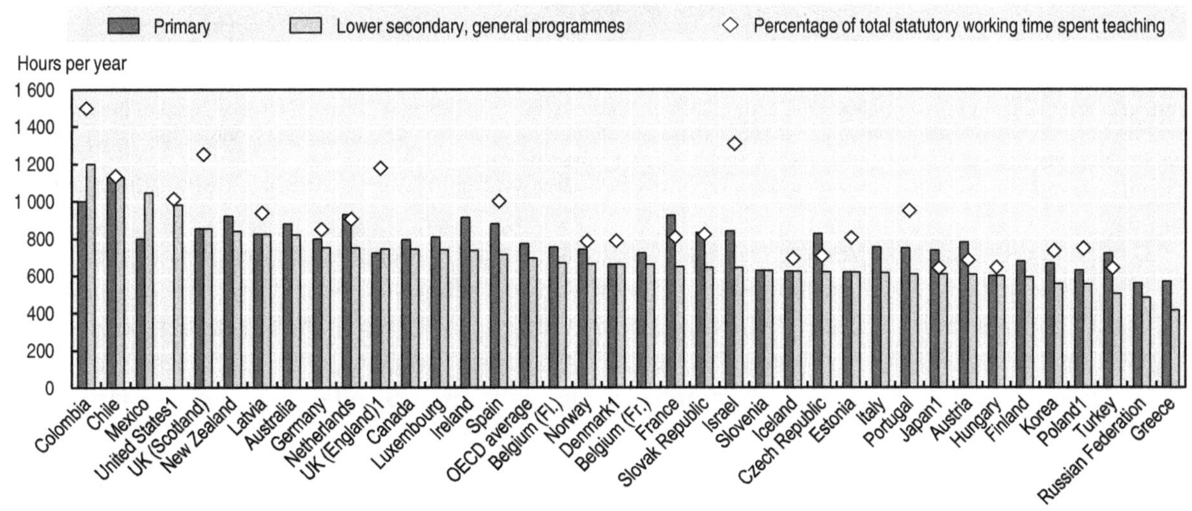

1. Actual teaching time.

Note: Net statutory contact time in public institutions. Countries are ranked in descending order of the number of teaching hours per year in lower secondary education.

Source: OECD (2014a), *Education at a Glance 2014: OECD Indicators, http://dx.doi.org/10.1787/eag-2014-en,* Table D4.1.

The OECD TALIS 2013 provides some information about the ways in which lower secondary teachers distributed their weekly working time prior to the introduction of a new framework for the utilisation of working hours. Lower secondary teachers reported to spend on average 18.9 hours per week teaching, around the TALIS average of 19.3 hours, and 7.9 hours on individual planning or preparation (either at school or out of school), slightly more than the TALIS average of 7.1 hours (see Figure 4.2). The TALIS average, however, masks significant differences between countries. Looking at other Nordic countries, for example, Finnish lower secondary teachers reported to spend more of their weekly working time on teaching (20.6 hours per week) and less time on preparation (4.8 hours per week) than their

Figure 4.2. **Distribution of teachers' working time, 2013**

Average number of hours lower secondary teachers report having spent on different activities during the most recent complete calendar week

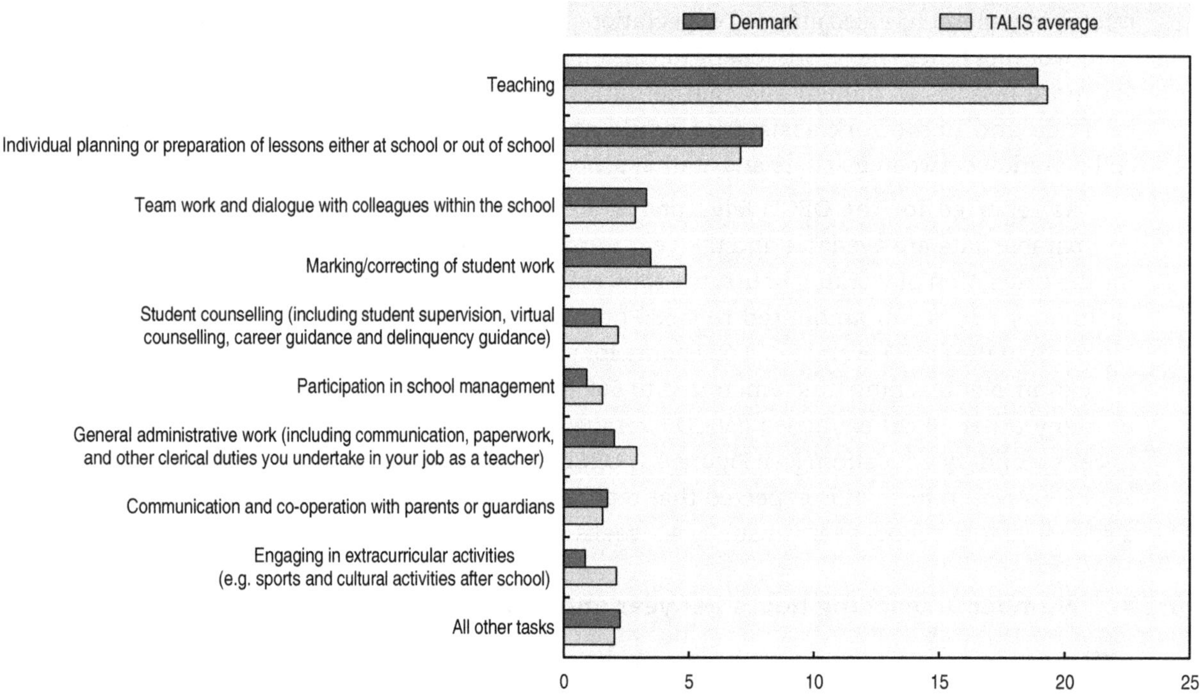

Note: A "complete" calendar week is one that was not shortened by breaks, public holidays, sick leave, etc. Also includes hours worked during weekends, evenings or other off-classroom hours. The sum of hours spent on different tasks may not be equal to the number of total working hours because teachers were asked about these elements separately. It is also important to note that data presented represent the averages from all the teachers surveyed, including part-time teachers.
Source: OECD (2014b), *TALIS 2013 Results: An International Perspective on Teaching and Learning*, *http://dx.doi.org/10.1787/9789264196261-en*.

Danish counterparts. In Norway and Sweden, lower secondary teachers reported to spend both, less working time on teaching and less working time on preparation than lower secondary teachers in Denmark (Norway: 15.0 and 6.5 hours per week respectively; Sweden: 17.6 and 6.7 hours per week respectively). The overall weekly working time reported by lower secondary teachers in Denmark was lower than in Sweden, but higher than in Norway and Finland (OECD, 2014b).

Considering the distribution of teachers' time on different tasks, since teachers in Denmark spent somewhat less time on teaching, they had more time available for preparation and other tasks. Following the 2014 *Folkeskole* reform and the introduction of a new arrangement for the utilisation of teachers' working time, teachers are expected to teach more hours. As a result, teachers experience less time for preparation and other tasks. Resources have overall been reprioritised from preparation and other tasks to teaching. This requires an adjustment from teachers to prepare for their lessons and work in another way (e.g. to a higher degree sharing teaching materials) to fulfil other tasks required of them by their school leadership.

Teacher appraisal, feedback and collaboration

There are no national requirements for teacher appraisal in Denmark. Teacher appraisal remains very much an internal school matter, is conducted on a voluntary basis and practices are defined locally, usually by the school with the possible influence of municipal requirements and/or guidelines. According to the *Folkeskole* Act, the school principal is responsible for the school's quality of teaching as well as the overall administrative and pedagogical management of the school. As a result, the main responsibility for designing, introducing and organising teacher appraisal procedures within the school lies with the school principal. Actual teacher appraisal practices in Danish schools are poorly documented, but they seem to be based on a culture of school leaders showing confidence in their teachers. Appraisal seems to be taken as a school-teacher or teacher-teacher dialogue and procedures are defined in collaboration with teachers (Shewbridge et al., 2011).

The 2014 *Folkeskole* reform aims to enhance collaboration between colleagues in schools. During school visits, teachers consistently expressed interest in working with other teachers in their school, receiving feedback on their teaching from them and working together towards common goals. In the OECD review team's discussions with teachers in Danish schools, teachers also reported collaborating with other teachers of the same subject and year level around what they are going to teach and working on their unit or lesson plans together. This included sharing plans and resources and seeking consistency across classrooms. Teachers did not report that they spent collaborative time discussing individual students and their learning although they expressed an interest in doing so. They reported that following the changes to their working day, collaborative time has, however, been increasingly difficult to find. In several schools visited during the review, specialised teachers, sometimes called coaches or impact coaches, had less teaching responsibilities and more time devoted to working with individual teachers on their teaching practice. This practice was largely voluntary and teachers experiencing this type of work expressed very positive feelings regarding their experiences.

Other staff in schools

There are other types of staff working in schools to support students in a variety of ways, including early childhood development trained pedagogues, behaviour, contact and wellbeing counsellors (*Adfærd-Kontakt-Trivsel*, AKT), and teacher's aides or assistants.

The profession of pedagogues is comparable to pre-school teachers in other countries. Pedagogues are trained in supporting all stages of human development from birth to old age and can be specialised in early childhood education and care, leisure and youth education (*Skolefritidsordning og Fritidshjem*, SFO), or other areas of particular interest in the school system. Depending on the context in which they work, they might be compared to recreational instructors, play workers or social workers. In all of their work, pedagogues focus on the importance of play and children's and young people's comprehensive development, which includes their intellectual, social, emotional, neuromuscular, ethical, moral and aesthetic development (BUPL, 2016).

AKT counsellors have been employed in the *Folkeskole* since the late 1990s. These specialist teachers focus on social processes in schools and constitute a central resource in areas related to behaviour, psychology and wellbeing. They can support individual students in and outside of classrooms and work together with teachers in the classroom to help offer differentiated teaching according to students' needs. AKT counsellors can also initiate training in schools related to social issues, the development of social skills and inclusive communities, or general health education with a focus on social wellbeing and the prevention of bullying and violence at school. A further task may be to understand and resolve conflicts and bullying in schools. AKT counsellors receive specific training and preparation for their role. The amount of time that AKT counsellors can dedicate to their role varies greatly between schools and municipalities. Schools can also employ other professionals, such as counsellors and psychologists (DCUM, 2016).

Teacher's assistants have less training and are often hired to support students with special needs within a school. The use of these differentiated types of staff varies greatly from school to school and municipality to municipality. This is likely a result of the autonomy that school principals have to staff their schools within the budget that the school has been allocated by the municipality. As the OECD TALIS 2013 indicates, there are overall 10.3 teachers to one pedagogical support staff in lower secondary education. This compares to a teacher-pedagogical support personnel ratio of 14.4 on average across TALIS countries, and 8.2 in Finland, 5.4 in Norway, and 7.1 in Sweden (OECD, 2014b).

School autonomy and school leadership

A hallmark of Denmark's education system is its decentralised nature that places a high degree of responsibility in resource decision-making at the local and school levels (also see Chapters 1 and 2). This is evident in the autonomy that school principals enjoy to manage their school budgets, including staffing. In visits with schools and with municipal officials, stakeholders described this autonomy. In some municipalities there are a minimum number of teachers required, based on the number of classes the municipality determines a school should have. Otherwise, however, the school principal can determine which types of and how many staff members are hired.

School principals in Denmark are seen as the management and extension of the local municipal government. Besides a teaching background, there is no formal education requirement to be eligible as a school leader in Denmark. School leaders are former teachers and may go on to take a diploma course, and then a master's degree, which are largely theoretical in nature. The Danish Association of School Leaders offers a three day course for newly appointed leaders. Several municipalities described how they worked with school leaders in a collaborative manner to support their on-the-job training in areas such as budgeting, school improvement planning and the monitoring and evaluation of school improvement initiatives. Municipalities are increasingly using management by means of objectives for their school principals. Results contracts, school principal agreements and other forms of contracting serve as a means to define the objectives for the individual school (and school principal), typically for a one- or two-year period. Consequently, monitoring and performance systems are used to continuously assess if the school is performing according to the set objectives. Even though these instruments are implemented as management tools as such, they are equally important to hold schools and school leaders accountable for performance (OECD, 2013b).

School self-evaluation and the use of data in schools

Schools in Denmark are often responsible for the completion of a biannual quality report to be submitted to the municipality to feed into the municipal quality report, but this depends on the municipality (also see Chapters 1 and 3). This report can become a stimulus for discussions between municipal education directors and school leaders. Schools have access to many forms of data, including student performance data, student wellbeing data and budget utilisation data and the development of a data warehouse by the Ministry for Children, Education and Gender Equality seeks to make the available data more easily accessible (also see Chapter 3). Most municipalities visited required schools to set improvement goals for school improvement plans based largely on their self-evaluation data and their student performance data. Municipal officials reported that these school improvement plans were usually discussed with the education director of the municipality once a year, but one municipality reported them being the basis for the professional development plans for the school leaders within an area or the municipality. Another municipality reported that school leaders were encouraged to use their school improvement plans as the basis for school leaders working together collaboratively on areas of need. There is no comprehensive overview of the instruments used to perform internal assessment of schools, but schools are likely to rely on various self-evaluation activities, which may involve a wide range of different methods of data collection (OECD, 2013b).

Strengths

A number of changes to strengthen initial teacher education

In recent years, a number of changes were implemented to strengthen initial teacher education in Denmark. These changes are expected to have a beneficial impact on the selection of candidates entering teacher education, the expertise acquired by teacher students throughout their initial education, and eventually the quality of teaching and learning in schools. The application process to initial teacher education programmes has undergone some changes to identify students who potentially would have difficulty completing the programme and the Ministry of Higher Education and Science reported that this had already somewhat reduced the dropout rate in initial teacher education.

Starting in 2013, the Bachelor of Education programme moved to a competency-oriented and outcome-based degree with objectives for each teaching practice. Institutions have standard competency examinations, but have some autonomy to create their own programmes leading to these competencies among their graduates and to design courses for experienced teachers to upgrade their competencies. These changes towards an outcome-based programme for teachers in many ways parallels changes in the curriculum and Common Objectives used for instruction in Denmark's schools. Teachers entering the profession are, then, used to honing in on the evidence that they have learned and can demonstrate certain skills and knowledge.

According to the typology of different models of teacher education put forward by Musset (2010), these changes indicate a desire to develop a model of "professionalisation" of teaching. Starting to promote this change in initial teacher education is well aligned with the move towards enhancing teacher professionalism in the last several years.

The central level has made available targeted funding for the professional development of teachers

As part of the 2014 reform of the *Folkeskole*, Denmark has set itself the goal to ensure that every teacher has the competencies and qualifications for the subjects they teach by 2020. To reach this goal, many teachers need to upgrade their skills through courses and written exams. The Danish government has committed itself to financing these courses (although not the teacher release time for participation) with earmarked resources allocated directly to municipalities amounting to DKK 1 billion. Schools can access this funding through their municipality. It is the responsibility of school principals to identify the competencies required within their school and to assign teachers to take these courses to meet the ministry's goal by 2020.

Most municipalities that the OECD review team visited reported that they relied on school leaders to determine the needs and to arrange for teachers at their schools to take the necessary exams and/or courses. University colleges have developed screening procedures for experienced teachers to define their competencies which are as yet uncertified. School leaders interviewed by the OECD review team reported that this was very helpful to them in planning their staff's future professional needs in the area of competency certification.

The introduction of a goal to fully qualify teachers in the *Folkeskole* for the subjects they teach and to enhance their general competencies together with the provision of earmarked funding to achieve this goal seems to address a need within the Danish education system. As data from the OECD TALIS 2013 suggest, a large proportion of Danish lower secondary teachers had completed a teacher education programme (93.5%, TALIS average: 89.8%), but more than one in three teachers reported that their formal education had only included content, pedagogy and practice in some rather than all of the subjects they were teaching.[2] If analysed by different subjects, 5.2% of lower secondary teachers currently teaching reading, writing and literature reported not having received any formal education or training or professional development in this subject (TALIS average: 5.7%). However, 10.7% of teachers reported a lack of initial training and professional development for the teaching of mathematics (TALIS average: 6.6%), 14.9% for the teaching of science (TALIS average: 5.7%), and 20.8% for the teaching of modern foreign languages (TALIS average: 10.5%) (OECD, 2014b).

There is a desire for and instances of collaborative work at the central, municipal and school levels

Representatives at all levels within the school system expressed their desire to build on collaborative work to foster the improvement of student achievement and wellbeing. This sentiment was strongest at the municipal level where education directors and their staff expressed such a desire in all visits conducted. There was a genuine attempt in more than one municipality to make school leader collaborative work the norm. Many school leaders and some municipal school education directors described their efforts to increase their knowledge of collaboration by visiting jurisdictions known for collaborative work and examining how this might better be incorporated within their own context. Visits to other countries, including in particular to Ontario, Canada, but also other contexts, such as New Zealand and the United States, were referenced with regularity.

At the school level, leaders and teachers recognised the value of having educators with expertise work directly with teachers with the aim of improving teaching practice. The most common practice was working with an expert teacher on supporting individual staff of the school. School leaders typically assigned fewer teaching hours to these individuals to accommodate the extra work load with their peers. Teachers expressed how much they valued this type of support and some thought feedback from these colleagues more valuable to their teaching than feedback from their school leaders. However, no studies have been completed to evaluate direct improvements in student achievement as a result of this type of collaborative work.

Emerging practices of collaboration, teamwork and peer learning were also identified in a previous OECD review on evaluation assessment in Denmark conducted in 2010 (Shewbridge et al., 2011). As Shewbridge et al. noted, "work in Danish schools is increasingly organised in a way that grants opportunities for teamwork. Schools more and more are structuring work around teams of teachers (e.g. class team, form team, section team, subject team) which share responsibility for organising their work". TALIS 2013 data provide further evidence for some teacher co-operation in Danish schools, which seem to be more developed than in other TALIS countries: only 11.4% of lower secondary teachers reported to never jointly teach as a team in the same class (TALIS average: 41.9%) and only 6.8% reported to never engage in joint activities across different classes and age groups (TALIS average: 21.5%), for example. However, classroom observations among peers are still rather rare: 45.0% of lower secondary teachers reported to never observe other teachers' classes and provide feedback (TALIS average: 44.7%) (OECD, 2014b).

Changes to the school day and scheduling autonomy of teachers' working time for schools provide opportunities to improve student learning

The introduction of longer school days as part of the 2014 *Folkeskole* reform coupled with the new framework for the utilisation of teacher working hours (Act no. 409) that typically also requires teachers to be present for a longer time at school provides some potential opportunities for schools and students that may contribute to improve student learning.[3] Greater teacher presence in schools may help students learn and facilitate greater collaboration between teachers and other staff. In several schools visited during the review visit, students reported a greater level of self-confidence and a feeling of being better prepared for class thanks to teachers being more available in schools to work with them on their homework, for example. The presence of teachers at school for a prescribed period of time each day also presents an opportunity for teachers to participate in collaborative activities with colleagues.

Changes to the way in which teachers' working time is organised and teachers distribute their time for different tasks and responsibilities also entail potential benefits if schools use their new autonomy in this respect well and if teachers adjust to the new realities (also see Chapter 2). The new framework for the utilisation of working hours (Act no. 409) also defines a yearly norm of working hours and gives school leaders the ability to assign teaching time and other duties within this timeframe to meet the needs of their school as they see fit as the working time arrangement no longer describe what teachers should do and when. This working time conception recognises that teachers' work entails a wide range of tasks beyond teaching. And it gives school leaders greater autonomy over the work schedules for all of their staff than was previously the case. School leaders now have the flexibility to organise their staff around the learning needs of their school's students and the competencies, strengths, weaknesses, and learning needs of their staff. Such an arrangement is also the case in the Flemish Community of Belgium, for example. Here, school leaders have considerable room to manage their teacher resources and to manage the teacher hours allocated to the school in the way they see fit. As a school resources review of the Flemish Community suggests, this autonomy gives school leaders the ability to select the optimal distribution of teacher resources across classes and students and across roles and tasks within the school, enabling schools to adapt the use of teacher hours to the schools' specific needs and the student characteristics of each school (Nusche et al., 2015).

The new autonomy gives school leaders a range of new possibilities. For instance, school leaders can assign less teaching time to their classroom teachers in favour of having them work with other teachers in their area of expertise. School leaders can also use their new autonomy in this regard to support beginning teachers in their school. In case a beginning teacher requires more preparation time, school leaders could make the decision to assign less teaching time and fewer classes to teach. As Jensen et al. (2012b) argued, it is likely to be inefficient to have teachers of different levels of effectiveness and levels of experience having the same teaching responsibilities. Giving more experienced teachers more teaching hours or more students or classes to teach and reducing new teachers' teaching hours so they can focus on developing their teaching skills at the beginning of their careers could improve teaching and learning. School leaders can also give consideration to teachers who may be teaching diverse subjects and require slightly more preparation time or to teachers taking on a leadership role at the form level or across the school. Alternatively, school leaders may assign more teaching time to teachers who are teaching several classes where very similar materials are delivered and who require less preparation, or to teachers who are receiving support of an expert teacher or who are co-teaching with another teacher who, as a result, may also require less preparation time.

In sum, then, this autonomy to organise teachers' working time is one more tool (along with data, support from expert teachers, time to work together, etc.) that schools can utilise to meet the needs of their students. Schools (teachers and leaders) must have the ability, then, to identify the most urgent student learning needs, connect those to the most urgent professional learning needs of their staff and of their leadership (school and perhaps municipal education leaders) and plan opportunities to work together towards meeting those needs. The elements are in place for this type of a change process to occur.

Experts and consultants are available at the central, municipal and school levels

The Ministry for Children, Education and Gender Equality has created a corps of learning consultants. These are experts in teaching and learning available centrally to support schools and municipalities in their school and system improvement efforts, if needed. Consultants are drawn from the school sector (mostly from schools and municipalities) and, after a period of time in the corps, they return to their respective municipality or school. This adds significant capacity to the Danish school system: it is a source of additional support to schools and municipalities during their tenure and a source of capacity building across the system as learning consultants go back to their original job with the experience they have gained in their role as a learning consultant. The requirement for learning consultants to return to municipalities and/or schools also ensures that good education professionals do not leave municipalities, schools and classrooms. It is also positive that municipalities seem to recognise the value of such a central body of experts and seem to have developed high levels of trust towards central learning consultants. Further potential benefits of the learning consultant corps include the creation of networks and peer-learning among schools through work in groups of schools; the creation of a circle of learning and evidence that brings knowledge to schools and municipalities, but also from the local to the central level; and links between initial teacher education and school practice.

Several municipalities visited by the OECD review team indicated that they had their own teaching and learning consultants or experts among their municipal staff. These were available to support schools and their teachers in the improvement of teaching and, ultimately, of the learning of their students. At the school level, several teachers and school leaders reported the use of staff teacher experts to support the learning of teachers within a school staff in a variety of ways. These varied from co-teaching with the class teacher and debriefing on the experience to sharing resources and strategies in discussion format.

Together with the increased opportunities and funding for teachers to advance in their professional learning and to acquire the necessary competencies, these support initiatives provide multiple opportunities to enhance the teaching skills of the workforce as well as opportunities for teacher to teacher collaboration around teaching strategies and individual teaching practices. Fullan et al. (2015) report that the combined power of capacity building of staff with collaborative inquiry yields great impact for improvements in student achievement.

Box 4.2. **The introduction of a learning consultant corps to support municipalities and schools**

The Danish Ministry for Children, Education and Gender Equality has introduced a national body of about 80 learning consultants in 2014 to provide support to municipalities and schools for quality development, to spread good practices, and to facilitate school networking and peer-learning. Both schools and municipalities can ask for the support of a learning consultant and schools can also work together in groups with a learning consultant. Learning consultants work in teams and analyse the challenges a school faces based on school data and information on student performance. They then develop a school development plan, a strategy for change management, and indicators for monitoring and evaluation. Learning consultants collaborate with a ministerial research centre to learn about the latest evidence and to feed into the knowledge available in the research centre. They also collaborate with teacher training institutions to develop links between theory and practice. Learning consultants have diverse backgrounds, from teaching and school leadership to local administration in a municipality. They receive training and capacity building for their role and meet on a monthly basis to learn about new methods and evidence and to reflect about their experiences and challenges. Learning consultants can work in different arrangements. For example, learning consultants can work for two days a week in their learning consultant role at the ministry and for three days a week in the field. Learning consultants are typically hired for two years after which they return to a school or municipality. This allows the ministry to adjust the number and profile of learning consultants depending on the demand and also helps spread knowledge more widely across the system. Some municipalities in Denmark, such as Copenhagen, have developed and implemented their own systems of learning consultants to facilitate leadership and specialist advice to schools from practitioners with high credibility.

Source: Interview during the country review visit, *http://uvm.dk/Uddannelser/Folkeskolen/Laeringskonsulenterne.*

There are a number of initiatives to improve teaching and learning for students with special needs and bilingual students

Initial teacher education has been adapted to include courses on teaching students with special educational needs and bilingual students. These changes, which have been introduced in response to a growing number of bilingual students and to the mainstreaming initiatives of students with special educational needs embarked on in Denmark, have meant that, since 2012, all graduating teachers should have a broader and deeper understanding of working with these two types of learners. There are also special programmes on offer for teachers wishing to develop a higher level of expertise in the area of supporting students with special educational needs as well as opportunities to develop this competency in teachers who do not feel competent enough to support the special needs of different students.

These are welcome initiatives in the current context of inclusion and considering that many Danish teachers feel inadequately prepared to support students with special educational needs. In the TALIS report for 2013, 27.7% of practicing Danish teachers in lower secondary education reported a high need for professional development with regard to supporting students with special needs in their classrooms. This proportion was above the TALIS average of 22.3%, and constitutes an increase since TALIS 2008 for which 24.6% of lower secondary teachers reported such a professional development need (OECD, 2014b). In all other areas of professional development represented in Figure 4.3, Danish teachers reported a less pronounced need for professional development than teachers on average across TALIS countries.

Figure 4.3. **Teachers' professional development needs, 2013**

Lower secondary education teachers reporting a high level of need for professional development in the following areas:

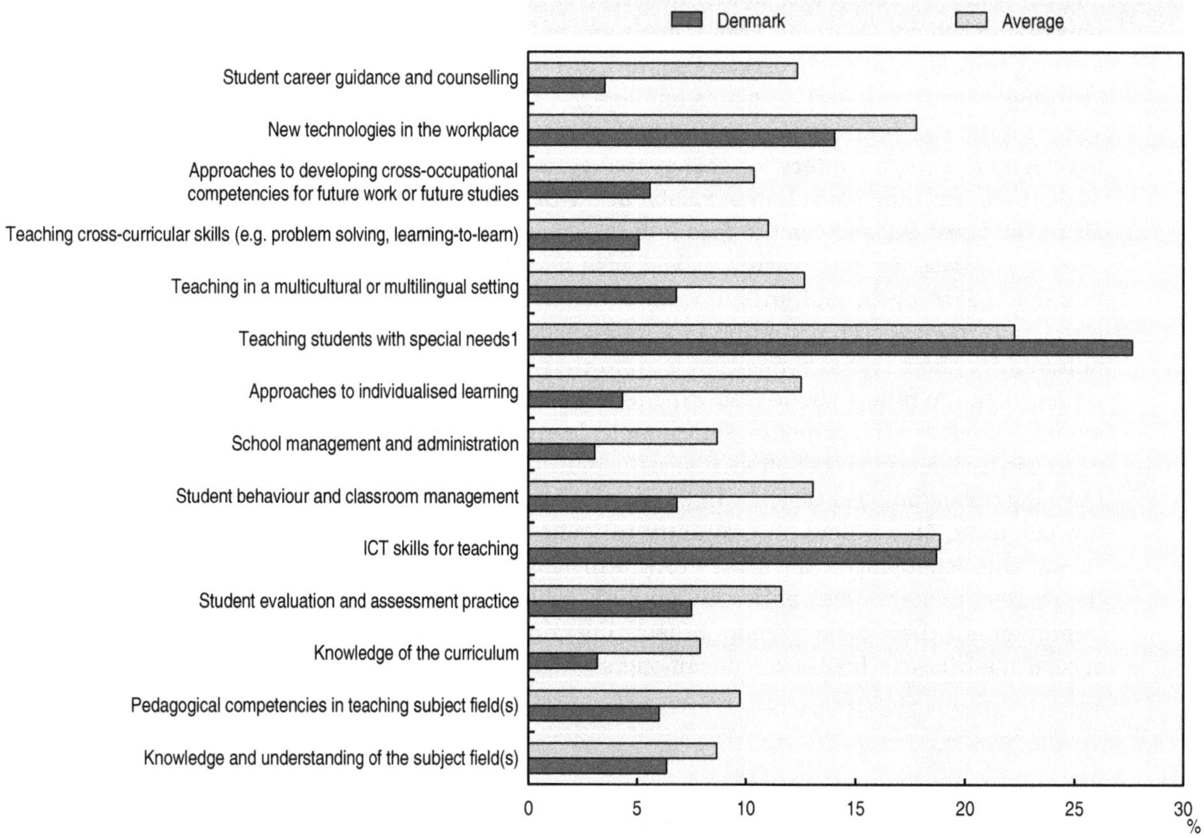

1. Special needs students are not well defined internationally but usually cover those for whom a special learning need has been formally identified because they are mentally, physically or emotionally disadvantaged. Often, special needs students will be those for whom additional public or private resources (personnel, material or financial) have been provided to support their education. "Gifted students" are not considered to have special needs under the definition used here and in other OECD work. Some teachers perceive all students as unique learners and thus having some special learning needs.

Source: OECD (2014b), *TALIS 2013 Results: An International Perspective on Teaching and Learning*, *http://dx.doi.org/10.1787/9789264196261-en*.

School hiring practices have traditionally created a broad range of staff members who work with students in the school. Typically, school communities have a mix of social workers, psychologists, pedagogues and AKT counsellors who are specialists in behaviour, social inclusion and wellbeing. This gives school leaders the opportunity to support both teachers of students with special needs and the students themselves with specialists in their school. If not available in a school, many types of these specialists seem to be working at the municipal level in the form of local educational-psychological advisory services (PPRs). Schools can call upon these services to provide learning support and advice. In addition, there is a central resource that schools and municipalities can seek advice from. The

National Board of Social Services (*Socialstyrelsen*), a government agency under the Ministry of Social Affairs and the Interior, promotes new developments and initiatives in social services and supports local authorities in providing services to children, young people, socially marginalised groups and disabled people. A specialised knowledge and counselling organisation (*Videns- og Specialrådgivningsorganisation*, VISO) within this board provides advice to municipalities, institutions and citizens across the country in the area of special needs education and rare special needs free of charge. VISO provides advice about methods to organise pedagogical frameworks and to create an inclusive learning environment and can also contribute to the diagnosis of a child's behaviour and special needs. Examples for the areas of expertise include, autism, cerebral palsy and diffuse brain injuries, hearing loss, and self-harm. Typically, teachers and school leaders should in the first instance discuss their needs with their local educational-psychological advisory service (PPR), which should then decide if VISO should become involved. Support can be provided to the PPR, education staff, the local authorities and parents. Even though VISO provides advice and recommendations only, there were, however, reports that municipalities may be reluctant to engage with these services as they may be concerned about the financial costs of the measures VISO recommends. At the time of drafting the report, the Ministry for Children, Education and Gender Equality was, furthermore, planning to establish an outgoing consulting unit that supports better inclusion in day care, school and leisure time facilities and a Centre for Inclusive Education and Special Needs Education.

There is a growing focus on pedagogy and goal-oriented teaching and learning

The conditions are in place for school staff and school leaders to focus on pedagogy which alters student learning outcomes (Chapter 3). The 2014 *Folkeskole* reform focuses the curriculum on outcomes for students and national student assessments give teachers and school leaders the ability to monitor the learning outcomes of their students (at the school or class levels), and municipalities a tool for monitoring the quality of education in their schools. In the spring of 2015, the results of the first student wellbeing survey were released that gave students the chance to report on their wellbeing and their sense of belonging at school. This new survey provides a voice for direct student feedback to the institutions serving them. Competency screening, coursework and exams are available to strengthen the expertise levels of the teaching staff. And evidence points to a growing willingness to dialogue around pedagogical needs at the municipal (education directors and school leaders), school (school leaders and staff) and national levels (e.g. introduction of a corps of learning consultants, development of a website of educational resources, and initiatives to share research).

Stakeholders also share a widespread willingness to embrace the reform goal of focusing on outcomes or what is learned instead of the input or the teaching. There are several conditions in place that indicate progress in this area. There are standardised outcomes established in subject areas at year levels throughout the system in the form of Common Objectives. There is an increasing availability of data at the municipal, school and individual student levels to use for different actors when setting goals and monitoring progress toward the achievement of these goals. And in several school and municipality visits, the team heard of trips that principals and municipal leaders had made to various jurisdictions around the world to learn from the experiences of professionals further along with the use of such data to support instruction. Municipal leaders and school leaders also reported that these visits focused on using data to increase the efficient use of resources to support their improvement efforts.

Challenges

The recent reforms of the education system have increased demands on teachers in terms of their practice (instruction and assessment of student learning), their time in the classroom and in the school, and the range of student needs to be met in regular classrooms. This section addresses the challenges and opportunities created by each of these changes in turn.

There are challenges in moving from a teaching focus to a learning focus

The Danish school system has undergone several major changes in the past few years. One of the most fundamental changes is the introduction of a set of Common Objectives which focus on student learning. In addition, several years ago the Danish Ministry for Children, Education and Gender Equality developed a set of national student assessments that have the potential to give teachers data with which to influence the planning of their teaching based on the class of students and the individual students they are teaching (see Chapters 1 and 3). This focus on working with data on individual student learning and progress stands in contrast to a focus on what is taught or the teaching. This shift, although articulated by teachers, school principals and municipal leaders, is, however, still in its infancy in terms of implementation in classrooms, schools and municipalities across the country.

While teachers described a beginning understanding of the meaning of the Common Objectives at each year level in each subject, they expressed more difficulties in using the national test results effectively for their teaching and linking these results to targeted improvement strategies for individual students. Discussions with teachers and school leaders varied somewhat, but overall teachers and school leaders did not seem to use these data systematically in their schools. Teachers identified a need to come to an understanding of this new goal-oriented way of working with the curriculum and how it changes their way of teaching and assessing students. As data from the OECD TALIS 2013 suggest, teachers in Denmark are also still reluctant to administer and use their own assessments. Only 56.2% of lower secondary teachers reported to develop and administer their own assessment (TALIS average: 67.9%) (OECD, 2014b). Enhancing the focus on improving student learning across the school system also brings new demands at the level of municipal and school leadership. Houlberg et al. (2016) report that many municipalities are still reluctant to follow up on school performance and goal attainment despite the fact that school performance is now more transparent. Similarly, their report finds that there is a tendency among school leaders to "apply more informal leadership strategies based on relationships and dialogue rather than utilising evaluation, documentation and other forms of data" (Houlberg et al., 2016).

These impressions are again substantiated through data from international surveys and assessments. For the OECD Programme for International Student Assessment (PISA) 2012, almost half of 15-year-olds were in a school whose principal reported to never use student results to develop the school's educational goals or at most one to two times during the year (47.0%, compared to an OECD average of 31.7%). And only slightly more than half of 15-year-olds were in a school whose principal reported to use assessments of students to monitor the school's progress from year to year (56.8%, OECD average: 81.2%). Similarly, only 65.6% of students were in a school whose principal reported that their school had a written specification of the school's curriculum and educational goals (OECD average: 86.2%), and only 37.8% were in a school whose principal reported that their school had a written specification of student performance standards (OECD average: 73.6%). These practices of having written specifications of the school's curriculum and educational goals and student performance standards are also substantially less common than in other Nordic countries (Finland: 94.1% and 75.3%, Norway: 96.7% and 73.0%, Sweden: 69.9% and 94.5% respectively). Concerning the use of assessment data at administrative levels, only 69.9% of students were in a school whose principal reported that achievement data was tracked over time by an administrative authority (OECD average: 72.1%) (OECD, 2013a).

Embedding a learning focus within practices at the classroom, school, local and central levels is a major cultural shift that will need to be implemented through a range of changes with regards to initial teacher education, professional development, performance management and leadership practices. The review team identified a number of challenges in these respects, as detailed below.

Targeting initial teacher education and professional development to the competency needs of schools and the education system and embedding professional learning in everyday practice

In terms of teacher initial and in-service education, establishing a learning focus means analysing evidence to identify student learning needs and recognising that these student learning needs indicate a teacher learning need (Katz and Dack, 2013).

While the 2014 *Folkeskole* reform sets a target for all teachers to have full qualifications in the subjects that they teach by 2020, there has been limited prognosis and forecasting in Denmark to determine the future competency needs of teachers. While this has occurred occasionally, there is no systematic approach to gap analysis or monitoring of needs over time (e.g. centrally within the Ministry for Children, Education and Gender Equality and the Ministry of Higher Education and Science). This means that there is no systematic knowledge on whether entry to initial teacher training is sufficiently geared to the needs of the system and no knowledge for institutions and authorities to formulate strategies for strengthening the recruitment into initial teacher education to meet the needs of the system.

There are also concerns about ensuring that teachers' continuing professional development responds well to learning needs in the system. Teacher professional development needs to be offered based on data and knowledge regarding learning needs of students. These data are needed at the classroom, school, municipal and system levels in order to plan against teacher expertise and qualifications. In order for this planning to happen, a systematic overview of the expertise of all groups of teachers needs to be in place. In Denmark, however, there are no systematic requirements for the professional development of teachers and in its visits to municipalities and schools the OECD review team did not hear about any systematic assessment at the local level of the gap between current specialisations of teachers and the need to meet qualification targets. Each of the municipalities visited had their own ideas for the development of offerings for their teachers, even if many were quite aware of the government's goals for the specialisation of teachers by the year 2020 and were encouraging and/or incentivising school leaders to develop these competencies among their school staff. Additional earmarked funding from the central government provides one source of support for teacher development and a tool for the central level to steer professional development (see above). However, stakeholders in schools and municipalities raised concerns that they lack support for the release of teachers in order for them to participate in learning opportunities. Teachers, the teacher union, the school leader association and municipal leaders perceived this as a serious barrier to using the funds for teacher development.

There are also concerns about professional development planning and use at the school level. Various school leaders had decided on a topic for their school-wide professional learning (e.g. "visible learning" based on the work of John Hattie [2012, 2009]) and schools were planning workshops that all teachers were to participate in. Challenges with this type of professional learning include a lack of differentiation based on teacher need, a lack of teacher ownership over their learning and often a lack of connection to the learning needs of students. More generally, as interviews during this and a previous OECD study as well as international data suggest, professional development is not always planned systematically at the school level, is not based on sound teacher evaluations and knowledge about teacher's development needs to better meet the needs of their students (more on this below), and lacks strong links with wider school development planning. A sizeable share of school leaders seems to not plan professional development with the school's needs and goals in mind. And at times, professional development may be more an individual teacher's choice (Shewbridge et al., 2011). For the OECD TALIS 2013, 27.4% of lower secondary school principals reported not to work on a professional development plan for the school (TALIS average: 20.9%) (OECD, 2014b). For the OECD PISA 2012, 38.2% of 15-year-olds were in a school whose principal reported to never or at most one to two times a year make sure that teachers' professional development activities are in accordance with the teaching goals of the school (OECD, 2013a).

Practices of ongoing learning and job-embedded practice that are connected to individual teachers' practices or problems within a school, some of the most powerful forms of professional learning, also seem to be in their infancy in Denmark. Research shows the most effective teacher learning activities help teachers to examine what they do in the classroom, what works for their students and why. Teachers learn best collecting, evaluating and acting on feedback to modify their teaching practices, working collaboratively with others to evaluate practice, and directly engaging and challenging tacit assumptions on teaching. Teachers also need to have opportunities to see evidence of the impact they are having over time. Integrating these opportunities for this form of learning into teaching is key to professional growth (Hattie, 2009; OECD, 2005; Timperley et al., 2007).

Enhancing teacher professionalism

Even if teachers' levels of self-efficacy as reported for the OECD TALIS 2013 are very high in Denmark (see Figure 4.4), there are several aspects of teacher professionalism which are still at the early stages of development as compared to other OECD countries. Considering the decentralised nature of education in Denmark, not all municipalities and schools may provide their teachers with the support they need to develop their practice.

Teaching standards: There does not appear to be a shared understanding of the standards of teacher practice. There is no discussion regarding excellent teaching within schools, municipalities or at the central level, and no benchmark to which teachers can self-assess or school or municipal leaders can assess against. This is different to many other OECD member countries. Clear, well-structured and widely supported teaching standards can be a powerful mechanism for developing the profession and for aligning the various elements involved in developing teachers' knowledge and skills. Teaching standards can guide the development of the teaching profession by clarifying expectations of what systems of initial teacher education and professional development should aim to achieve, offering a credible reference for making judgments about teacher competency, guiding teacher

Figure 4.4. **Teachers' self-efficacy, 2013**

Lower secondary education teachers reporting to feel they can do the following tasks "quite a bit" or "a lot":

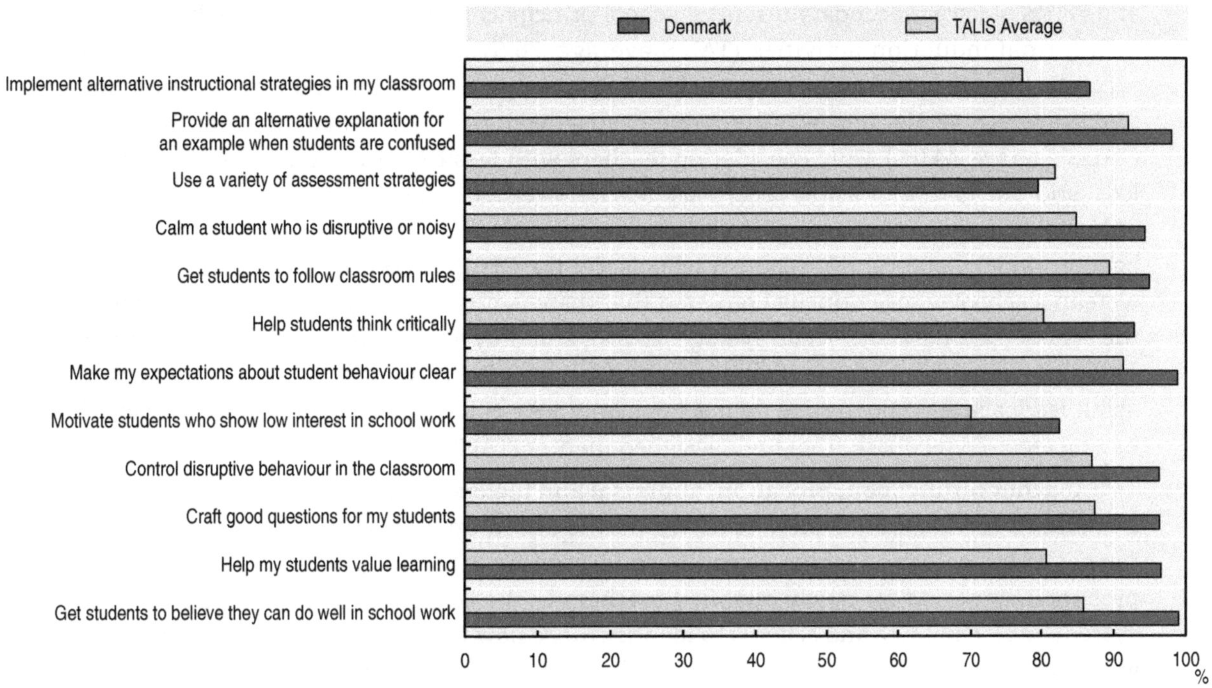

Source: OECD (2014b), *TALIS 2013 Results: An International Perspective on Teaching and Learning*, *http://dx.doi.org/10.1787/9789264196261-en.*

professional development, and providing the basis for career advancement (OECD, 2013b; OECD, 2005). And teaching standards can strengthen horizontal accountability by clearly setting out and providing a reference for the professional practices that teachers should be able to meet (Hooge, 2016).

Induction and mentoring: As research indicates, new teachers are likely to struggle with issues such as classroom management and student discipline in the early years of their career. New teachers' experience in the first years of their career is a crucial influence on teachers' decisions to leave the profession and a difficult start to the career may also reduce new teachers' confidence and influence their long-term effectiveness. This may imply high costs for both individual teachers as well as schools and students who do not benefit from the fresh ideas and enthusiasm that new teachers can bring. New teachers, particularly those in disadvantaged school, should, therefore, benefit from additional support, e.g. through induction or mentoring opportunities (Jensen et al., 2012b; OECD, 2005). In Denmark, there is no formal and systematic induction of beginning teachers into the teaching profession. Instead, the availability of induction processes depends on local contexts and there appears to be a wide range of practices in this regard. Some municipalities and schools pay special attention to new or beginning teachers (e.g. through some informal mentoring by school staff and school leaders to having new teachers teach less and work with an experienced staff member for periods of time). And, as pointed out above, the new framework for the utilisation of teacher' working hours will provide more opportunities for school leaders to take the particular needs of new teachers in the organisation of working time in their school into account (e.g. new teachers could have less teaching hours and, therefore, more time to prepare). However, as yet, such practices appear to be the exception rather than the norm.

For the OECD TALIS 2013, 55.7% of lower secondary teachers' school principals reported that all new teachers had access to a formal induction programme (TALIS average: 43.6%) and 78.3% of lower secondary teachers' school principals reported that teachers had access to informal induction activities (TALIS average: 76.5%). However, only 26.6% of lower secondary teachers themselves reported having taken part in a formal induction programme (TALIS average: 48.6%), and 39.5% reported having taken part in informal induction activities (TALIS average: 44.0%). Only considering teachers with less than five years of experience or less, still only 39.9% of lower secondary teachers reported having taken part in a formal induction process (TALIS average: 51.9%). As far as mentoring is concerned, mentoring could be more widely established in Danish schools. For the OECD TALIS 2013, one in four teachers were in a school whose principal reported that there is no mentoring system for teachers in the school (Denmark and TALIS average: 25.8%), and only 4.2% of lower secondary teachers reported having a mentor assigned to support them (TALIS average: 12.8%). When asked about feedback and appraisal in their school, only 5.6% of lower secondary teachers reported having received feedback from their assigned mentor (TALIS average: 19.2%) (OECD, 2014b).

Teacher certification, probation, appraisal and feedback: In Denmark, there is neither a standard certification of new teachers that is based on a specific set of criteria nor a formal appraisal of a teacher's readiness to assume a teaching role. There is also no probationary period for newly qualified teachers in the *Folkeskole*, which would allow the system, municipalities and schools to identify those new teachers who struggle to perform well on the job or who find that teaching does not meet their expectations (Shewbridge et al., 2011). And while there are teacher appraisal practices at a local level, performance appraisal of practicing teachers in Denmark is not mandatory. Occasionally, municipalities require their school leaders to appraise their teaching staff, but no formal appraisal process appears to be occurring systematically. As a result, not all teachers in the *Folkeskole* receive appraisal on their practice and feedback on how to improve.

This was also the impression of a previous OECD review on evaluation and assessment in Denmark. As Shewbridge et al. (2011) pointed out, "there is no expectation that each teacher in the *Folkeskole* has his or her practice appraised and receives feedback for improvement. The existing teacher appraisal practices are the initiative of individual schools (in some cases in the context of municipality's requirements) and depend essentially on the endeavour of the school principal and the evaluation ethos created in the school". While emerging practices of joint planning and teamwork are evident in many Danish schools, the observation and evaluation of teaching and learning by managers or peers – followed by feedback, discussion and possibly coaching – is the exception rather than the rule. However, teachers during this and the previous review visit reported a desire to receive feedback from their school leaders to improve their teaching and the learning of their students and teachers conveyed their appreciation for the time school principals took to provide them with feedback.

Data from the OECD TALIS 2013 similarly suggest that teachers could benefit more systematically from appraisal and feedback practices which are based on classroom observation and have strong links to teacher and school development to ultimately improve student learning. For TALIS 2013, 91.0% of Danish lower secondary teachers were in schools whose principal reported that teacher appraisal was conducted, but in the same report about one in four teachers reported never having received feedback in their current school (22.3% compared to a TALIS average of 12.5%). Only 43.7% of lower secondary teachers responded that they received feedback from their school principal, compared to 54.3% on average across

TALIS countries. In addition, the involvement of other members of school management teams in teacher appraisal is particularly low in Denmark, with only 14.9% of lower secondary teachers reporting that they received feedback from members of the management team, compared to 49.3% on average across TALIS countries (see Figure 4.5).

Figure 4.5. **Teachers' feedback from principals and school management team, 2013**

Lower secondary education teachers who report receiving feedback from members of the school management team and the school principal

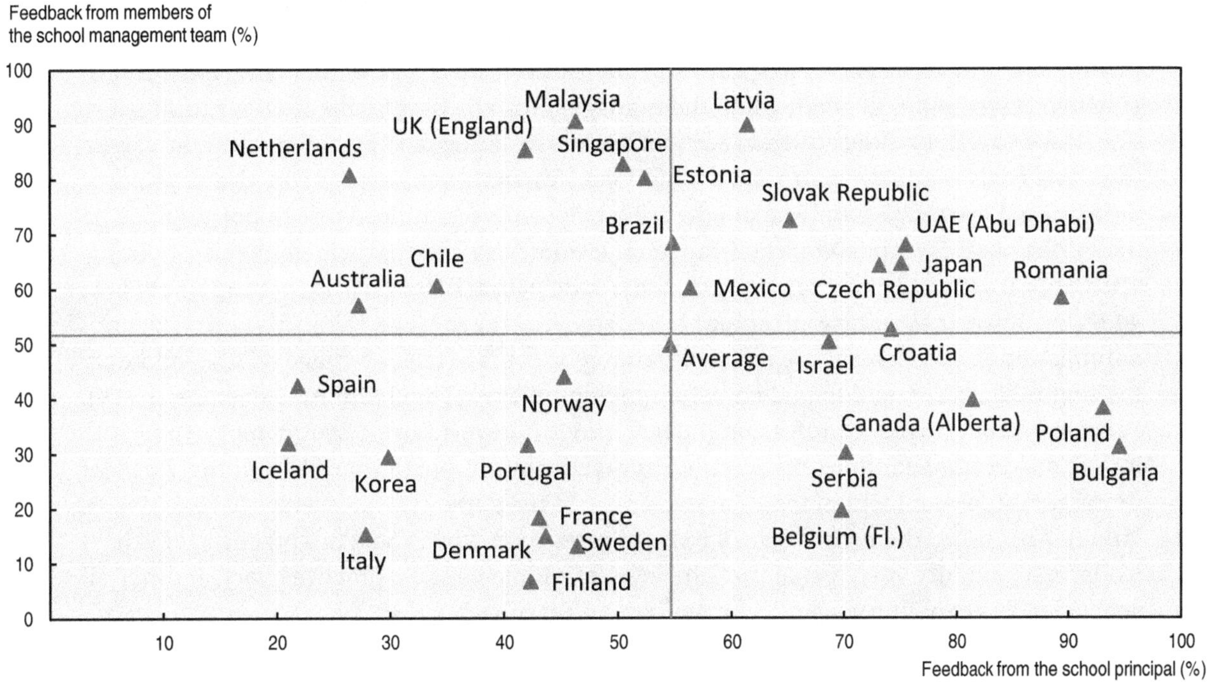

Source: OECD (2014b), *TALIS 2013 Results: An International Perspective on Teaching and Learning*, *http://dx.doi.org/10.1787/9789264196261-en*.

Also, if teacher appraisal takes place, it does not always seem to involve classroom observations and to not always have substantial impact on teaching practices: only 57.7% of lower secondary teachers reported that they had received feedback following a classroom observation (TALIS average: 78.8%), only 22.6% of lower secondary teachers agreed or strongly agreed that feedback is provided to teachers based on a thorough assessment of their teaching, and only 49.9% of lower secondary teachers reported that appraisal and feedback had a moderate or large impact on their teaching practices (TALIS average: 62.0%). As was already pointed out above, appraisal also seems to have weak links to professional development: only 40.5% of lower secondary teachers agreed or strongly agreed that a development or training plan is established to improve their work as a teacher (TALIS average: 59.1%) (OECD, 2014b).

A lack of systematic and effective teacher appraisal and feedback that involves classroom observations and has strong links to professional development raises the concern that underperformance of a teacher may not be detected and, therefore, may not be addressed, to the detriment of students (OECD, 2013b).

Strengthening pedagogical leadership focused on improving teaching and learning

School leadership is another area that should be further developed and strengthened in Denmark. As research has highlighted, pedagogical leadership in schools is essential for teaching and learning. This provides a strong rationale for implementing policies that ensure the effective management and development of the school leadership profession (Pont et al., 2008, Day et al., 2009, Louis et al., 2010).

The management of the school leadership profession in Denmark reveals a number of deficits, which should be addressed to further develop pedagogical leadership. First, effective school leadership, like teaching, is not defined by a framework or descriptive profile that highlights school leaders' pedagogical role. As a result, there is no common understanding of effective leadership that could guide the management and development of the profession. This leads to a lack of clarity among school leaders in terms of expectations and on how to improve their leadership practice. This was, for instance, evident in the myriad of professional learning school leaders described. Second, school leaders are not required to undertake specific training for their function, even if they may participate in such training. The OECD TALIS 2013, however, suggests that participation in leadership training is very low: 44.6% of lower secondary principals reported to never have taken part in a school administration or principal preparation training or course (TALIS average: 15.2%), and only 3.3% who did take training, did so before taking up their position (TALIS average: 25.4%). Participation in ongoing professional development, nevertheless, seems more common: 89.3% of lower secondary principals reported having participated in some form of professional development in the 12 months prior to the survey (TALIS average: 90.5%) (OECD, 2014b). And, third, the review team's visit suggests that, while there are practices of school leader performance management at the level of municipalities, practices vary and not all school leaders benefit from sufficient support and feedback.

Representatives of the Danish Association of School Leaders expressed to the OECD review team that there was a great deal of focus on pedagogical leadership as well as a desire on the part of school leaders to carry out this work. The association also highlighted its own support initiatives they had developed for leaders in the form of a publication on classroom observation and feedback. However, school leaders felt that they were lacking training and experience to work in this manner and the review team gained the impression that school principals could devote more attention to their pedagogical leadership role. As pointed out above, there is still little evidence of critical school self-evaluation beyond professional dialogue and observation-based teacher appraisal practices, for example. Also according to data from the OECD TALIS 2013, school leaders in Denmark are still less active in pedagogical leadership than school leaders in other OECD countries. Danish school principals in lower secondary schools reported to spend half of their time on administrative and leadership tasks and meetings, and less than one-fifth of their time on curriculum and teaching-related tasks. They also reported to engage less in practices related to pedagogical leadership than principals in other countries, including classroom observations (see Figures 4.6 and 4.7) (OECD, 2014b). This raises concerns regarding the quality of school improvement efforts overall and specifically how effective leaders are at developing the competency of the teaching staff in individual schools.

The lack of strong leadership is also of concern considering the significant changes the Danish education system is undergoing with the implementation of the 2014 *Folkeskole* reform, the introduction of a new framework for the utilisation of teachers' working hours

Figure 4.6. **Principals' working time, 2013**

Average proportion of time lower secondary education principals report spending on the following activities:

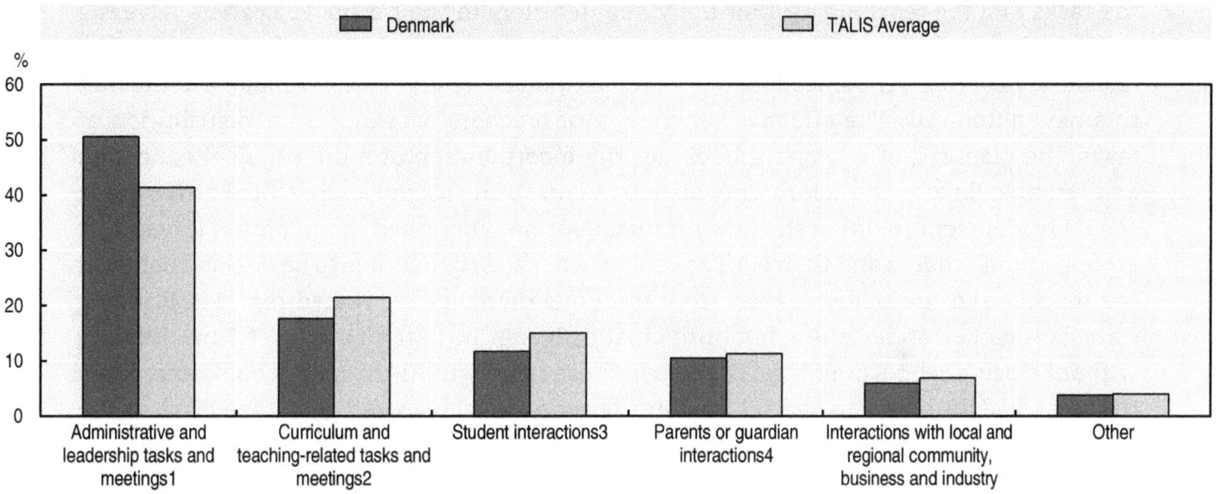

1. Including human resource/personnel issues, regulations, reports, school budget, preparing timetables and class composition, strategic planning, leadership and management activities, responding to requests from district, regional, state, or national education officials.
2. Including developing curriculum, teaching, classroom observations, student evaluation, mentoring teachers, teacher professional development.
3. Including counselling and conversations outside structured learning activities.
4. Including formal and informal interactions.

Source: OECD (2014b), *TALIS 2013 Results: An International Perspective on Teaching and Learning, http://dx.doi.org/10.1787/9789264196261-en.*

Figure 4.7. **Principals' leadership, 2013**

Lower secondary education principals who report having engaged "often" or "very often" in the following leadership activities during the 12 months prior to the survey:

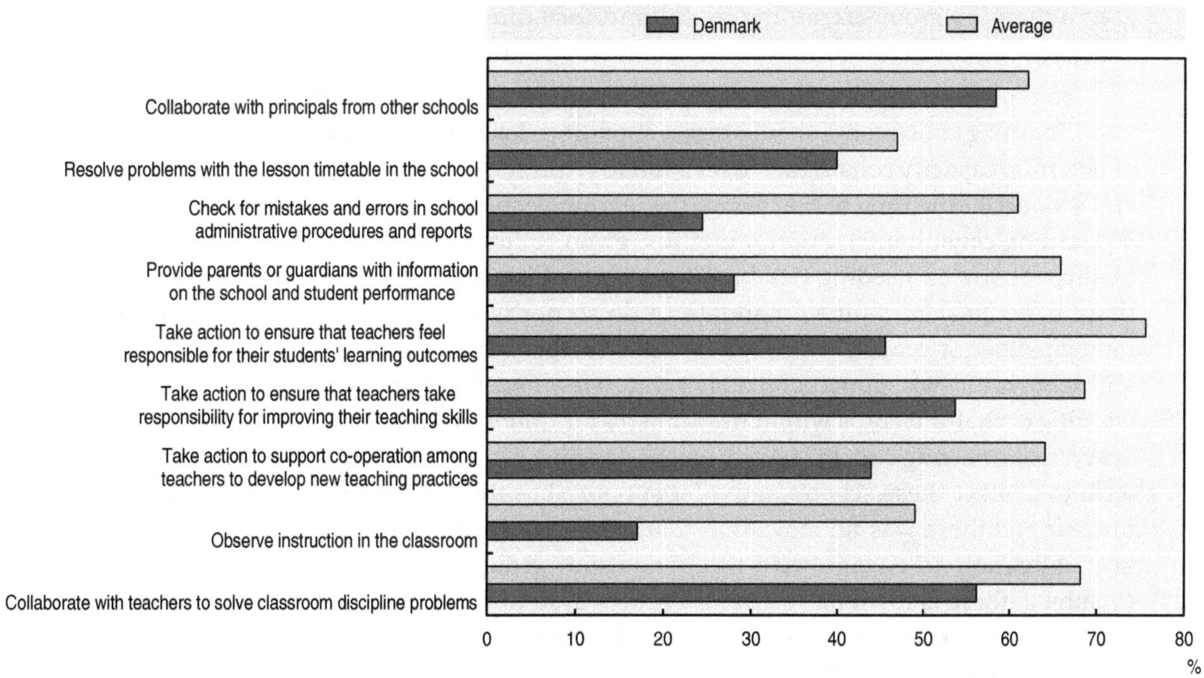

Source: OECD (2014b), *TALIS 2013 Results: An International Perspective on Teaching and Learning, http://dx.doi.org/10.1787/9789264196261-en.*

(Act no. 409), and school consolidation in some municipalities. The legislative changes to working conditions for teachers have given school leaders much more latitude in assigning the tasks and the teaching load for individual teachers in their schools. Leaders have the opportunity to assign teaching based on the needs of the school, its student body, and its teachers. However, school leaders need the competencies and tools to make the most of this new autonomy. The effective scheduling of teachers' working time, distribution of tasks, the planning of a longer school day, the incorporation of more physical education and stronger links to the community all depend on strong school leadership. Furthermore, school leaders reported that the new arrangement had increased the potential for conflict among school leaders and their staff as each teacher's assignment is to be decided between the teacher and the school leader. More than one municipality visited reported bringing schools together under one school principal or leader in part as a way of consolidating without closing school buildings. Leaders in these larger, multi-campus schools expressed that they had little time to be in classrooms observing teachers and giving feedback as the administrative demands of the job changes.

Targeting support provided by the central learning consultants at schools and municipalities with different needs

The Ministry for Children, Education and Gender Equality has developed a plan of hiring experts in various aspects of pedagogy from across the country (see Box 4.1). This central group of consultants is currently available to municipalities and schools to advise on school improvement and professional development of the teaching staff and school leaders, for example. As elaborated above, this initiative has the potential to contribute to greater capacity at the local and school levels. However, this highly competent group of educators could be better targeted at certain defined problems within the school system, even if there is a group of learning consultants focussing on special needs education which is highly relevant in the current context of inclusion, for example.

From discussions and the background report prepared for this review (Houlberg et al., 2016), learning consultants should target support to lower performing schools, also in light of potential capacity constraints to respond to requests by a large number of municipalities and schools (at the time of the review, the learning consultant corps had employed around 80 learning consultants). Priority is, thus, given to low performing schools identified in quality reports as needing risk-based support which are guaranteed support. However, there is no clear or defined mandate to do so nor is there any consistent outreach to municipalities or schools which fall into this category. It is essentially up to municipalities and schools to seek support and advice. Interview partners from the unit in charge of this learning consultant corps within the Ministry for Children, Education and Gender Equality described reviewing data to identify low performing schools and indicated that it was their wish to contact these schools and offer support, but the criteria for low performing were unclear and there was no indication that, when contacted, a municipality or school had any obligation to engage with the consultant group. Also, as elaborated further in Chapter 3, there is room for the Danish school system to pay more attention to excellence and to the further improvement of schools that are already performing well. The learning consultant initiative could contribute to supporting excellence, but does not seem to have considered this dimension in its work yet.

Education systems that have implemented system leadership roles and structures could provide some ideas for how to further develop Denmark's learning consultant initiative, to ensure it is well targeted to the needs of schools with different contexts and performance levels and embedded in broader improvement strategies. The London Challenge and City Challenge programmes in England, United Kingdom, and the Focused Intervention Partnership in Ontario, Canada, provide two interesting examples for targeted support for schools of different levels of performance as well as the use of consultants and school-to-school collaboration in broader improvement initiatives (see Box 4.3).

Box 4.3. **London Challenge and City Challenge and Ontario Focused Intervention Partnership**

London Challenge and City Challenge

In England, United Kingdom, the Department for Education and Skills introduced London Challenge, a programme to improve education in London. While the programme focused on supporting secondary schools in London between 2003 and 2008, it was expanded as City Challenge to work with primary schools and in two further geographical areas, Greater Manchester and the Black Country, between 2008 and 2011.

Building on the London Challenge experience, the City Challenge programme pursued three clear objectives: to reduce the number of underperforming schools; to increase the number of good and outstanding schools; and to improve educational outcomes for disadvantaged children. The programme included a number of elements: "Keys to Success" identified underperforming schools that would require most support; interventions targeted at satisfactory schools and others to support good schools in becoming outstanding; programmes designed to support schools in narrowing attainment gaps between disadvantaged pupils and their peers; providing schools with data about their intake, so-called "Families of Schools" data, and encouraging schools to work with other schools in their Family; capacity building work with local authorities; leadership strategies led by the National College for School Leadership, including the designation of National and Local Leaders of Education, and professional development programmes in teaching schools; and various local interventions in each area. The programme did not promote a single view of what schools needed to do to improve, but all interventions were based on local decisions involving key stakeholders, including school principals and local authority officials.

As Hutchings et al. (2012) highlighted in their evaluation of the programme, it was helpful that City Challenge had objectives relating to good and outstanding schools as well as to underperforming schools, as this reinforced the message that all schools need to work to improve. Strategies for school improvement provided different forms of support depending on school performance. Inadequate and underperforming schools benefited from support from experts. Satisfactory schools worked with two or three other schools with similar intakes, led by the principal of a school that was further along its school improvement journey (but not necessarily outstanding). And good and outstanding schools benefited from a wide range of opportunities to share practice and learn from other schools with outstanding practice in specific areas. They also benefited from supporting weaker schools.

Source: Baars, S. et al. (2014), *Lessons from London Schools: Investigating the Success*, *http://centreforlondon.org/publication/lessons-london-schools*; Kidson, M. and E. Norris (2014), *Implementing the London Challenge*, *www.instituteforgovernment.org.uk/sites/default/files/publications/Implementing%20the%20London%20Challenge%20-%20final_0.pdf*; Hutchings, M. et al. (2012), *Evaluation of the City Challenge Programme*, *www.gov.uk/government/publications/evaluation-of-the-city-challenge-programme*.

Ontario Focused Intervention Partnership (OFIP)

In Ontario (Canada), the Focused Intervention Program (OFIP) provides targeted support to primary schools that have "experienced particular difficulties in achieving continuous

Box 4.3. **London Challenge and City Challenge and Ontario Focused Intervention Partnership** *(cont.)*

improvement" since 2006/07. These schools are identified through results on provincial assessments of reading, writing, and mathematics in Years 3 and 6. In 2006/07, schools qualified for OFIP support if less than 34% of students reached provincial standards in Year 3 reading. In addition, since 2009/10, resources from the OFIP programme were extended to over 1 100 schools in which less than 75% of students met provincial standards in the Years 3 and 6 assessments. Once identified a capacity building approach is used to build upon the assets of the students, staff and community to meet the specific learning needs of students and increase student achievement. OFIP funds are used for professional development, additional student and professional learning resources, literacy and numeracy coaches, and teacher release time for collaboration and additional training. The improvement efforts in these schools were supported by the Ministry of Education through student achievement officers as well as learning supports from the school boards involved. From 2002/03 to 2010/11, the number of schools with fewer than 34% of students achieving at provincial standard in Year 3 reading was reduced by two-thirds (from 19% to 6%), showing significant success in reducing the number of primary schools in which students fail.

Source: Ontario Ministry of Education (2016a), *Ontario Focused Intervention partnership for Elementary Schools, Capacity Building Series, http://learnteachlead.ca/projects/capacity-building-2/?pcat=2412.*

Although a different process, differentiated and risk-based approaches to school evaluation may provide further inspiration for how support could be better targeted. For instance, Chile has been in the process of introducing external school evaluations since 2009 with the creation of an Education Quality Assurance Agency and a Superintendence of Education. The Education Quality Assurance Agency is responsible for the implementation of school evaluations that focus on pedagogical processes in schools. School evaluations follow a proportional approach focussing on low-performing schools. Schools are ranked on the basis of their performance in standardised national student assessments and in other indicators of education quality, including academic self-esteem and motivation; school climate; participation and citizenship education; habits for a healthy life; school attendance; grade repetition; gender equity; and graduation in a technical-professional field, taking the schools' socio-economic context into account. Based on these indicators, schools are classified in one of four categories (high, average, average-low and unsatisfactory). Schools classified as showing unsatisfactory performance are evaluated at least every two years and are obliged to seek public or private technical-pedagogical support from providers that are similar to Denmark's learning consultants. Schools classified as showing average-low performance are evaluated at least every four years, and schools classified as average at the Agency's discretion. Schools showing high performance receive so-called "learning visits" to identify and spread good practices (Santiago et al., forthcoming). School supervision in the Netherlands provides a further example (see Box 3.4 in Chapter 3).

There are concerns about the new organisation of teachers' working time

Considering the role of the quality of daily classroom instruction for student learning and achievement (e.g. Katz and Dack, 2013), and particularly so for students from a disadvantaged backgrounds, the effective use of teachers and other staff and the quality of their instruction in classrooms is essential. As highlighted above, the introduction of a new framework for the utilisation of teachers' working hours and the new autonomy for school leaders to manage and distribute work among staff within their organisation entails the potential benefit to adjust the use of staff time to local needs. However, different stakeholders voiced also various concerns, even if they indicated support for the overall goals of the *Folkeskole* reform at the same time (also see Chapter 2).

Representatives of the teacher union and the school leader association expressed concerns that the expectation that all teachers would, on average, teach more classroom hours would, in fact, reduce the local autonomy of municipalities and schools. It was argued that if every teacher (on average) is to teach a certain number of hours, the local authority would have less flexibility to differentiate staffing and the use of time based on perceived student and teacher needs and circumstances. Accountability requirements have also increased, which gives a sense of a more rigorous monitoring of these working conditions and overall school improvement. The possibility for schools to adjust the scheduling of teachers is, furthermore, limited in small schools in rural areas, as interview partners pointed out during the review visit.

Teachers, school principals and representatives of the teacher union and school leader association also voiced concerns about a lack of clarity regarding the process of changing the organisation of working arrangements and working time within schools. Most teachers reported a lack of understanding regarding the flexibility school principals had to assign their teaching hours. And school principals and their member association reported a lack of knowledge examples of effective ways to use their new flexibility to allocate and manage their staffs' working and teaching time according to the needs of the student population. Some school principals did report that they used expert teachers to act in a coaching role with less experienced or less qualified teachers, thus giving them more teaching hours per week and then assigning fewer classes to newer teachers, but they also reported having no way to monitor the effectiveness of such organisation of the teaching workforce at the school.

In all of the schools visited, the review team was told by teachers that they felt they had less preparation time now and that they taught more than they used to. They reported that they were not allowed to take any preparation work or marking home with them as had been their practice and that this cut their preparedness for the lessons they were assigned to teach. As teachers saw it, their ability to collaborate with their peers had been hampered by the new working conditions making it more difficult to meet and plan together as same level or same subject teachers. And they apparently faced a lack of time to seek out and prepare for the needs of all students in their classrooms, especially those with special needs. While it was the government's intention that teachers should change their way of working, such a change in work organisation is likely to take more time.

There are concerns about the inclusion process and the quality of learning for students with special educational needs (SEN)

Following the national agreement to work towards inclusion (see Chapter 1), there have been significant changes to the funding models for how students with special educational needs (SEN) access education (also see Chapter 2). Prior to these changes, separate special needs schools were funded to provide classes to special needs students. While these separate special schools still exist at the level of municipalities and regions, municipalities provide schools with financial incentives for the increased integration of students into regular schools and classrooms. As such, the inclusion of students with special needs in regular schools and classrooms has become much more common over time.

Stakeholder groups interviewed by the OECD review team, however, expressed concerns regarding the inclusion process and the adequacy of support for special needs students in Denmark. The Disabled People's Organisation (DPOD) reported to the OECD review team that there was evidence showing that many students with dyslexia did not learn to read and write in the *Folkeskole*. An evaluation report of inclusion suggests that 70% of parents are worried that the needs of their children with special needs are not being met in the regular classroom. A small scale survey conducted by Autism Denmark among 200 parents of children with autism reports that over 30% of them were keeping their children with autism at home due to school refusal. There is also anecdotal evidence that suggests students are often shifted from one school to another and that students who had been integrated to a regular school were being taught in separate classes with little contact to regular students. Breaks were also organised separately in some schools visited as part of the review.

There are concerns if schools are prepared to ensure the successful inclusion of children with special needs. Both staff in regular and special education schools expressed a lack of relevant competencies to improve learning outcomes for special needs students. This was evident in discussions with teachers in every school visited by the team. As elaborated further in Chapter 3, for instance, teachers indicated that it was not clear to them how the national learning goals could be used and adapted for their students with special needs. A lack of competencies and preparedness is also evident in international survey data. As mentioned above, in the OECD TALIS 2013, Danish teachers reported a high level of need for professional development with respect to teaching special needs students (Figure 4.3), and the data show that they receive less training in this area than the average of OECD surveyed countries (25.3% of lower secondary teachers participated in training in this area in the twelve months prior to the survey, compared to 31.7% on average across TALIS countries). Also school leaders perceive a lack of competencies among their staff to meet the needs of children with special needs. For the OECD TALIS 2013, 40.5% of lower secondary teachers were in a school whose principal reported that a shortage of teachers with competencies in teaching students with special needs hindered the school to offer quality instruction (TALIS average: 48.0%). In addition, despite the availability of different specialist staff in schools and municipalities (e.g. AKT teachers and PPRs), 48.3% of lower secondary teachers were in a school whose principal reported that a shortage of support personnel hindered the school to offer quality instruction (TALIS average: 46.9%) (OECD, 2014b). Furthermore, school leaders and teachers stressed during school visits that parents and students are also not always ready to support the successful inclusion of children with special needs. Schools and municipalities may thus need greater support to make inclusion happen and to use available support services described above more effectively.

Further concerns that emerged during the review visit concerning the inclusion of students with special needs include the challenge related to maintaining a well-functioning separate special school system in a context of increasing inclusion. This entails the risk of losing sight of the ongoing needs of separate special schools and the performance and wellbeing of children in these schools (e.g. about the impact of the 2014 *Folkeskole* reform on special needs schools and how special needs schools can successfully implement the required changes; the particular challenge to get parents involved in special needs schools as a result of a lack of proximity), and a lack of attention to the need to ensure successful transitions of students with special needs across the education system, in particular from the *Folkeskole* to upper secondary education.

Policy recommendations

Develop a vision for teacher professionalism

Many changes to the education system in Denmark have left teachers struggling with what it means to be an excellent teacher. Teachers have been asked to teach towards outcomes, to meet the needs of students with special needs in regular classrooms, to work with expert teachers within their schools, to use data and evidence to plan instruction and they have had their working conditions redefined by legislation, not negotiation. Teachers by and large reported that they were struggling with some of these changes, but that they were working hard to implement all of them simultaneously. They generally voiced support for the changes in expectations around teaching and learning in the classroom and the school.

To support teachers, school leaders and municipal leaders in understanding and supporting the implementation of these changes, Denmark should consider developing a national teacher profile, vision or standards of practice. Such a national teacher profile would communicate the new expectations regarding teacher practice (e.g. collaboration and team work in schools, mentoring and peer feedback and observation, continuous professional development, reflective practice, and use of student assessment data, etc.). The expectations for teachers as laid out in such standards would put the conditions in place for many of the changes of the 2014 *Folkeskole* reform. They could aid those in the education sector to implement and monitor the effect of the reforms on teacher practice, and establish a foundation for teachers to explore their practice and for schools to develop their improvement initiatives. The professional standards would also set out teachers' required competencies in the use of evidence, data and assessments.

While initial teacher education already provides different competency profiles following the shift towards a competency-based teacher education, a national teacher profile would help to provide a framework to guide the development of the profession as whole. It could guide initial teacher education, teachers' ongoing professional development, teacher feedback and appraisal, and teachers' career advancement. In a decentralised system like Denmark, a national teacher profile could be particularly relevant to promote a shared vision and expectations. Teachers' work and expected knowledge and skills must reflect the student learning objectives that schools are aiming to achieve. The preparation of a profile of teacher competencies should, thus, be based on the Common Objectives, the objectives for student learning in Denmark. The profile should reflect the sophistication and complexity of what effective teachers are expected to know and be able to do; be informed by research and evidence; and benefit from the ownership and responsibility of the teaching profession (OECD, 2013b; Shewbridge, 2011). A national teacher profile should outline expectations for teachers to continually improve their teaching practice by knowing their students' individual learning needs, by increasing their professional knowledge around pedagogy, assessment and evaluation, and by using this knowledge to meet the learning needs of their students. The key is to communicate the expectation that teachers use opportunities to enhance their professional knowledge to improve their teaching practice to increase the learning outcomes for students. Denmark could investigate Ontario's College of Teachers Standards of Practice (Box 4.4).

Organise initial teacher education based on the competency needs of the system

As a starting point, a more systematic approach to gap analysis is recommended in order to understand the current demographics of teaching professionals including subject

Box 4.4. **Ontario's College of Teachers Standards of Practice**

Commitment to Students and Student Learning: Members are dedicated in their care and commitment to students. They treat students equitably and with respect and are sensitive to factors that influence individual student learning. Members facilitate the development of students as contributing citizens of Canadian society.

Professional Knowledge: Members strive to be current in their professional knowledge and recognise its relationship to practice. They understand and reflect on student development, learning theory, pedagogy, curriculum, ethics, educational research and related policies and legislation to inform professional judgment in practice.

Professional Practice: Members apply professional knowledge and experience to promote student learning. They use appropriate pedagogy, assessment and evaluation, resources and technology in planning for and responding to the needs of individual students and learning communities. Members refine their professional practice through ongoing inquiry, dialogue and reflection.

Leadership in Learning Communities: Members promote and participate in the creation of collaborative, safe and supportive learning communities. They recognise their shared responsibilities and their leadership roles in order to facilitate student success. Members maintain and uphold the principles of the ethical standards in these learning communities.

Ongoing Professional Learning: Members recognise that a commitment to ongoing professional learning is integral to effective practice and to student learning. Professional practice and self-directed learning are informed by experience, research, collaboration and knowledge.

Source: Ontario College of Teachers (n.d.), *Standards of Practice*, *www.oct.ca/-/media/PDF/Standards%20Poster/standards_flyer_e.pdf*.

specific education and additional qualifications, so that the content of teacher initial teacher education can be targeted to the needs of the system. In Ontario, Canada, the College of Teachers holds continuous data on teacher initial qualifications and additional qualifications earned throughout a teacher's career. Thanks to these data, the province can anticipate teacher qualification needs and gear admissions accordingly. Box 4.5 provides some other examples from Ontario for the identification of system teacher needs.

Box 4.5. **Targeting entry to initial teacher education based on system needs**

In Ontario, the Ontario College of Teachers (OCT) provides an annual report called Transitions to Teaching based on a survey conducted with its members. This report provides information to the education sector to describe demographic characteristics of the current workforce. The Ontario Ministry of Education also partners with OCT to collect information about registration in additional qualification courses. As a result, the province is more aware of how teachers are engaging in professional learning, how this might serve to meet system needs, and how to best allocate human and financial resources. For the 2014 report, see Ontario College of Teachers (2014).

The Higher Education Quality Council of Ontario (HEQCO) is an independent organisation that was established with a mandate to assist the government of Ontario (and the Minister of Training, Colleges and Universities in particular) through the provision of impartial research and policy advice for improving the accessibility, accountability, and quality of

Box 4.5. **Targeting entry to initial teacher education based on system needs** *(cont.)*

Ontario's colleges and universities. Reaching out to independent research organisations to conduct evaluations for identifying system needs is another possible approach to forecasting for future teacher recruitment needs.

Source: Ontario College of Teachers (2016), *Transition to Teaching, www.oct.ca/becoming-a-teacher/transition-to-teaching*; Higher Education Quality Council of Ontario (2016), HEQCO Website, *www.heqco.ca/Pages/wel.aspx* (accessed 4 February 2016).

An additional strategy could include a targeted recruitment of applicants who hold specialised post-secondary education degrees in such areas as science, technology, engineering, and mathematics. Incentives could include: subsidised professional learning; greater experience recognition on a salary grid; or signing bonuses for those teachers with specialised subject knowledge to increase retention rates in order to meet system needs (OECD, 2005).

Denmark should also consider monitoring the quality of initial teacher education, including the extent to which teacher education programmes prepare students for changing needs of schools, such as greater diversity in classrooms. Norway provides an example for monitoring the quality of teacher education as part of a wider monitoring framework of an initiative to raise the status and quality of the teaching profession (GNIST). The monitoring system was implemented in 2008 and contains five target areas (recruitment, quality in education, quality in teaching, quality in school leadership, improved status for the profession) with 23 indicators to monitor improvement. The basic approach is to make use of existing information available nationally, but to highlight this information in a coherent set of indicators. At the same time, the monitoring framework for GNIST has used some first-hand research, e.g. via the administration of surveys to teacher educators, school principals and teachers on their perception of quality in education (OECD, 2013b; Nusche et al., 2011).

Improve the planning of teacher professional learning and strengthen job-embedded learning in schools

While it is important to determine future recruitment and qualification needs, it is also essential to address the professional learning needs of the current workforce. Ontario has had much success with system improvement through the implementation of ministry-funded initiatives. Targeted initiatives are focused on professional learning for increasing the effectiveness of instruction. The Ministry of Education of Ontario allocates human and financial resources to support professional learning in areas that target system needs in literacy and numeracy. Many of these initiatives also support the use of collaborative teacher inquiry with the intention of moving away from system-wide professional development towards professional learning that is both job-embedded and focused on being more responsive to local needs (Ontario Ministry of Education, 2007a, 2010, 2014a, 2014b, 2014c, 2015).

Findings from Darling-Hammond (2000) "indicate that measures of teacher preparation and certification are by far the strongest correlates of student achievement in reading and mathematics, both before and after controlling for student poverty and language status." However, in Denmark, there have been limited studies that document a link between teacher subject specialisation and student outcomes. One study conducted by Calmar Andersen and Winter (2011) found no significant association between supplementary education to teachers and students' educational performance, however, they did find that it has a positive effect on students' wellbeing. They also found that collaboration and ongoing discussion among teachers about teaching and learning tended to be accompanied by higher student performance and wellbeing. This study provides support for job-embedded professional learning as one effective approach to responding to system needs.

National teacher and school leader profiles (see above and below) would help set clear expectations in this regard, both for teachers and their school leaders, and help gear school level planning processes to focus on this type of teacher learning and development. For teachers, it would communicate that teaches should continuously assess, review and improve their practices and build on peer observation, demonstration and feedback. For school leaders, it would communicate that it is one of their core responsibilities to help their staff develop in this way. Municipalities should set incentives and hold their school leaders accountable, and so should school leaders for their teachers. The national corps of learning consultants could support municipalities and schools to focus on this kind of learning.

Schools should also pay greater attention to the development of professional learning communities (within schools or across schools) and opportunities for mentoring to support job-embedded learning and development. Education systems such as Japan, Shanghai and Singapore use professional learning communities as a key vehicle for teacher growth and development, for example. Teachers work together to set learning goals, research and try new approaches, observe others, receive feedback, and assess evidence of impact in the school. Such groups tend to have strong leadership to guide others through the continuous improvement process (Jensen et al., 2012a). Professional learning communities could also help develop teachers' capacities for using assessment and data in a non-threatening environment.

As far as structured professional development is concerned, schools should make greater use of student assessment data and information from teacher appraisal to identify teacher development needs and goals. Stronger links between teacher appraisal and feedback, teacher professional development and school development will also depend on the extent to which Denmark is successful in strengthening the school leadership profession (more on this below).

Provide opportunities for teachers and school leaders to collaborate

Teachers

Teachers in Denmark are familiarising themselves with the Common Objectives that they teach towards and working to implement this outcome-based curriculum. Currently, they need more opportunities to work with other teachers at their level and in their subjects to come to a shared understanding of the meaning of the objectives, to understand how the national tests reflect the attainment of the objectives in each subject at each level and to explore and test teaching strategies to improve student competency overall. Why engage teachers as collaborative learners? Earl (2010) found that through collaborative inquiry, teachers integrate new knowledge and understanding of student learning and classroom instruction into their existing knowledge of professional practice. For those involved in inquiry, the process can serve to expand and refine their personal knowledge base about what it means to be a teacher (Earl, 2010). Collaboration enables learning from close observations of knowledge exchange and teaching exchanges and helps to build up trust and social capital in schools that enables the unlearning of old assumptions and habits, the development of new understandings and practices, and the possibility to solve collective action problems (Burns and Cerna, 2016). Opportunities for collaborative learning, then, have the potential to set teachers on a course of continuous improvement of their teaching practice related to the needs of the students in their classes and schools.

Hattie (2015) dispels the myth that one simple intervention can be defined and structured from near the top of the political system, but that rather a system focus on learning and an understanding of the type of teaching that supports student learning is required. Fullan et al. (2015) describe this work as building the professional capacity of teachers and define it as "human capacity (the quality of the individual), social capacity (the quality of the group) and decisional capital (the development of expertise and professional judgment of individuals and groups to make more and more effective decisions over time)". In order to engage in this type of work, teachers need time, the commitment of their school leaders to the process and to themselves engaging in the process, and the belief of their municipal leaders that this work will make the difference to student learning.

Providing more opportunities for this type of work (see Box 4.6 for teacher collaboration practices in Ontario, Canada) can be accomplished in many ways. As is done in Ontario, Canada, timetabling in schools can have teacher collaborative groups free from teaching duties at the same time for a period of time each week. This time can, then, be dedicated to collaborative inquiry and can be facilitated by teacher subject experts from the teaching staff. School leaders have the flexibility to assign teaching responsibilities so that this time is available. A school leader may decide that a particular group of teachers needs more time to focus on teaching and learning within their level and subjects and schedule slightly less teaching time to make a period for continued collaboration among those teachers over time. This would need to be based on the school improvement plan, as developed from the evidence of learning within the school. A group of teachers may also require expertise both in content (subject) and pedagogy (teaching strategies, etc.). In some schools this can be provided by staff teacher expertise, municipal consultants (if available) or also the ministry's corps of learning consultants. To facilitate greater collaboration and new working practices among teachers in Denmark, it will be key to support school leaders in the organisation and scheduling of time for staff and the differentiation of the workloads for teachers to perform specialised functions on top of regular classroom teaching roles. This could include training and the development of templates and examples for timetabling and scheduling.

England in the United Kingdom provides some examples for initiatives that use teacher collaboration and peer networks to engage teachers in research and to promote evidence-informed professionalism. Funding for school based research consortia and Networked Learning Communities were two successive, early national initiatives that had some success in building a networked infrastructure for the support of teacher use of research. Teaching Schools constitute a concept in more recent initiatives seeking to achieve similar momentum within a more self-directing system. The National Teacher Union's "Teacher2Teacher" programme provides a further interesting initiative (see Box 4.7) (Cordingley, 2016).

Schools and municipalities should also pay particular attention to collaboration between teachers and pedagogues to make the most of this additional resource. In kindergarten classrooms across Ontario, Canada, a team teaching model is supported where one classroom teacher and one early childhood educator (whose education and skills are quite similar to pedagogues) work together to provide a nurturing environment to support the unique needs of each student. Early childhood educators have training in observing,

Box 4.6. **Types of teacher collaboration in schools in Ontario, Canada**

1. Co-teaching classes – this process involves a pair of teachers to a small group of teachers co-planning a lesson, co-teaching that lesson with assigned roles and co-reflecting on the student learning outcomes of the learning experience, including naming evidence of the impact on student learning.
2. Teaching Learning Critical Pathway – a process of inquiry involving the gathering of data, its analysis to determine area of greatest need, identifying relevant curriculum, reviewing current practice, determine assessments to be used to monitor student learning, planning a teaching block of time (approximately six weeks), sharing evidence of student learning with other teachers, developing and administering a culminating task, engaging in teacher moderation of student work from the task and reflect on what has been learned, what the next steps are in teacher learning (see Teaching-Learning Critical Pathway, 2008).
3. Moderation of student work – is a process that involves educators in a collaborative discussion of student work based on common assessment criteria.
4. Deconstructing curriculum – examining curriculum expectations in order to understand what is written as it might be translated into what students learn.
5. Examining the student learning journey – deconstructing a curriculum concept from when a child enters schools through many grades or levels to understand what a student is expected to learn at each level of the system.
6. Monitoring marker students – pick a small number of students in a class, at a year level or in a school and share their assessment results with others in the school. Document the use of teaching strategies against the outcomes of learning for these students.
7. Review assessment data (data walls) – making more public the achievement data of marker students in a class, a grade or a school.
8. Teacher collaborative inquiry cycle – plan, act, observe and reflect – on teaching practice and learning outcomes of students.
9. Share and explore pedagogical documentation of student learning.

Source: Ontario Ministry of Education (2007b, 2008a, 2008b, 2010, 2013b, 2014a, 2014c, 2015), LearnTeachLead, *http://learnteachlead.ca/*.

Box 4.7. **The "Teacher2Teacher" programme to support teacher collaboration and networks to engage in research and to foster evidence-informed professionalism in England, United Kingdom**

At the beginning of the 21st century, the National Union of Teachers (NUT), the biggest English professional association at the time, developed a professionally-driven approach to build the capacity of teachers by engaging in and with research through networks involving both peers and researchers. The NUT's "Teacher2Teacher" programme involved pairs of teachers working together over a sustained period to develop and evaluate emerging practice based on intense working with leading edge researchers over 24 hours. The topics for "Teacher2Teacher" programmes arose from requests for NUT members, the views of NUT policy officers about system level issues causing teachers concern and the views if their substantial body of members who were also school leaders. Leading edge researchers were identified and recruited on the basis of their research publications and after considerable desk research and consultation across NUT's extensive network of researchers.

Box 4.7. **The "Teacher2Teacher" programme to support teacher collaboration and networks to engage in research and to foster evidence-informed professionalism in England, United Kingdom** *(cont.)*

During the initial 24-hour residential workshops teachers were immersed in illustrations of new approaches, in experimenting with tools and resources that nest them in classroom practices and in planning to experiment with them, over three cycles of experimentation and reflection that spanned roughly 12 weeks. During the initial residential, the teachers learned about the evidence about collaborative coaching and built structured, formal Learning Agreements. The objective was to shape their expectations of how they would work, the evidence they would collect about how their learning connected with student learning and the ways teachers would support each other's, sometimes quite different, projects. After approximately 12 weeks the teachers came together for another intense workshop focused on analysing how each other's experiments had worked, exploring together changes in student learning and work, photographs and videos of lessons, lesson plans and changes in their thinking and understanding. This reflection and analysis was facilitated by the original specialists. The final stage of the programme involved the teachers planning how to translate their own learning into learning experiences for their colleagues, role-playing the initial stages and considering how they would be able to i) continue their own learning as part of the process of supporting others and ii) how they would know their own and their colleagues' learning had been successful.

Some of these teachers went on to write up their learning experiences and others used this embedded form of engagement with and in research as a springboard for embarking on more explicit research for doctorate and master's degree programmes. NUT itself then established a series of scholarship projects focused on key NUT priorities such as Thinking Skills and improving the quality of talk which enabled teachers to progress to a more formal mode of engagement with and in research and several other "graduates" of these programmes subsequently supported and promoted teacher engagement in and with research by, for example, and serving as members of teacher research groups including the National Teacher Research Panel. During the first 10 years, NUT ran these programmes for between 8 and 12 different groups of teachers and focused on a wide range of different priorities. It is still continuing over a decade since it started, in this instance in relation to development education.

Source: Cordingley, P. (2016), "Knowledge and research use in local capacity building", in *Governing Education in a Complex World, http://dx.doi.org/10.1787/9789264255364-9-en.*

planning and supporting early learning that promotes each child's physical, cognitive, language, emotional, social and creative development and wellbeing; and teachers have training in elementary curriculum, assessment, evaluation and reporting, and child development (Ontario Ministry of Education, 2012). The OECD notes that many schools in Denmark are also using this model to support early learners with "integrated school start" programmes (OECD, 2006). While it may not always be possible to fund this team teaching model, the skills and expertise of pedagogues may be leveraged more explicitly in scheduling at the school level. The Danish government describes that activity lessons "may be planned and executed by teachers, other pedagogical staff or staff with other types of qualifications" (Danish Ministry of Children and Education, 2012). Activity lessons could be play-based, inquiry-based, or serve to support/supplement academic learning such as independent practice time with opportunities for homework assistance. Activities that focus on physical and mental health and wellbeing should also be encouraged. The structure could potentially include a model where teams of teachers could supervise students while others take time to co-plan and collaborate. Again, the Danish government notes that "schools must take advantage of whatever formation and grouping of classes best fit the different types of activities. The activity lessons could be planned across classes and form levels".

School leaders

The power of collaborative inquiry for school leaders is the opportunity to reflect on, investigate aspects of and improve their practice. In terms of teacher collaborative inquiry, research indicates that school leaders learning visibly and publicly alongside their staff in school is likely to have beneficial effects on teaching practice and enhanced student achievement (Katz and Dack, 2013). These are compelling reasons for school leaders to engage in collaborative inquiry, among themselves in networks, but also with the staff of their schools.

Recent research highlights the importance of school leader groups engaging in their own collaborative inquiry. Kasl and Yorks (2010) demonstrate the difference between traditional inquiry questions posed by school leaders to teachers, and questions focused on school leaders' own individual learning. For example, a traditional inquiry question posed by principals might be more likely to highlight what teachers will do: "How can we improve the way that teachers use technology in the classroom?" In contrast, the question posed by the same group with a focus on their own learning would be, "How can we improve our ability as administrators to influence the way that teachers use technology in the classroom?" The difference between the two questions "may seem minor", but, in fact, "points to a radical distinction". The first implies that administrators are "taking action on the system", while the second suggests "that the change they seek is in themselves" (Kasl and Yorks, 2010). According to City et al. (2009), it is important that school leaders individually develop their own theory of action, but it is equally important that they shape their inquiry so it "relates concretely to the work of teachers and students in the classroom" (City et al., 2009). Powerful connections to the school's professional community are formed when a principal's inquiry is parallel to and in support of teacher and student learning and inquiry (Katz, 2013).

What applies to school leaders working with teachers also applies to municipal education leaders regarding participating with groups of school leaders in their collaborative inquiries around their practice. These same municipal leaders could capitalise on the networking opportunities they have established in order to conduct their own collaborative inquiries based on their practice with school leaders and schools. The same principles apply and the same benefits can accrue.

It is recommended that municipal education leaders provide time and facilitation for school leader learning teams to come together and collaborate concerning the issues of school organisation, differentiated staffing and scheduling. The first phase of this collaboration may need to be support for school leaders in identifying within their data what student needs are evident and need addressing. School leaders then need an opportunity to work in teams with leaders with similar school needs to share strategies and problem solve regarding the needs identified. Over the course of a school year the work would need to focus on monitoring strategies to gauge effectiveness of addressing the needs identified. Performance management processes that involve peer-evaluators and school self-evaluations that involve critical friends can also provide opportunities for school leaders to learn from each other as long as school leaders are prepared and trained for such roles (OECD, 2013b).

The London Challenge and City Challenge initiatives in England, United Kingdom, provide a concrete example for encouraging school to school and school leader collaboration and learning (Box 4.4). The various activities and interventions of these initiatives were built around a belief that school-to-school collaboration has a central role to play in school improvement; the recognition of the importance of school leadership; and a belief in the usefulness of data-rich approaches to tackling issues and sharing learning. As an evaluation of the City Challenge programme by Hutchings et al. (2012) suggests, arrangements that enabled school leaders and teachers to share effective practice proved to be extremely beneficial. These included conferences at which practice was shared; a stronger school supporting a weaker one; groups of three schools led by the principal of a more successful school; "Families of Schools" which had similar intakes; hub schools or knowledge centres; and the Improving and Outstanding Teacher Programmes. Both principals and teachers argued that they learned most effectively from seeing good practice or hearing about it from those who had undertaken it. The most effective strategies to improve teaching and learning took place in schools, and involved observing excellent teaching; opportunities to reflect with colleagues; and coaching in the teacher's own classroom. This sector-led approach to school improvement was of benefit not only to the recipient schools but also to home schools since the partnership relationships created an enhanced environment for reflection on school effectiveness. However, as Baars et al. (2014) suggest, school-to-school support requires careful management. In particular, local and national leaders of education as consultant leaders needed very careful selection, training and quality assurance, as there is no guarantee that a good principal will make for a good consultant leader. Box 4.8 provides further specific examples for ways to encourage and facilitate collaboration between school leaders and schools in the Flemish Community of Belgium and New Zealand.

Box 4.8. **Networks for schools and school leaders**

Flemish Community of Belgium

In 1999, the authorities of the Flemish Community of Belgium launched a policy to encourage school collaboration through the establishment of "school associations" (*scholengemeenschappen*) in secondary education. From 2003, school associations were also introduced in the primary sector. School associations are collaborative partnerships between schools in the same geographical area. On average, school associations comprise between 6 and 12 schools. In 2010, the vast majority of schools (96.7%) belonged to a school community, and most of the schools that have not joined a school community provided special needs education. The key goal of this initiative is to strengthen schools' organisational and leadership capacities through increased co-operation. In secondary education, the policy also aims to improve the co-operation of schools in the supply of study options, career guidance and efficient use of resources. Joining a school association is voluntary, but the Flemish Ministry of Education and Training provides incentives for schools to join an association by attributing resources to the association, and granting more organisational flexibility in the case of secondary schools. School associations receive a package of points for the management and support staff in their schools, which are then redistributed among the individual schools in the community based on a repartition system agreed between the schools forming the community. In elementary education, some of these points may be used to appoint a co-ordinating director of the school community, and in secondary education, the school community can retain up to 10% of the points to ensure its own functioning.

Source: Nusche, D. et al. (2015), *OECD Reviews of School Resources: Flemish Community of Belgium 2015, http://dx.doi.org/10.1787/9789264247598-en.*

Box 4.8. **Networks for schools and school leaders** *(cont.)*

New Zealand

New Zealand has initiated "Learning and Change Networks" to establish a web of knowledge-sharing networks among schools, families, teachers, leaders, communities, professional providers and the Ministry of Education. Network participants work collaboratively to accelerate student achievement in Years 1 to 8 and to address equity issues. Learning and Change Networks address three big agenda items – schooling improvement, blended learning and digital technologies, and cultural responsiveness – holistically instead of creating projects that deal with those agendas separately. Design work on the strategy commenced in October 2011 and five pilot networks representing 55 schools (*kura*) were established. The strategy went live in October 2012 with 57 networks established involving 373 schools (*kura*) (approximately 15% of New Zealand schools [*kura*]), with an average of 6 to 7 schools per network. There is a particular focus on priority groups traditionally under-served by the system – Māori, Pasifika, those from lower socio-economic groups, and those with special education needs – along with their families (*whānau*), teachers, school and community leaders. As some of the distinctive features, Learning and Change Networks put an explicit and prominent focus on an applied theory of making professional learning communities and networks work so as to achieve outcomes that individual schools and teachers cannot readily do by themselves and on a sophisticated set of leadership and management arrangements that puts the onus on action and change on the networks and their members, while embedding these in regional and national structures of support. A central role is given to evaluation, generating learning evidence at school, network, regional and system levels and a strong connection to international experience and networks. Learning and Change Networks also recognise the importance of engaging learners, their parents, families (*whānau*) and communities in powerful learning-focused partnerships.

Source: OECD (2015b), *Schooling Redesigned: Towards Innovative Learning Systems*, *http://dx.doi.org/10.1787/9789264245914-en*.

Support the development of effective teaching through systematic formal and informal teacher feedback and appraisal

The effective monitoring and appraisal of teaching is central to the continuous improvement of schools. It can be a key lever to increase the focus on teaching quality and continuous professional learning for teachers, in line with a widespread recognition of the impact of teaching performance on student learning outcomes. It can help teachers develop their competencies by recognising strengths on which they can build and identifying weaknesses to be addressed by suitable professional development (OECD, 2013b). While there are local appraisal practices in Denmark, there is significant potential to further develop formal teacher appraisal systems and informal teacher feedback in schools and municipalities. This is a recommendation that should be developed concurrently with recommendations on teacher and school leader collaboration as just described and on the development of pedagogical school leadership as elaborated further below.

Formal appraisal and feedback

It is recommended that Denmark strengthen formal teacher performance appraisal focused on the continuous improvement of teaching practice. Teacher appraisal would serve both as a form of developmental feedback for teachers and as a mechanism for feedback for schools, municipalities and potentially the Ministry for Children, Education and Gender Equality on the effective use of targeted funds for teacher development. In a previous OECD review of evaluation and assessment in Denmark, Shewbridge et al. (2011) provided some directions for how this could be accomplished. As Shewbridge et al. suggested, developmental appraisal could be a school-internal process carried out by line managers, senior peers, and the school principal (or members of the management group). It could draw on the professional teaching standards that Denmark once these have been developed, but also take school-based indicators and criteria as well as school objectives and contexts into account. It can be low-key and low-cost, and include self-appraisal, peer appraisal, classroom observation, and structured conversations and regular feedback by the school principal and experienced peers. It could be organised once a year for each teacher, or less frequently depending on the previous assessment by the teacher. The main outcome would be specific feedback on teaching performance as well as on the overall contribution to the school which would lead to a plan for professional development. Such a system would need to go hand in hand with a shift in school culture towards continuous improvement based on student learning. Guidelines for schools could be provided as part of a practical toolkit for all aspects of school evaluation (Chapter 3).

A large degree of local autonomy to develop and implement formal teacher appraisal can help generate trust, commitment and professionalism and encourage collaborative practices (OECD, 2013b). At the same time, as pointed out in the sections on challenges, there are concerns about the lack of systematic teacher appraisal practices at the local level. Teachers in Denmark are entirely dependent on local capacity and willingness to benefit from appraisal and feedback to improve their practice. In order to guarantee the systematic and coherent application of developmental evaluation across Danish schools, it would, therefore, be important to undertake the external validation of the respective school processes. Municipalities have a key role to play in ensuring that schools develop effective developmental appraisal processes (e.g. by auditing school-level processes, holding school leadership accountable, and documenting practices in biannual quality reports) (Shewbridge et al., 2011). The development of a national sample programme of external reviews of schools through the Ministry for Children, Education and Gender Equality could be a further instrument of external validation (see Chapter 3). The new corps of learning consultants can provide a further source of support to municipalities and schools for the development of effective formal internal teacher appraisal. Municipalities and schools should also be encouraged to co-operate and disseminate good practice through networks and partnerships to build capacity across the system (OECD, 2013b).

An alternative approach entails the introduction of stronger national parameters and regulations that suggest a range of tools and guidelines for implementation of formal teacher appraisal. To give an example from another school system, the province of Ontario, Canada, has developed a Teacher Performance Appraisal System based on the "Standards of Practice for the Teaching Profession" (Box 4.5). Under this legislated requirement school boards are responsible for having the principal of each school complete two performance appraisals for each new teacher during the first year of employment. One formal performance appraisal is required for each experienced teacher the first year they enter the board and once each five years thereafter. The ministry provides many resources for boards and principals as they plan this support for teacher development. The requirements and the resources and supports are available at the ministry's website (*www.edu.gov.on.ca/eng/teacher/appraise.html*). Concurrent with this appraisal system and linked to it Ontario teachers complete an annual learning plan (ALP) each year which includes the teacher's professional growth objectives, proposed action plan, and timelines for achieving those objectives. This is linked to a teacher's performance appraisal in years where formal appraisals occur.

Support for new teachers

As noted in the challenges section, support for beginning teachers varies considerably across the Danish education system. Most often reported was that these teachers' needs were taken into consideration by the school leader. This support often involved varying their teaching assignments somewhat along with appointing expert teachers in the school to work with new teachers to support their development. These relationships between new and expert or highly experienced teachers could be a significant source of feedback for new teachers if there is time for observing the new teacher while they are teaching or co-planning and co-teaching lessons with the new teacher. Feedback and plans for professional learning can be part of the reflection process.

In Ontario, the "New Teacher Induction Program" (NTIP) is both required by legislation and supported financially by the Ontario Ministry of Education. It provides a variety of supports for new teachers, including: orientation for all new teachers by the school and school board; mentoring for new teachers by experienced teachers; on-the-job training in areas such as classroom management; communication with parents; and other activities aligned with current ministry initiatives. For more information, see the ministry's website (*www.edu.gov.on.ca/eng/teacher/induction.html*).

Informal teacher feedback

When a culture of learning and continuous improvement is established in a school, a group of schools or a municipality there are many ways for teachers to receive informal feedback aimed at improving their teaching practice. School leaders would often be engaged in classrooms in the school giving feedback to teachers on observations made. If teachers are engaged in a series of co-planned, co-taught lessons they critique their own teaching, the lesson they planned and provide feedback to their co-teacher on their teaching. If a teacher is assigned to work part of the time with an expert or coach on staff they would receive continuous feedback for improvement throughout these lessons. Most collaborative teacher activities mentioned earlier in this chapter include an element of feedback to teachers and quite often teacher self-assessment of their practice. Setting an expectation of continuous improvement through standards of practice for the profession would help put the conditions in place that encourage teachers to reflect on their practice. Strengthening pedagogical leadership in schools, which should include improving school leaders' skills for classroom observation, feedback and coaching, and encouraging the further distribution of leadership and teacher leadership would also help establish informal feedback in schools, including from teachers' peers.

Develop the school leadership profession and provide systematic support for school leaders and their deputies

As research has established, school leaders' actions and practices are an important contributor to student learning, directly after the impact of the teacher's actions in the classroom. Considering the small size of the school leadership profession, measures that target this group can, furthermore constitute highly cost-effective measures for improving teaching and learning in schools (Pont et al., 2008; Day et al., 2009; Louis et al., 2010).

In Denmark's decentralised education system, school leadership plays a particularly important role. School principals and their deputies have a broad range of responsibilities for the effective functioning of their schools. School leaders are responsible for all aspects of the school budget, school staffing (including administrative and care taking staffing), maintenance and operation of the school facility, parent and community outreach and consultation, teacher professional learning, teacher performance appraisal and feedback, and pedagogical leadership. The changes the Danish school system is currently undergoing as a result of initiatives like the 2014 *Folkeskole* reform, the introduction of a new framework for the utilisation of teachers' working time, and the inclusion of children with special needs, among others, further increase the importance of school leadership. A number of the policy options just described to develop the teaching profession (e.g. the planning of teacher professional learning, teacher collaboration and teacher feedback and appraisal) depend to a great extent on effective leadership.

Denmark should, therefore, pay particular attention to the development and management of its school leadership profession, from recruitment and initial training to professional development and evaluation/performance management. This includes both the Ministry for Children, Education and Gender Equality and the individual municipalities as the employers of school leaders. A few education systems have developed comprehensive school leadership development strategies that could inspire new initiatives in Denmark (see Box 4.9). Both municipalities and schools should be supported to develop school leaders' skills and practices, for instance through the Ministry of Children, Education and Gender Equality (and its learning consultant corps), LGDK, or others. Denmark's school leader association should be thoroughly involved in the process of developing the profession.

Box 4.9. Comprehensive school leadership development strategies

New Zealand

New Zealand has invested considerably in developing school leadership competencies across its education system. New Zealand's school leadership improvement efforts include a research-based model of effective pedagogical leadership, the Kiwi Leadership for Principals framework; the Educational Leadership Practices survey, a formative tool to help school principals analyse their leadership in schools; and a Professional Leadership Plan offering professional development opportunities for school principals at different stages of their career.

Source: OECD (2013b), *Synergies for Better Learning: An International Perspective on Evaluation and Assessment*, *http://dx.doi.org/10.1787/9789264190658-en*; New Zealand Ministry of Education (2016), Educational Leaders, *www.educationalleaders.govt.nz* (accessed 4 February 2016).

Ontario, Canada

The province of Ontario, Canada, has identified successful school and system leadership as a core element of its efforts to achieve the province's three core educational goals: i) high levels of student achievement; ii) reduced gaps in student achievement; and iii) increased public confidence in publicly funded education. To this end, Ontario has developed and implemented a comprehensive school and system leadership strategy, the Ontario Leadership Strategy (OLS), to support student achievement and wellbeing by attracting and developing skilled and passionate school and system leaders. As part of this strategy, several tools and support mechanisms (e.g. The Ontario Leadership Framework 2012, and Core Leadership Capacities) have been developed to streamline and focus efforts to support

Box 4.9. **Comprehensive school leadership development strategies** *(cont.)*

school principals and vice-principals, to refine leadership skills and to put advanced leadership concepts and practices to work on a daily basis to meet educational targets and achieve concrete results. A province-wide Principal/Vice-Principal Performance Appraisal (PPA) system focused on goals that promote student achievement and wellbeing constitutes a key component of the OLS. It is designed to support the strategy's two overarching goals: i) to attract competent people to school leadership roles; and ii) to develop the best possible instructional leaders.

Source: OECD (2013b), *Synergies for Better Learning: An International Perspective on Evaluation and Assessment, http://dx.doi.org/10.1787/9789264190658-en*; Institute for Educational Leadership (2013), *The Ontario Leadership Framework 2012, A School and System Leader's Guide to Putting Ontario's Leadership Framework into Action, http://iel.immix.ca/storage/6/1345688999/Final_User_Guide_EN.pdf*; Ontario Ministry of Education (2016b), Leadership development, *www.edu.gov.on.ca/eng/policyfunding/leadership/index.html* (accessed 4 February 2016).

The first step in the further development of the profession should be the creation of a framework to guide the work of school leaders (both formal school leaders and informal teacher leaders) (see Box 4.10 for examples). Such a framework, which should be collaboratively developed with the school leaders' association, would serve to:

- Facilitate a shared vision of leadership in schools.
- Promote a common language that fosters an understanding of leadership and what it means to be a school leader.
- Identify the practices, actions, and traits or personal characteristics that describe effective leadership.
- Guide the design and implementation of professional learning and development for school leaders.
- Aid in the recruitment, development, selection and retention of school leaders.

Box 4.10. **Professional school leadership standards**

Chile

In Chile, different sets of school leadership standards provide guidance for school leaders about the role they should fulfil. In a shift from the traditionally administrative and managerial role of school leaders, all of these frameworks and standards emphasise school leaders' role as pedagogical leaders. A first set of standards, the Good School Leadership Framework (*Marco para la Buena Dirección*) published in 2005 was updated with a new set of standards in 2015 (*Marco para la Buena Dirección y el Liderazgo Escolar*). The new school leadership standards have been designed to support school leaders in their self-reflection, self-evaluation and professional development; to establish a common language around school leadership that facilitates reflection of school leadership within the school community; to guide the initial preparation and professional development of school leaders; to provide a reference for the recruitment and evaluation of school leaders; to facilitate the identification of effective school leaders and to spread good practices; and to promote shared expectations about school leadership and provide a reference for professional learning. They are not prescriptive, but should be a common reference for adaptation to local contexts. To reflect the contextual nature of school leadership, the standards distinguish conceptually between practices and competencies, and describe

Box 4.10. **Professional school leadership standards** *(cont.)*

practices, personal resources, competencies and knowledge that form the basis of successful school leadership. Practices entail five dimensions: i) constructing and implementing a shared strategic vision; ii) developing professional competencies; iii) leading processes of teaching and learning; iv) managing the school climate and the participation of the school community; and v) developing and managing the school. Personal resources comprise three areas: i) ethical values; ii) behavioural and technical competencies; and iii) professional knowledge.

Source: Santiago, P. et al. (forthcoming), *OECD Reviews of School Resources: Chile*, OECD Publishing, Paris.

Victoria, Australia

The state of Victoria, Australia, has developed a Developmental Learning Framework for School Leaders, as a fundamental element of its 2006 Learning to Lead Effective Schools strategy. The framework is intended to strengthen the leadership skills of school principals and teachers. It can be used in various ways, e.g. for self-assessment, performance and development reviews, school leader selection, coaching and mentoring and leadership induction and planning. The Victoria leadership framework breaks new ground in being applicable to leadership throughout the school at all levels in the school, showing where a teacher or school leader is located on a leadership continuum and what they need to know and be able to do in order to improve. As such, the Victoria framework is based on the core belief that leadership is learnable. The framework describes development within five leadership domains: i) technical; ii) human; iii) educational; iv) symbolic; and v) cultural. Within each of these leadership domains, the framework lays out typically five progressive levels of competency and related capabilities. It defines what effective leadership looks like in practice at each of the different stages of development and growth and provides a clear direction about what it means to develop as a leader.

Source: OECD (2013b), *Synergies for Better Learning: An International Perspective on Evaluation and Assessment*, *http://dx.doi.org/10.1787/9789264190658-en*; Department of Education Victoria (2007), The Developmental Learning Framework for School Leaders, *www.education.vic.gov.au/Documents/school/principals/profdev/developmentallearn.pdf.*

New Zealand

New Zealand has developed a Kiwi Leadership for Principals (KLP) model that provides a statement of the expectations of school principals. Built on a core conceptualisation of educational leadership and stressing the need of building effective relationships as well as school leaders' attention to their particular contexts, KLP defines Leading Change and Problem-Solving as the two key leadership areas for school principals. The KLP model, further, identifies four areas of practice (culture; pedagogy; system; partnerships and networks) to reach these two objectives. Four educational leadership qualities underpin school leaders' ability to lead their schools: *manaakitanga* (leading with moral purpose), *pono* (having self-belief), *ako* (being a learner), and *awhinatanga* (guiding and supporting). In alignment with this leadership framework, two sets of professional standards for primary and secondary school principals provide a baseline for assessing satisfactory performance within each area of practice (culture; pedagogy; system; partnerships and networks). New Zealand has been in the process of developing two further parts of the overall leadership strategy: Kiwi Leadership for Senior and Middle Leaders and Leadership for Māori-medium Leaders.

Source: OECD (2013b), *Synergies for Better Learning: An International Perspective on Evaluation and Assessment*, *http://dx.doi.org/10.1787/9789264190658-en*; New Zealand Ministry of Education (2008), *Kiwi Leadership for Principals, Principals as Educational Leaders*, *www.educationalleaders.govt.nz/content/download/45029/377177/file/Kiwi%20Leadership%20for%20Principals%20(2008).pdf.*

Considering the importance of pedagogical leadership for teaching and learning, the framework should have a clear focus on competencies related to this leadership style, but also recognise that successful school leadership is always context-dependent (OECD, 2013b, Pont et al., 2008). Once it has been developed, a Danish leadership framework could serve as a basis for continued collaboration among school leaders, as a reference point for school leadership consultants, as a catalyst for the development of personal learning objectives with a learning plan for individual school leaders and a basis for reflection and introspection on the part of individual school leaders.

Denmark should also consider developing a more strategic approach to the training of school leaders. The ministry's plan to introduce a national programme for the training of principals and the provision of funding for the training of school leaders as part of the 2014 *Folkeskole* reform point into the right direction. Although the research evidence on the impact of training and development on school leaders is limited, the effective preparation and ongoing training of school leaders is essential to enable school leaders to be successful in such a challenging role. Research suggests that leadership development should ideally be a continuum and be available at and targeted to the different stages of a school leaders' career. This is not yet the case in Denmark. Training should ideally begin with teachers and continue for beginning as well as long-standing school principals. Taster courses can help identify and prepare future school leaders. As just highlighted, opportunities for collaboration, coaching and mentoring between school leaders can also provide useful support and enable school leaders to gain new expertise (Pont et al., 2008). England, United Kingdom, provides an example for a more strategic approach at school leadership development that targets school leaders at different stages of their career. The Department for Education introduced new National Professional Qualifications for head teachers, senior school leaders and middle leaders. In addition, the department provides funding for targeted programmes that seek to develop excellent middle and senior leaders that work in challenging schools. The Teaching Leaders charity works to improve the quality of subject and year-group leaders of schools in disadvantaged communities. The Future Leaders charity seeks to develop the leadership skills of teachers who want to work as head teachers in disadvantaged communities. A Talented Leaders programme seeks to recruit outstanding school leaders for areas that face recruitment challenges. These programmes act as a pipeline for young, aspiring school heads who want to gain leadership responsibility, and are keen to do so in those schools that need them the most.[4]

The wide range of tasks and responsibilities that school leaders are often expected to fulfil bear a risk of placing too high expectation on school leaders (Pont et al., 2008). School leaders interviewed by the OECD review team in Denmark expressed concerns that some of the management aspects of their diverse roles within their school limited their ability to focus on student learning and teacher practice affecting student learning. This is similar to other countries in which school leaders hold a large degree of autonomy for the management of their school. In such contexts, it is especially important that school leaders have the support they need from their employer as well as distributed leadership structures. During the review visit, some municipalities reported that support for some of the more managerial roles was being co-ordinated at the municipal level so that school leaders had more time to concentrate on the teaching and learning environment and practice in their schools as expected of them in the 2014 *Folkeskole* reform. The aim of these changes was to still allow flexibility at the school level to meet the particular needs of the learning community while at the same time removing some tasks from the role of the school leader. Such approaches could be useful to enable school leaders to focus on their pedagogical leadership role and should be shared between municipalities. As Shewbridge et al. (2011) already pointed out, the concept of shared leadership also needs to be more firmly embedded in schools, to support existing principals and allow them to concentrate on their pedagogical role.

Further developing school leader performance management in municipalities is another area for possible policy development. While the evidence base on school leader appraisal is still rather limited, effective performance management can ensure that school leaders themselves receive external feedback and targeted support to improve practice. Individual appraisal constitutes a tool to set clear expectations and to hold principals accountable for their performance (OECD, 2013b; Radinger, 2014). The Danish Ministry for Children, Education and Gender Equality could consider providing further support and materials for municipalities on how to organise school leader appraisal effectively that does not add to school leaders' workload and stress levels, but that is a meaningful exercise. These materials could form part of a comprehensive national toolkit for school evaluation suggested in Chapter 3, which does not necessarily preclude the possibility that municipalities might elect to use their own alternative approaches, or perhaps adapt and customise the national approach to suit their own circumstances. Municipalities could be encouraged to work together to ensure sufficient capacity to implement good appraisal processes, to learn from each other and to share best practices.

Support effective teaching and learning for all students in a context of inclusion

As the inclusion of students with special educational needs is becoming the norm in Denmark, one recommended strategy in supporting effective learning in diverse classrooms is for regular school to partner with centres of excellence in working with children of differing exceptionalities. These organisations would likely be able to highlight effective inclusive practices and resources for teachers to maximise the learning and development for students with special educational needs. Both municipal and regional special schools can play a key role in this process by taking on a new function of supporting both students with special needs being educated inclusively in regular schools and teachers providing inclusive education in these schools. Drawing on the experience and expertise of teachers from special needs schools is also important when planning transitions from special schools into the regular school system. This would involve leveraging support and information provided by staff who has previously worked with the student.

Turning special schools into methodological centres providing support to mainstream schools, however, is a highly complex process of institutional change. The process requires serious adaptive capacities from special needs professionals and schools and it can be implemented only slowly and gradually through pilot development projects based on voluntary participation and through spreading successful practices. The example of countries, such as Germany, where the number of special schools is high, and the growing demand for mainstream placements has led to rethink the role of special schools' staff, might be relevant for Denmark. In Germany an increasing number of special schools' teachers are spending part of their working time in mainstream schools not only directly supporting children but also providing consultancy to class teachers (NESSE, 2012). The process of transforming the function of special schools could also draw on Denmark's participation in the work of the European Agency for Special Needs and Inclusive Education which collected a significant amount of experience and examples of good practice in the field of turning schools into institutions that are capable of providing genuine inclusive education. Expertise in services like VISO (*Videns- og Specialrådgivningsorganisation* – Specialised Knowledge and Counselling Organisation) and municipal PPRs (*Pædagogisk Psykologisk Rådgivning* – Local Educational-Psychological Advisory Services) also has a key role to play in facilitating the inclusion process in regular schools and these services should be easily accessible to municipalities and schools. Learning from other sectors of the education sector with long-standing experience of inclusion, like early childhood education and care, as well as channels for schools and municipalities to share promising practices and knowledge could constitute further mechanisms to support inclusion.

Professional learning for educators is an essential and ongoing next step. Professional learning around how to adapt Common Objectives and learning goals for students with special needs is one area to focus on in Denmark (also see Chapter 3). In diverse classrooms, it is particularly important that teachers use multiple methods and pathways to achieve learning goals, because no single method will be able to reach all students. An example from Ontario, Canada, may serve well to highlight success with inclusionary practices for students with special education needs. In 1998, Ontario legislation (Reg. 181) was enacted to ensure that "the first consideration regarding the placement of an 'exceptional pupil' be placement in a regular classroom with appropriate supports, when such placement meets the student's needs and is in accordance with parents' wishes". Today, classrooms in Ontario are filled with students with diverse learning needs. A universal design for learning (UDL) approach is one that reflects a belief that teaching strategies, instructional resources, tools, and accommodations that are used to support students with special needs, may also be beneficial for all learners (Ontario Ministry of Education, 2013a).

The synthesis of available evidence and research and practice in Denmark regarding successful inclusive practices and goal-oriented teaching for students with SEN, for example through a thematic review carried out by the Ministry for Children, Education and Gender Equality or the Danish Evaluation Institute (EVA) could be a further element to support inclusion (see Chapter 3).

Notes

1. Denmark reported actual teaching time, that is the annual average number of hours that full-time teachers teach a group or a class of students, including overtime, while most OECD countries reported statutory teaching time.
2. According to TALIS 2013, 36.3% of lower secondary teachers reported that their education had only included content of some of the subjects they were teaching (TALIS average: 22.6%). Similarly, 35.3% of lower secondary teachers reported that their education had included pedagogy for some of the subjects they were teaching (TALIS average: 22.7%) and practice in some of the subjects they were teaching (TALIS average: 22.0%) (OECD, 2014b).
3. While the number of student hours per year is regulated, municipalities are free to decide to have a longer school year and less vacation. The schedules are decided at the school level with a high degree of variation.
4. For further information see *www.gov.uk/government/publications/2010-to-2015-government-policy-teaching-and-school-leadership/2010-to-2015-government-policy-teaching-and-school-leadership*. The website of the Teaching Leaders charity can be accessed here *www.teachingleaders.org.uk*; the website of the Future Leaders trust is available here *www.future-leaders.org.uk*.

References

Baars, S. et al. (2014), *Lessons from London Schools: Investigating the Success*, CfBT Education Trust, Centre for London, LKMco. Ltd., Reading, London, Cambridge, *http://centreforlondon.org/publication/lessons-london-schools*.

BUPL (2016), *Pedagogy in Denmark – a Danish Concept*, *www.bupl.dk/english/pedagogy_in_dk?opendocument*.

Burns, T. and L. Cerna (2016), "Enhancing effective education governance", in *Governing Education in a Complex World*, OECD Publishing, Paris, *http://dx.doi.org/10.1787/9789264255364-13-en*.

Calmar Andersen, S. and S.C. Winter (eds.) (2011), *Ledelse, Læring og Trivsel i Folkesko-Lerne (Rapport 11:47)* [Leadership, Learning and Wellbeing in Schools (Report 11:47)], *SFI – Det Nationale Forskningscenter for Velfærd* [SFI – The National Centre for Social Research], Copenhagen, *https://pure.sfi.dk/ws/files/254638/1147_Ledelse_laering_trivsel.pdf*.

City, E. et al. (2009), *Instructional Rounds in Education: A Network Approach to Improving Teaching and Learning*, Harvard Education Press, Cambridge, MA.

Cordingley, P. (2016), "Knowledge and research use in local capacity building", in *Governing Education in a Complex World*, OECD Publishing, Paris, *http://dx.doi.org/10.1787/9789264255364-9-en*.

Danish Ministry of Children and Education (2012), *How to Make a Good School Even Better – An Improvement of the Standards in the Danish Public School*, Danish Ministry of Children and Education, Copenhagen, *www.eng.uvm.dk/~/media/UVM/Filer/English/PDF/130325%20How%20to%20make%20a%20good%20school%20even%20better.pdf*.

Darling-Hammond, L. (2000), "Teacher quality and student achievement", *Education policy analysis archives*, Vol. 8 (1), Arizona State University, AZ.

Day, C. et al. (2009), *The Impact of School Leadership on Pupil Outcomes: Final Report*, University of Nottingham, *http://dera.ioe.ac.uk/11329/1/DCSF-RR108.pdf*.

DCUM (2016), *Leksikon: AKT*, Danish Centre of Educational Environment, *http://dcum.dk/undervisningsmiljoe/akt*.

Department of Education Victoria (2007), The Developmental Learning Framework for School Leaders, *www.education.vic.gov.au/Documents/school/principals/profdev/developmentallearn.pdf*.

Earl, L. (2010),"Educators as knowledge leaders", in J. Robertson and H. Temperley (eds.), *Leadership and Learning*, Sage Publishing, Thousand Oaks, CA.

European Commission/EACEA/Eurydice (2015), *The Teaching Profession in Europe: Practices, Perceptions, and Policies*, Publications Office of the European Union, Luxembourg, *https://webgate.ec.europa.eu/fpfis/mwikis/eurydice/index.php/Publications:The_Teaching_Profession_in_Europe:_Practices,_Perceptions,_and_Policies*.

Eurydice (2016), *European Encyclopedia on National Education Systems: Denmark, Eurypedia*, Eurydice, *https://webgate.ec.europa.eu/fpfis/mwikis/eurydice/index.php/Denmark:Redirect*.

Følgegruppen for ny læreruddannelse (2012), *Deregulering og Internationalisering – Evaluering og Anbefalinger om Læreruddannelsen af 2006* [Deregulation and Internationalisation – Evaluation and Recommendations on Teacher Education 2006], *Følgegruppen for ny læreruddannelse* [Follow-up Group for New Teacher Education], *Uddannelses- og Forskningsministeriets* [Ministries for Education and Research], Copenhagen, *www.ft.dk/samling/20111/almdel/fiv/bilag/93/1066885.pdf*.

Fullan, M., S. Rincon-Gallardo and A. Hargreaves (2015), "Professional capital as accountability", *Education Policy Analysis Archives*, Vol. 23(15), Arizona State University.

Hattie, J. (2015), *What Works Best in Education: The Politics of Collaborative Expertise*, Open Ideas at Pearson, Pearson, London.

Hattie, J. (2012), *Visible Learning for Teachers: Maximizing Impact on Learning*, Routledge, London, New York.

Hattie, J. (2009), *Visible Learning: A Synthesis of Over 800 Meta-Analyses Relating to Achievement*, Routledge, London, New York.

Higher Education Quality Council of Ontario (2016), HEQCO Website, *www.heqco.ca/Pages/wel.aspx* (accessed 4 February 2016).

Hooge, E. (2016), "Making multiple school accountability work", in *Governing Education in a Complex World*, OECD Publishing, Paris, *http://dx.doi.org/10.1787/9789264255364-7-en*.

Houlberg, K. et al. (2016), *OECD Review of Policies to Improve the Effectiveness of Resource Use in Schools: Country Background Report for Denmark, Det Nationale Institut for Kommuners og Regioners Analyse og*

Forskning (KORA) [Danish Institute for Local and Regional Government Research], Copenhagen, *www.oecd.org/edu/school/10932_OECD%20Country%20Background%20Report%20Denmark.pdf.*

Hutchings, M. et al. (2012), *Evaluation of the City Challenge Programme*, Institute for Policy Studies in Education, London Metropolitan University, London, *www.gov.uk/government/publications/evaluation-of-the-city-challenge-programme.*

Institute for Educational Leadership (2013), *The Ontario Leadership Framework 2012, A School and System Leader's Guide to Putting Ontario's Leadership Framework into Action,* Toronto, ON, *http://iel.immix.ca/storage/6/1345688999/Final_User_Guide_EN.pdf.*

Jensen, B. et al. (2012a), *Catching Up: Learning from the Best School Systems in East Asia*, Grattan Institute, Melbourne, *http://grattan.edu.au/wp-content/uploads/2014/04/129_report_learning_from_the_best_main.pdf.*

Jensen, B. et al. (2012b), *The Experience of New Teachers: Results from TALIS 2008*, OECD Publishing, Paris, *http://dx.doi.org/10.1787/9789264120952-en.*

Kasl, E. and L. Yorks (2010), "Whose inquiry is this anyway? Money, power, reports and collaborative inquiry", *Adult Education*, Vol. 60(4), Sage Publications, Thousand Oaks, CA.

Katz, S. (2013), *Leaders in Educational Thought*, Ontario Ministry of Education, Toronto, ON, *http://learnteachlead.ca/project_category/leaders-in-educational-thought.*

Katz, S. and L. Dack (2013), *Intentional Interruption: Breaking Down Learning Barriers to Transform Professional Practice,* Corwin, Thousand Oaks, CA.

Kidson, M. and E. Norris (2014), *Implementing the London Challenge*, Institute for Government, London, *www.instituteforgovernment.org.uk/sites/default/files/publications/Implementing%20the%20London%20Challenge%20-%20final_0.pdf.*

Louis, K.S. et al. (2010), *Investigating the Links to Improved Student Learning – Final Report of Research Findings*, University of Minnesota, University of Toronto, a report commissioned by the Wallace Foundation, *www.wallacefoundation.org/knowledge-center/school-leadership/keyresearch/Documents/Investigating-the-Links-to-Improved-Student-Learning.pdf.*

Musset, P. (2010), "Initial Teacher Education and Continuing Training Policies in a Comparative Perspective: Current Practices in OECD Countries and a Literature Review on Potential Effects", *OECD Education Working Papers*, No. 48, OECD Publishing, Paris, *http://dx.doi.org/10.1787/5kmbphh7s47h-en.*

NESSE (2012), "Education and disability/special needs: policies and practices in education, training and employment for students with disabilities and special educational needs in the EU", an independent report prepared for the European Commission by the NESSE network of experts, *www.nesse.fr/nesse/activities/reports/activities/reports/disability-special-needs-1.*

New Zealand Ministry of Education (2016), Educational Leaders, *www.educationalleaders.govt.nz* (accessed 4 February 2016).

New Zealand Ministry of Education (2008), *Kiwi Leadership for Principals, Principals as Educational Leaders*, *www.educationalleaders.govt.nz/content/download/45029/377177/file/Kiwi%20Leadership%20for%20Principals%20(2008).pdf.*

Nusche, D. et al. (2015), *OECD Reviews of School Resources: Flemish Community of Belgium 2015*, OECD Publishing, Paris, *http://dx.doi.org/10.1787/9789264247598-en.*

Nusche, D. et al. (2011), *OECD Reviews of Evaluation and Assessment in Education: Norway 2011*, OECD Publishing, Paris, *http://dx.doi.org/10.1787/9789264117006-en.*

OECD (2015a), *Education at a Glance 2015: OECD Indicators*, OECD Publishing, Paris, *http://dx.doi.org/10.1787/eag-2015-en.*

OECD (2015b), *Schooling Redesigned: Towards Innovative Learning Systems*, OECD Publishing, Paris, *http://dx.doi.org/10.1787/9789264245914-en.*

OECD (2014a), *Education at a Glance 2014: OECD Indicators*, OECD Publishing, Paris, *http://dx.doi.org/10.1787/eag-2014-en.*

OECD (2014b), *TALIS 2013 Results: An International Perspective on Teaching and Learning*, OECD Publishing, Paris, *http://dx.doi.org/10.1787/9789264196261-en.*

OECD (2013a), *PISA 2012 Results: What Makes Schools Successful (Volume IV): Resources, Policies and Practices*, OECD Publishing, Paris, *http://dx.doi.org/10.1787/9789264201156-en.*

OECD (2013b), *Synergies for Better Learning: An International Perspective on Evaluation and Assessment*, OECD Publishing, Paris, *http://dx.doi.org/10.1787/9789264190658-en*.

OECD (2006), *Starting Strong II: Early Childhood Education and Care*, OECD Publishing, Paris, *http://dx.doi.org/10.1787/9789264035461-en*.

OECD (2005), *Teachers Matter: Attracting, Developing and Retaining Effective Teachers*, OECD Publishing, Paris, *http://dx.doi.org/10.1787/9789264018044-en*.

Ontario College of Teachers (2016), *Transition to Teaching*, Ontario College of Teachers, Toronto, *www.oct.ca/becoming-a-teacher/transition-to-teaching*.

Ontario College of Teachers (2014), *Transitions to Teaching*, Ontario College of Teachers, Toronto, *www.oct.ca/-/media/PDF/Transition%20to%20Teaching%202014/EN/Main_report_eng.pdf*.

Ontario College of Teachers (n.d.), *Standards of Practice*, Ontario College of Teachers, Toronto, *www.oct.ca/-/media/PDF/Standards%20Poster/standards_flyer_e.pdf*.

Ontario Ministry of Education (2016a), *Ontario Focused Intervention partnership for Elementary Schools, Capacity Building Series*, Ontario Ministry of Education, Toronto, *http://learnteachlead.ca/projects/capacity-building-2/?pcat=2412*.

Ontario Ministry of Education (2016b), *Leadership development*, *www.edu.gov.on.ca/eng/policyfunding/leadership/index.html (accessed 4 February 2016)*.

Ontario Ministry of Education (2015), *Pedagogical Documentation Revisited, Capacity Building Series*, Ontario Ministry of Education, Toronto, *http://learnteachlead.ca/wp-content/uploads/2015/02/Pedagogical-Documentation-Revisited-Looking-at-Assessment-and-Learning-in-New-Ways1.pdf*.

Ontario Ministry of Education (2014a), *Collaborative Inquiry in Ontario – What Have We Learned and Where Are We Now, Capacity Building Series*, Ontario Ministry of Education, Toronto, *http://learnteachlead.ca/wp-content/uploads/2014/12/CBS_CollaborativeInquiry.pdf*.

Ontario Ministry of Education (2014b), *Principals as Co-Learners: Supporting the Promise of Collaborative Inquiry, Capacity Building Series*, Ontario Ministry of Education, Toronto, *http://learnteachlead.ca/wp-content/uploads/2014/12/CBS_PrincipalsCoLearners.pdf*.

Ontario Ministry of Education (2014c), *A Model to Guide Collaborative Inquiry, Capacity Building Series*, Ontario Ministry of Education, Toronto, *http://learnteachlead.ca/wp-content/uploads/2014/12/CBS-ModelGuideCollaborativeInquiry.pdf*.

Ontario Ministry of Education (2013a), *Learning for All: A guide to effective assessment and instruction for all students, K-12*, Ontario Ministry of Education, Toronto, *www.edu.gov.on.ca/eng/general/elemsec/speced/LearningforAll2013.pdf*.

Ontario Ministry of Education (2013b), *Dynamic Learning, Capacity Building Series*, Ontario Ministry of Education, Toronto, *http://learnteachlead.ca/wp-content/uploads/2014/10/CBS_DynamicLearning_AODA.pdf*.

Ontario Ministry of Education (2012), *Pedagogical Documentation-Leading Learning in the Early Years and Beyond, Capacity Building Series*, Ontario Ministry of Education, Toronto, *http://learnteachlead.ca/wp-content/uploads/2014/10/CBS_Pedagogical_AODA.pdf*.

Ontario Ministry of Education (2010), *Teacher Collaborative Inquiry, Capacity Building Series*, Ontario Ministry of Education, Toronto, *http://learnteachlead.ca/wp-content/uploads/2015/01/CBS_Collaborative_Teacher_Inquiry1.pdf*.

Ontario Ministry of Education (2008a), *Teaching-Learning Critical Pathways, Capacity Building Series*, Ontario Ministry of Education, Toronto, *http://learnteachlead.ca/wp-content/uploads/2014/10/Teaching-Learning-Critical-Pathways-One-Model-for-Ontario-Professional-Learning-Communities-.pdf*.

Ontario Ministry of Education (2008b), *Using Data to Improve Student Achievement, Capacity Building Series*, Ontario Ministry of Education, Toronto, *http://learnteachlead.ca/projects/capacity-building-2/?pcat=2412*.

Ontario Ministry of Education (2007a), *Professional Learning Communities: A Model for Ontario Schools, Capacity Building Series*, Ontario Ministry of Education, Toronto, *http://learnteachlead.ca/wp-content/uploads/2015/01/TLCP-Professional-Learning-Communities.pdf*.

Ontario Ministry of Education (2007b), *Teacher Moderation: Collaborative Assessment of Student Work, Capacity Building Series*, Ontario Ministry of Education, Toronto, *http://learnteachlead.ca/wp-content/uploads/2014/10/Teacher-Moderation-Collaborative-Assessment-of-Student-Work-.pdf*.

Pont, B., D. Nusche and H. Moorman (2008), *Improving School Leadership, Volume 1: Policy and Practice*, OECD Publishing, Paris, *http://dx.doi.org/10.1787/9789264044715-en*.

Radinger, T. (2014), "School leader appraisal – A tool to strengthen school leaders' pedagogical leadership and skills for teacher management?", *European Journal of Education*, Vol. 49(3), Wiley-Blackwell, Hoboken, NJ, pp. 378-394, *http://onlinelibrary.wiley.com/doi/10.1111/ejed.12085/abstract*.

Santiago, P. et al. (forthcoming), *OECD Reviews of School Resources: Chile*, OECD Publishing, Paris.

Shewbridge, C. et al. (2011), *OECD Reviews of Evaluation and Assessment in Education: Denmark 2011*, OECD Publishing, Paris, *http://dx.doi.org/10.1787/9789264116597-en*.

Timperley, H. et al. (2007) *Teacher Professional Learning and Development: Best Evidence Synthesis Iteration*, New Zealand Ministry of Education, Auckland, *www.educationcounts.govt.nz/__data/assets/pdf_file/0017/16901/TPLandDBESentireWeb.pdf*.

ANNEX A

The OECD Review of Policies to Improve the Effectiveness of Resource Use in Schools

The ***OECD Review of Policies to Improve the Effectiveness of Resource Use in Schools*** (also referred to as the *School Resources Review*) is designed to respond to the strong interest in the effective and equitable use of school resources evident at national and international levels. It provides analysis and policy advice on how to distribute, utilise and manage resources to improve the quality, equity and efficiency of school education. School resources are understood in a broad way, including financial resources (e.g. expenditures on education, the school budget), physical resources (e.g. school buildings, computers), human resources (e.g. teachers, school leaders) and other resources (e.g. learning time).

Fifteen education systems are actively engaged in the review. These cover a wide range of economic and social contexts, and among them they illustrate quite different approaches to the use of resources in school systems. This allows a comparative perspective on key policy issues. Participating countries prepare a detailed background report following a standard set of guidelines. Some of the participating countries have also opted for a detailed review undertaken by a team consisting of members of the OECD secretariat and external experts. Insofar, the participating countries are (in bold those that have opted for an individual review): **Austria, Belgium (Flemish Community)**, Belgium (French Community), **Chile**, the **Czech Republic**, **Denmark**, **Estonia**, Iceland, **Kazakhstan**, **Lithuania**, Luxembourg, the **Slovak Republic**, Slovenia, Spain, Sweden and **Uruguay**. A series of comparative reports bringing together lessons learned from the different country reviews is planned for 2017 to 2018.

The project is overseen by the Group of National Experts on School Resources, which was established as a subsidiary body of the OECD Education Policy Committee in order to guide the methods, timing and principles of the review. More details are available from the review website: *www.oecd.org/education/schoolresourcesreview*.

ANNEX B

Composition of the OECD Review Team

Torberg Falch, a Norwegian national, is Professor of Economics at the Department of Economics, Norwegian University of Science and Technology, and currently serving as Vice-Dean for Education. He has published in several international journals, including the leading field journals in labour economics and economics of education. His research is on aspects of the teacher labour market, school spending determination, skill formation, school dropout, and the political economy of resource allocation. He has been project leader on several projects on education policy issues financed by different governmental sources. He is currently a member of the think tank European Expert Network on Economics of Education sponsored by the European Commission and co-editor of Education Economics.

Deborah Nusche, a German national, is a Policy Analyst in the OECD Directorate for Education and Skills, where she has been since 2007. She currently leads the country-specific work on Austria, Belgium and Denmark for the OECD School Resources Review. Prior to this, she conducted policy analysis for three major cross-country studies at the OECD: a review of school leadership policy and practice leading to the two-volume publication "Improving School Leadership" (2008); a review of migrant education leading to the OECD publication "Closing the Gap for Immigrant Students" (2010); and a review of evaluation and assessment in education, leading to the OECD publication "Synergies for Better Learning" (2013). She also conducted thematic education policy reviews in 15 OECD countries leading to country-specific analysis and policy advice. She has previous work experience with the United Nations Educational, Scientific and Cultural Organization (UNESCO).

Thomas Radinger, a German national, is a Junior Policy Analyst with the OECD Directorate for Education and Skills. He joined the organisation in September 2011 to contribute to the OECD Review on Evaluation and Assessment Frameworks for Improving School Outcomes. Thomas is a co-author of the project's final synthesis report *Synergies for Better Learning: An International Perspective on Evaluation and Assessment* (2013) and took the lead in the analysis of school leader appraisal. Between October 2012 and January 2015, he was involved in the development of the OECD Education GPS, an online platform to disseminate OECD data and research on education to a broader audience.

Bruce Shaw, a Canadian national, is currently the Director, Leadership and Implementation Branch, Student Achievement Division in the Ontario Ministry of Education. This branch supports teacher and leadership professional learning around student learning and teaching pedagogy to support high levels of student achievement. Implementation and monitoring of change initiatives at the system level is a focus, Kindergarten to Grade 12.

He directs field teams of student achievement officers in each area of the province, as well as having responsibility for professional learning resource development, finance and human resources for the branch. Bruce has served in education as a teacher and a school administrator in the elementary and secondary panels, a superintendent of schools K-12 and a senior executive at the Ministry of Education, Student Achievement Division.

ANNEX C

Visit programme

Wednesday, 22 April 2015, Copenhagen	
09:00-09:30	Ministry of Education, National Co-ordinators
09:30-10:00	Permanent Secretary of State Jesper Fisker
10:00-12:00	Ministry of Education, Heads of Divisions and Senior Advisors • Division for the Policy and Legislation of Primary and Lower Secondary Education • Division for Capacity Building • Division for International Affairs • Division for Analysis and Implementation
12:45-13:45	Ministry of Higher Education and Science
14:15-15:00	Ministry of Social Affairs
15:00-16:00	Ministry of Finance and Ministry for Economic Affairs and the Interior
16:00-17:00	Students' organisation
17:00-18:00	Disabled People's Organization Denmark
Thursday, 23 April 2015, Copenhagen	
09:00-10:00	Copenhagen City Authorities
10:30-13:00	**School visit 1: Peder Lykke Skolen, Copenhagen**
14:00-15:00	Teacher Union (DLF)
15:00-16:00	Danish Association of School Leaders
16:15-17:00	Parents' organisation
17:00-18:00	Danish Union of Early Childhood and Youth Educators
Friday, 24 April 2015, Birkerød, Copenhagen	
09:10-10:10	Rudersdal Authorities
10:30-13:00	**School visit 2: Skovlyskolen, Rudersdal**
14:00-15:00	County and Municipal Organizations (organisation of administrative leaders/directors at the municipality level)
16:00-17:00	Local Government Denmark
Monday, 27 April 2015, Copenhagen, Odense, Middelfart	
08:15-10:45	**School visit 3: Fensmarkskolen, Special school, Copenhagen**
12:45-13:45	Meeting with Odense City Authorities
14:00-16:30	**School visit 4: Ejerslykkeskolen, Odense**
17:15-18:15	Meeting with Middelfart Authorities
Tuesday, 28 April 2015, Tønder, Esbjerg	
08:30-11:00	**School visit 5: Møgeltønder filialskole, Tønder**
11:15-12:15	Meeting with Tønder Authorities
13:30-16:00	**School visit 6: Hjerting Skole, Esbjerg**
16:15-17:15	Meeting with Esbjerg Authorities

Wednesday, 29 April 2015, Copenhagen	
09:00-13:00	Review team meeting
13:00-14:00	Danish Evaluation Institute
14:00-16:00	Researcher seminar • Senior researcher Kurt Houlberg, KORA • Senior researcher Vibeke Normann Andersen, KORA • Senior researcher Jørgen Søndergaard, SFI • Professor Anders Vind, SFI • Professor Niels Egelund, IUP • Lektor Camilla Dyssegaard, IUP
16:00-17:00	Preliminary impressions by the OECD review team

ORGANISATION FOR ECONOMIC CO-OPERATION AND DEVELOPMENT

The OECD is a unique forum where governments work together to address the economic, social and environmental challenges of globalisation. The OECD is also at the forefront of efforts to understand and to help governments respond to new developments and concerns, such as corporate governance, the information economy and the challenges of an ageing population. The Organisation provides a setting where governments can compare policy experiences, seek answers to common problems, identify good practice and work to co-ordinate domestic and international policies.

The OECD member countries are: Australia, Austria, Belgium, Canada, Chile, the Czech Republic, Denmark, Estonia, Finland, France, Germany, Greece, Hungary, Iceland, Ireland, Israel, Italy, Japan, Korea, Latvia, Luxembourg, Mexico, the Netherlands, New Zealand, Norway, Poland, Portugal, the Slovak Republic, Slovenia, Spain, Sweden, Switzerland, Turkey, the United Kingdom and the United States. The European Union takes part in the work of the OECD.

OECD Publishing disseminates widely the results of the Organisation's statistics gathering and research on economic, social and environmental issues, as well as the conventions, guidelines and standards agreed by its members.

OECD PUBLISHING, 2, rue André-Pascal, 75775 PARIS CEDEX 16
(91 2016 10 1 P) ISBN 978-92-64-26239-3 – 2016

www.ingramcontent.com/pod-product-compliance
Lightning Source LLC
Chambersburg PA
CBHW061211240926
51846CB00006B/1188
9789264262393